Yacht Designs II

BY WILLIAM GARDEN

© Copyright 1992 Mystic Seaport Museum
50 Greenmanville Ave.
Mystic, CT 06355-0990

This book is printed by The Courier Companies, Inc.

Design by Clare Cunningham

Photo Credits:

Page 4:   Blackburn image from *Lone Voyager* by
               Joseph E. Garland, courtesy of the author
Page 25:   Roy Montgomery
Pages 28-29:   Christopher Cunningham
Page 65:   Courtesy of Peabody Museum of Salem
Page 78:   Ray Krantz
Page 86:   Courtesy of Connie Horder
Page 145:   Ray Krantz, top and bottom
Page 150:   Courtesy of Studio West Photography
Pages 154-155: Neil Rabinowitz
Page 156:   Neil Rabinowitz
Page 165:   Neil Rabinowitz
Page 174:   Courtesy of Capt. Walrus
Page 186:   Models and photos courtesy of Paul Gartside

All other photographs courtesy of William Garden

Garden, William, 1918 -
       Yacht Designs II / by William Garden
    xii, 196 p. illus.; 29.5 cm.

1. Yacht-building.   2. Naval architecture --
Designs and plans. I. Title.
VN 331.G37

ISBN 0-913372-61-7

PLAN NUMBERS FOR YACHTS IN THIS BOOK

CONTENTS

FOREWORD

In a brief but brilliant preface to his first book of yacht designs, William Garden noted that while fiberglass and other cost- and time-saving construction methods and materials have helped fuel an exponential increase in the pleasure-boat population, the range and variety of boat types and models have undergone a dramatic decline.

True enough, many of the boats in this diminished field offer the consumer performance features and amenities — and an overall durability — that were all but unobtainable in an earlier day. But that gain has been largely offset by the production-line sameness and predictability of what remains. The prevailing conformity is apparent not merely in stock boats and one-designs. It is also found in such rarefied and expensive corners of the market as maxis and custom cruiser-racer sailboats to the latest measurement rule, and one-off megayachts to the latest megafashion.

There is nothing unusual about the tendency of the human animal to conform. But that conformity becomes remarkable when it is expressed in yachts in the 100- to 200-foot range that are clones with as little real appeal or interest as a condo in Times Square. As for the current crop of America's Cup challengers and defenders, their price tag keeps going up, but their contirubtion to the welfare of the sport of yachting is as low as it can get.

In the rising tide of big money and bigger horsepower, the little fellow who dreams of putting to sea in a good little boat of timeless design has been all but pulled under. As a matter of fact, even the big fellow who dreams of putting to sea in a good big boat of timeless design (but bigger horsepower) is having trouble staying afloat.

And why is this? Because, as Bill Garden has written, we keep forgetting the all-important truth that ". . . our yachts are toy boats . . . the glint on a lovely brief bubble of time, a time of leisure and affluence for the middle class. A boat's importance as an escape from reality, as a change of pace, as a theme for reflection, and as an art form gives it worth or value."

When a yacht ceases to be a worthy theme for reflection, it does not cease to be a yacht. But it most certainly ceases to be a worthy yacht. And when a yacht fails to help us escape from the prison of everyday life and experience, it becomes just another prison — and a damned expensive and confining prison at that.

William Garden began his career in naval architecture and marine engineering in 1938. During the past 55 years he has drawn the lines for more than 1,000 vessels, ranging in size from prams and skiffs and pocket cruisers to 195' motor yachts, and 240' grain and oil barges. Upwards of 6,000 individual boats have been built to these plans.

Himself a lover of traditional wooden construction, Bill Garden has with equal facility and success designed yachts and workboats for construction in steel, fiberglass, aluminum, and composite materials. Himself an incurable devotee of the gaff topsail rig and of fast, easily-driven cruising sailboats with easily-handled sailplans, he has probably created a greater number of custom power yachts in all sizes and of all types than any other individual designer of our time.

Yet not one of his designs, whether sail, motor sail, or power, whether out-and-out sailing racer or pure workboat, could be the work of any designer other than William Garden. And not one of his designs lacks character and substance.

Do you think of Garden only in connection with his trademark trawler yachts? Then look at chapter 39 and his wonderful 62' dory commuter

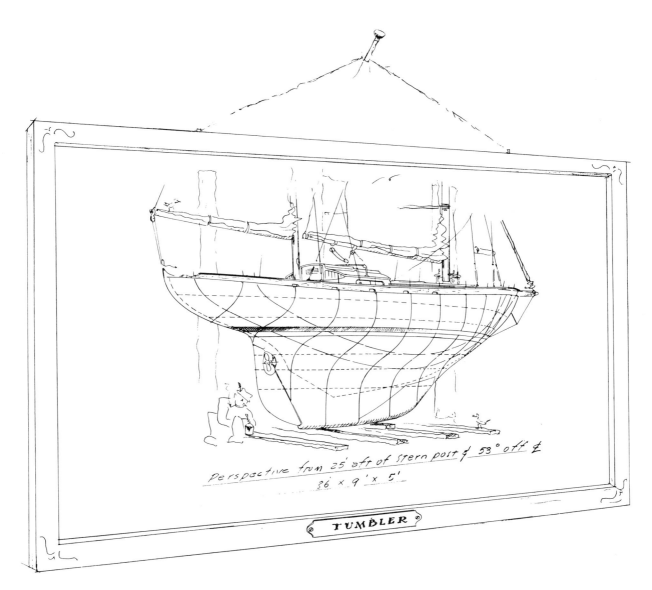

Perspective from 25' aft of stern post & 53° off ₵
36' x 9' x 5'

TUMBLER

Tlingit — or *Tlingit*'s big sisters. Is your picture of a Garden design the clipper-bowed steel schooner *Sequin*, complete with rolled-home poop and great cabin? Then maybe you should study his plans and commentary for the recent 92' express cruiser *Katherine*. From such yachts at flank speed Catherine the Great would have been delighted to throw spent lovers to the sharks.

But while the unexpected is the usual with Bill Garden, and while versatility is his stock in trade, what gives Garden designs their enduring worth and appeal is something that cannot be taught at school, derived from a computer program, or acquired for cash money. I speak of course of integrity: the wholeness and soundness of the self.

No more than anyone else has Bill Garden escaped failure and disappointment. Not all his designs reach perfection. "Everything we do,"

Garden notes in his preface a few pages from here, "can be done again with improvement."

But it is not Bill's way to look back with regret or to blame the other guy. Given the choice, he prefers to laugh, not cry. There is a lot of laughter in the text that follows, a generous portion of it directed at himself. And there is joy throughout this book — the joy of an artist in love with boats.

Bill's boats have character and integrity. They are happy ships. Not surprisingly, their owners tend to be repeat customers (often lifelong customers) of this designer, and devoted friends as well. And so today, more than half a century after the first boats to his design began capturing hearts in the Pacific Northwest, the work of the master expresses the dreams of boat lovers throughout the world.

— *Llewellyn Howland III*

INTRODUCTION

The articles here were compiled over a period of years as amusement, and for inclusion one day in a second book of yacht designs. At one time I thought it would be ready long since — but the more pressing and interesting job of designing new boats has been a constant interference and a necessity to pay the grocer and keep my own little fleet afloat.

For the past 50 years I've run a branch of Santa's Workshop for older boys, since the design practice for the latter part of these years has trended more toward yachts and away from the work boats that had been produced before.

Yachts are always interesting to develop — pure romance in many cases as compared to the more rigid restrictions of commercial work — but both are absorbing, and occasionally a work boat will slip into the book. Along this line, the old *Pacific Motor Boat* magazine always had a good mix of work and pleasure boats, but in those days the work boats had a more boaty shape than the ones today. They seemed to look the part of something that could go to sea. Going through the commercial publications in the 1990s, the development is toward wave-piercing catamarans, surface-effect craft, and all sorts of space-age machines as we slide into our more homogenized existence.

The past years, I'm sure, will finally be seen to have been the most fun, and in a way it's good to

see the clock run down and be able to sidestep galloping progress. Reality today takes some holding onto. Last week the copy of a purchase order came across the desk for a pair of 3000-hp engines going into a boat on the board. This is one and a quarter million bucks, which despite today's shrinking dollar will still require a lot of effort in the accumulation, a big sum particularly in the perspective of the first 2-cycle gas engine that I purchased in the mid-1930s for three dollars. Admittedly my three-dollar engine was in parts and in a gunny sack.

But back to the boats. A few of these you may have already seen in one of the periodicals, since the hope of ever getting the time to put them all together into a book often has seemed remote. For these I apologize, but in all cases here I've included more detailed plans and information.

The pure sailboat or auxiliary-powered sailboat section of this second book of yacht designs will start with a little fellow, the sloop *Capt. Blackburn*, since the Captain himself seems to have been resurrected again by some good articles in the press, and the details of his boats are of interest.

Some disappointment always results when exhuming most old boats and developing a new design from the original concept. Everything we do can be done again with improvement. With the *Blackburn* sloop, I've tried to develop the original

model into a more contemporary boat while maintaining some of the character of the original.

From the plan files we'll go through a variety of boats that you might find of interest. Several bins are full of plans, and I've picked a few that might appeal. Over the years a lot of drawings have been jettisoned for lack of file room, but lots are left to fish out if there's time to do yet another of these books.

Despite their high retail prices, books of this sort are losers financially. This is particularly true of books with many illustrations, since the author must put the drawings together via contact prints and write the text as time allows. The net return for this non-thriller, no-sex product ends up at a small percentage of the retail price. After production costs have been paid, it's a minimum-wage effort but it's interesting to put the thing together. Outside there is a cold drizzle today, and a book is a pleasant ego gratification while on the way to the poorhouse.

— William Garden,
Toad's Landing, Victoria, B.C., Canada

PART ONE

Sailboats

1

The Cutter/Sloop *Capt. Blackburn*

LO Deck:	27'0"
LWL:	22'0"
Breadth:	8'6"
Displacement:	8,500 lbs.
Ballast:	3,400 lbs.
Sail Area:	490 sq. ft.

In 1897 Capt. Howard Blackburn, the famed Grand Banks fisherman and doryman, in command of the Gloucester schooner *Hattie I. Phillips*, set sail for Cape Horn and the Alaska Gold Rush. On board were a party of Klondike enthusiasts, and in the hold was a cargo of coal to help defray expenses. After what Blackburn called a "rough and tumble" experience, including a beat through the Straits of Magellan, they arrived in San Francisco. The passage took 127 days. In San Francisco, Capt. Blackburn injured his knee so badly that he had to leave the schooner and return to Gloucester for an extended recuperation on crutches. Blackburn had retired long before; but this San Francisco voyage had fired him up to get to sea again.

Those familiar with the story will recall that during the winter of 1883 Blackburn lost all his fingers and toes after being adrift off the coast of Newfoundland with a shipmate while dory fishing from the schooner *Grace L. Fears*. Losing all hope of being found by the schooner, Blackburn rowed West and finally came ashore in Newfoundland.

The icy row ashore, with his hands frozen to the oars and his companion frozen to death on the floorboards, was an epic adventure of the time.

In Gloucester, after returning from the San Francisco voyage and when his knee had healed, Blackburn built a neat little sloop, which he named *Great Western*, and in which he planned to sail across the Atlantic to Gloucester, England. *Great Western* was 30' from the transom to the end of the fiddle head, about 27' on deck, 8'-6" breadth extreme, 4'-4" depth of hold, and 4.77 tons measurement. She was a flush-decker, with 7" bulwarks, a short cockpit, and a sliding hatch to the hold, which Blackburn referred to as a roomy cabin. Below was a bunk with barely sitting headroom, a 50-gallon water tank, room for stores, an oil stove for cooking, plus lockers for chronometer, sextant, taffrail log, and all the bits and pieces required for the voyage.

Great Western was rigged as a low gaff sloop, with the jib out to the bowsprit end and fitted with a bonnet for reducing its area, plus a flying jib carried above and hoisted to a short spike

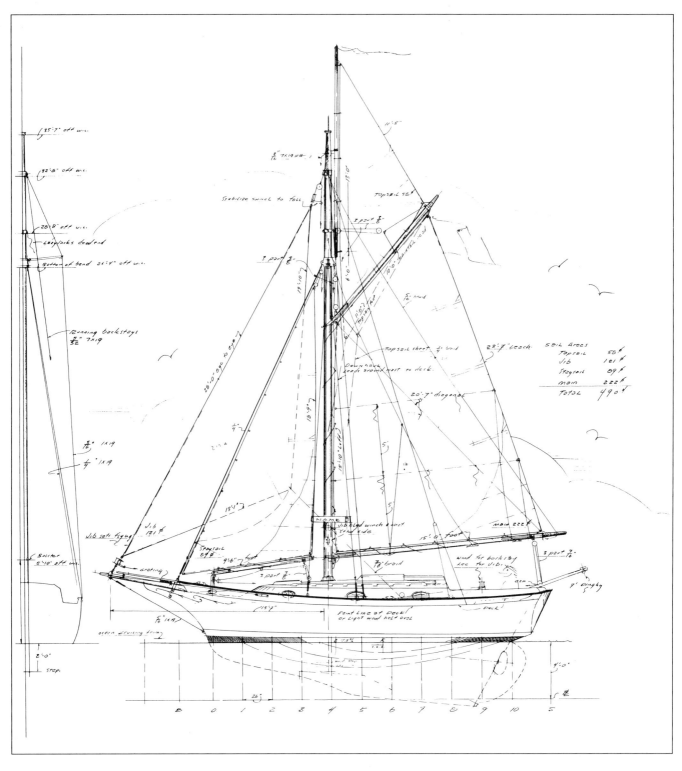

topmast. A gaff topsail also was fitted, but reported to be seldom used.

From clipper bow to elliptical stern, her photos indicate a nice little vessel with graceful sheer, somewhat along the lines of a Friendship Sloop but higher-sided. Blackburn himself described *Great Western* as a "clipper sloop," along the lines of the small Boston or Gloucester sloop boats of that time.

Before we get to the details of the 1980s devel-

opment of the sloop *Blackburn*, you will wonder how a man without fingers could handle sails. Capt. Blackburn led all halyards aft to the cockpit. In swaying up the sails he would take a turn of the halyard around his body and then fall back, repeating the process until the sail was up. Then he would stoop down until the halyard rested on the cockpit coaming, where he held it down with one palm until he could cleat it with the other palm. To haul in the sheets, he would take a turn

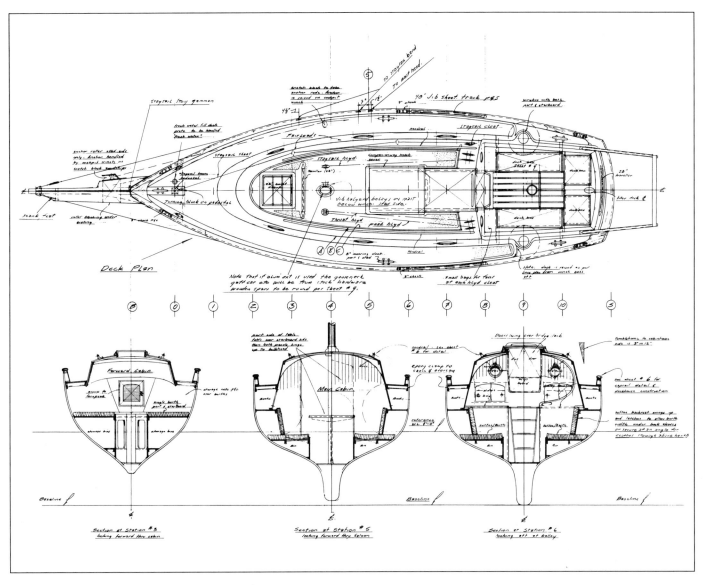

Deck Plan

Section at Station #3
looking forward thru cabin

Section at Station #5
looking forward thru Saloon

Section at Station #6
looking aft of Galley

on the cleat and then sway on the sheet between block and cleat, taking in the slack with his teeth.

Sailing from Gloucester, Massachusetts, on June 18, 1899, Blackburn made the singlehanded passage to England in 61 days.

An old *Rudder* magazine article about this voyage became the inspiration for the little sloop *Capt. Blackburn* — designed more or less as a replica, but built in a more modern way, and with more reasonable accommodations.

The new *Capt. Blackburn*'s rig is that of a simple gaff cutter — or let's call her a "cutter-rigged-sloop," like the *Saucy Sally* in Dr. Doolittle's first voyage to Africa. The new rig is generally similar to *Great Western*'s but with a higher-peaked main and a staysail set up to the fiddle head rather than to the bowsprit end, so she is properly a cutter. The jib now is on a roller furler, which Capt. Blackburn would have blessed. *Great Western*'s spike topmast is deleted for simplicity, and our

sprit topsail is taken aloft by one halyard. The topsail luff is set up with a downhaul from the tack. The downhaul leads down, around the mast, and to a pin on the main boom jaws or to a cleat on deck. This forward lead to a topsail or a fisherman staysail's tack allows proper control of the sail's draft. Altogether it's a snug rig and a pleasant change from the triangular efficiency of the modern "me-toos."

On deck, the deep bulwarks give a shipshape feel, and will keep the loose gear and coconuts aboard. Much as I would love to give her a short trunk ending just abaft the mast, the longer trunk seems to suit the layout below and to be more practical. The skiff slung aft is also handy on a small cruiser. Steering is by wheel, and modern gear is used throughout.

For power a little Bukh diesel is shown. It turns a 16"x10" propeller through a 2-1/2:1 reduction gear, for 5 knots in flat water. This

The GREAT WESTERN
Capt. HOWARD BLACKBURN.
DIMENSIONS: Length over all 30 feet.   Breadth of Beam 8 ft. 6 in.   Depth of Hold 4 ft. 6 in.
Sailed from Gloucester, Mass., June 18th, 1899. Arrived at Gloucester, Eng.,
August 19th, 1899. Time of voyage 62 days.

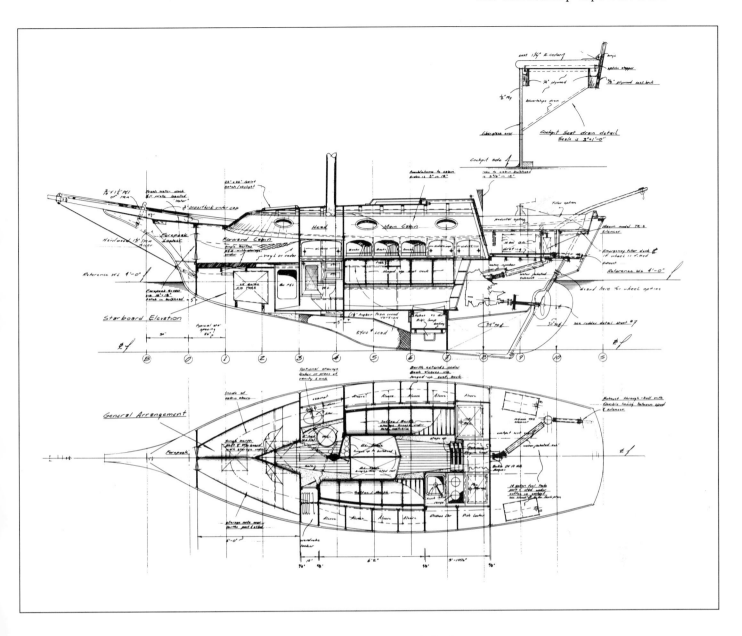

would have pleased Blackburn and saved him some days of rolling around in calms. In performance under sail the newer version will have an easy edge on all counts.

Traditional colors would be a dark bottle-green hull and black bulwarks, with a 1/2" gold cove at the deck line. The boot would be white or red lead, and the bottom would be green or red anti-fouling paint. The decks and trunk would be sand-colored or white to set it off, and the mast and spars would be varnished or spar-color painted.

The plans for *Capt. Blackburn* are available only from *Woodenboat* magazine, and consist of 11 sheets that show her construction in either foam core or cold-moulded wood. The plans list covers the following drawings:

1 Sail plan
2 Lines and offsets
3 Rudder details
4 General arrangement
5 Deck plan and sections
6 Construction section and tanks
7 Construction jig for foam core
8 Construction plan in wood and ballast details
9 Spar plans in wood with moments of inertia noted for matching stock sections in aluminum
10 Boom jaw details — wooden boom
11 Gaff jaw details — wooden gaff

A good little ship for the lone mariner or for use as a family cruising yacht.

2

A 32' Double-ended Cutter

LOA:	32'0"
LWL:	27'0"
Breadth:	11'8"
Draft:	5'0"
Sail Area:	645 sq. ft. (main, jib & staysail)
Displacement:	21,500 lbs.
Ballast:	7,500 lbs.

In building a small yacht the absence of mechanical items can cut costs substantially, working on the premise that the first rule of economy is deletion and the second rule is substitution. Substitution often can be accomplished by using a more primitive wooden component — perhaps one cobbled together at home — rather than a more sophisticated part that carries profits for manufacturing and distribution, with tax on top. So let's look into a boat that can be built mainly from the wood lot.

When we take this course we immediately face the likelihood of inside ballast in small pieces, in order to utilize scrap metal. Keel castings of lead or iron for a boat of this size will equal the price of a small used automobile.

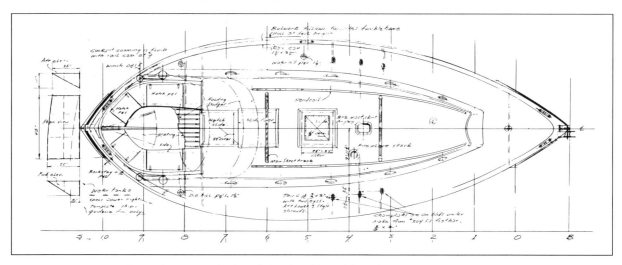

Lots of room on deck with 11'-8" of breadth and a narrow trunk cabin.

The jib-headed cutter rig with an optional motor-sailer deckhouse is a good choice for off-season cruising.

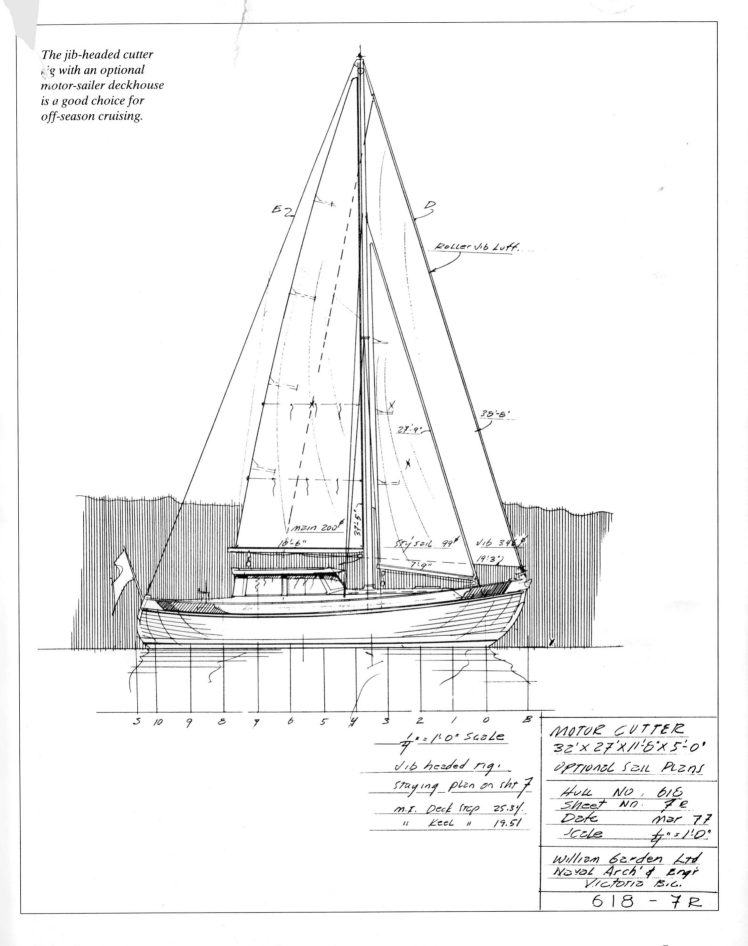

E2   D

Roller Jib Luff.

35'-6'

27'-9'

37'-5'

main 200□

16'-6"

Sty'sail 99□   Jib 34□□

7'-9'   19'3')

S 10 9 8 7 6 5 4 3 2 1 0 B

$\frac{1}{4}$" = 1'-0" Scale

Jib headed rig.

staying plan on sht 7

m.r. Deck Step 25.34

" Keel " 19.51

MOTOR CUTTER
32' X 27' X 11'-6" X 5'-0'
OPTIONAL SAIL PLANS

Hull No.	618
Sheet No.	7 R
Date	mar 77
Scale	$\frac{1}{4}$" = 1'0'

William Garden Ltd
Naval Arch't & Eng't
Victoria B.C.

618 - 7R

The Armstrongs explore a northern British Columbia inlet with Kishanina, *the family cutter.*

Inside ballast made from scrap iron or lead embedded in concrete usually can be half-scrounged, with the rest procured at small cost.

With inside ballast the keel bolts are deleted and the backbone assembly simplified, since the keel members won't be subjected to the deeper wringing weight of an outside ballast keel. On the dry side of the mudflat are the reduced right-ing moment because of inside ballast's higher center of gravity, the loss of outside ballast's resistance to damage when grounding, and the casting's denser concentration of weight. Inside ballast will also raise the cabin-sole height. But for a simple cruising boat it will get one afloat with cost savings.

A wooden structure is always appealing. Wood

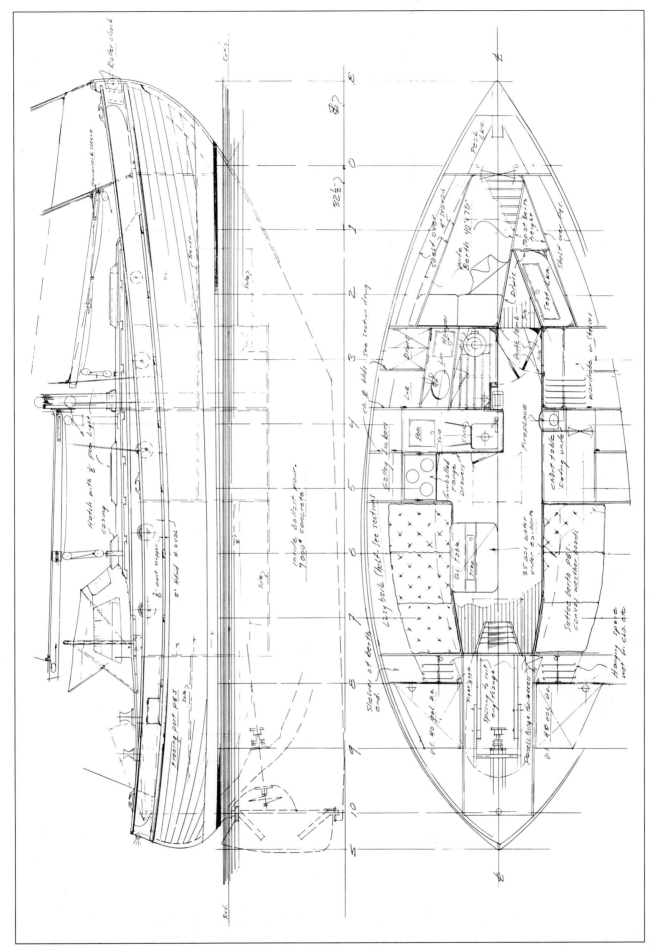

The jib-headed cutter rig seems to fit best with the trunk-cabin layout.

9

grows on trees, is easily worked, and is sympathetic to handling. Wood floats, smells good and takes coatings, and upon completion of the boat wood helps to insulate us in a cocoon sort of structure safe from the disturbing polyester reality of change.

I suppose that resistance to change has been at least partly responsible for long hair and old-man beards, 1890s get-ups on young people, and the revival of all sorts of period lifestyles. The year 1870 with penicillin is perhaps an ideal dream, so along with our 19th-century wooden structure let's put in an old-time engine — maybe only 50 years old, but with petcocks to prime and brass fittings to please the bewhiskered sailors.

Many of these engines are still around. For aesthetics, next to a good pair of oars they might be the most pleasing match for this simple boat. A 1- or 2-cylinder Atlantic or Palmer, a 10-14-hp Easthope, a jewel-like 12-15-hp Sterling — or, best of all, an 8-12-hp Vivian — would be ideal.

Sheet 1 shows a profile and arrangement plan with our simple little yacht rigged as a jib-headed cutter. This rig works well on the boat, but unfortunately requires some costly hardware.

The layout is practical and affords a good feeling of spaciousness belowdecks. The same plan is used for the pilothouse version, but with the sole raised and larger tanks under.

The photo and plan show one of the boats with the jib-headed, all-inboard rig plus pilothouse, which seems essential for Northwest off-season cruising. This particular boat was a three-year backyard project by Laurie Armstrong and his family here in British Columbia.

The boat is designed and set up for strip construction and inside ballast. From the trunk cabin plan and layout it's apparent how far aft the engine can go in a short-ended hull. The deck and trunk layouts indicate the amount of leg room on deck, due to the chainplates being set well inboard to facilitate fore and aft passage. The good working deck is fitted with ample bulwarks to give a feeling of security.

Despite every effort to economize, however, any way you approach it a boat of this size is a costly undertaking. Estimates in times of shrinking dollars won't do unless we tie them to something more tangible. Perhaps two years' carpenter's wages will be a guide to the cost of materials,

plus another two years — or about 3,500 or 4,000 man-hours — to complete the job. The time and material costs will vary with how elaborately the boat is built and outfitted, and with one's ability and experience in woodworking.

The size seems to be a good one for the home builder. Strip construction is straightforward, with the hull planked over the moulds prior to bending or laminating in frames to tie together the floor timbers, shell, and bulkheads.

Decks are plywood with fiberglass over, surrounded in turn by a real ship bulwark. Laid-wood decking is an option.

The long cabin trunk affords headroom for the full length of the cabins. On one of the models shown, a pram-type hood aft is fitted for cockpit shelter. As an alternative, the boat can be built with a pilothouse extending from Station 5 aft to the cockpit.

For a 27' waterline length, these boats have lots of room for accommodations. The galley and chart space can be amidships as shown, or the berth-settees can be shifted forward to the toilet room bulkhead and the galley placed at the companionway. Breadth is sufficient to fit pilot berths above and outboard of the settees if desired.

Forward, a double berth can be fitted, or an optional vee-berth arrangement will accommodate two singles with chain stowage between. The cabin-sole width is generous, and the boat has a feeling of real space belowdecks.

The breadth of 11'-8" contributes to initial stability, so she will sail at a reasonable angle of heel and be less tiring than a narrower boat. The keel is of gum, iroko, or ironbark, for impact resistance should she take a grounding.

The rig shown is a simple jib-headed cutter with a sail area of 645 square feet. The jib is on roller furling or reefing. For the purist, a 3' bowsprit, double headsails, and a gaff cutter rig can be fitted.

If you're more practical than romantic and decide to give up your search for an 8-12-hp Vivian, a modern engine can be used. A diesel engine of about 100-cubic-inch piston displacement, or a gasoline engine of 130-160-cubic-inch piston displacement, would work well. The pilothouse model carries the engine forward under the pilothouse for maximum accessibility and use of space.

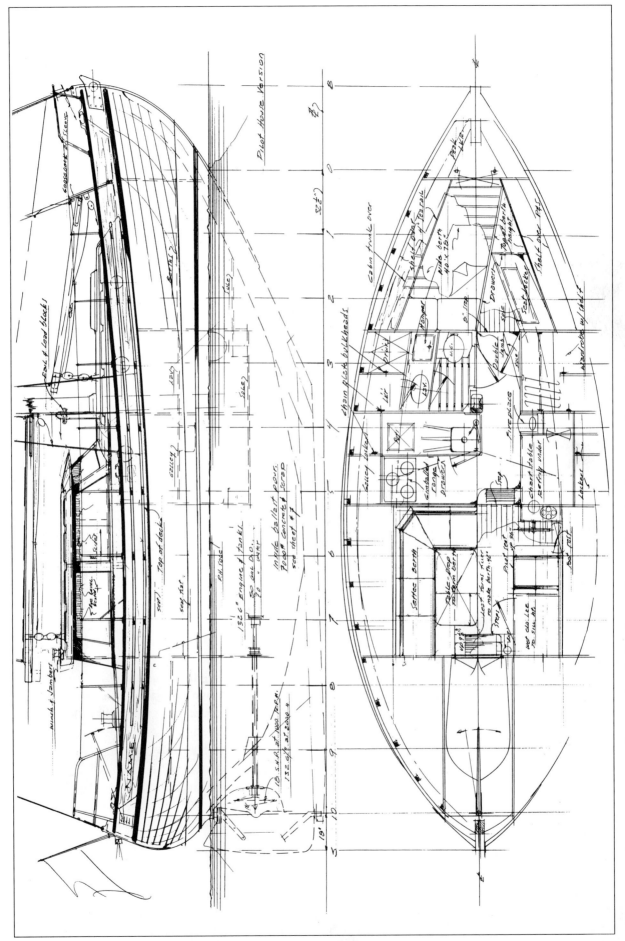

The sunken deckhouse has particular appeal in the Northwest climate of occasional summer calms and rain.

11

3

Saanich Beagle

LOA:	28'0"
LO Deck:	24'4"
LWL:	20'9"
Breadth:	9'5"
Draft:	4'
Displacement:	8,300 lbs.
Ballast:	2,500 lbs.
Sail Area:	361 sq. ft.

Saanich Beagle was built by Bent Jespersen to house a couple of friends and their dogs. She is about the smallest full-headroom cruising yacht practical for use as a floating summer home, and since she is a little ship that has given all of us pleasure in her development and completion, a discussion in depth might help round out her theme.

Perhaps most boatmen who decide to build a new yacht do so to fulfill an inborn need, either for escape or to create something they envision, imaginary or actual. While almost any reasonably practical floating platform might get them across the water, a great band of purists are obsessed with the style of their going. Nothing will suffice but a particular ship modeled after their own dreaming. A more practical plastic yacht won't do at all. Perhaps the off-the-shelf boat is too much someone else's boat, too commonplace. Whatever the reason, the deviation required to put together a new design is the course chosen. It is a course filled with vexation and problems, but one with added interest so important to many of us: creating something from the lumber pile on up.

The first owners of this boat were Beaglers, which accounts for half the name — the other half, *Saanich*, being the Indian name for our local peninsula. Beaglers belong to a different group of people. This is probably due to the nature of beagles, which fact can't be fully appreciated until a half-day has been spent chasing a tireless and suddenly deaf beagle across endless acres of wild land and shoreline, while the fair tide is being lost, an onshore gale is developing, air-

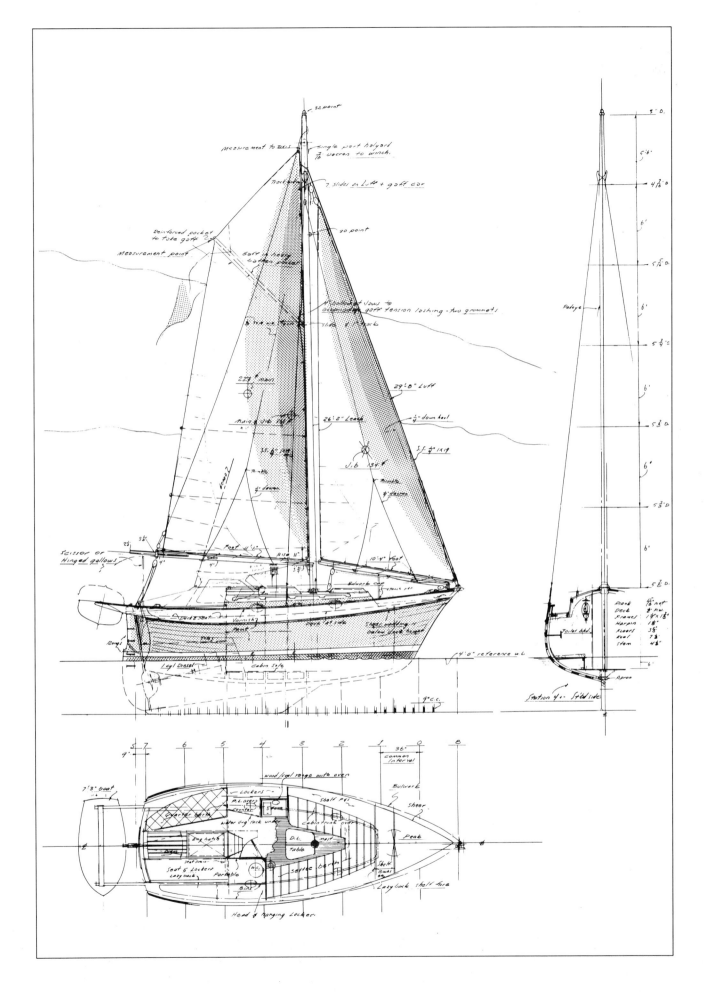

13

planes are being missed, and in some insidious way an adverse domino effect is tumbling right down the schedule to eventual near-disaster, all set in motion by a galloping damn beagle, ignorant to all whistles and entreaties, bound to do his own bloody-minded thing.

To put up with this, the Beagler seems to possess more than one person's share of patience, decency, and compassion — perhaps compassion in large measure — plus the good humor not to pull the trigger and send the galloping little son-of-a-bitch to the happy hunting ground. I've found Beaglers to be at the top of the scale of interesting people and good clients — and bless them they need some compensation.

For this boat, a couple sketches that seemed to match the owners' needs and personalities were roughed out first. No.1, whose sketch is included here for general interest, was found to be over budget. While the layout and size in general had to fit a big man, they still wanted a minimum yacht, with the thought that pleasure often grows inversely with size. *Multum in parvo*, if I remember any Latin — "Much in little" — plus a beagle bunk in the stern.

The smaller "as built" plan is illustrated in some detail. The general layout of the larger boat was retained, but scaled down to match the budget. "Motor sailer" is a reasonably accurate term for a boat of this model. In this case an engine of only modest power was requested, so a single-cylinder Faryman diesel was worked in. It pushes the boat along at a fair cruising speed, but like all small diesels it is a fair thumper. The fuel tank is placed abaft the engine on the centerline.

On deck our *Saanich Beagle* is shipshape, with the frameheads carried up above deck and sealed inboard to form a secure and easy-to-scrub bulwark. There is ample deck space, and the cockpit will seat a fair crowd. Boom gallows at the aft end of the cockpit serve the dual purpose of boom rest and a support for a person climbing into the dinghy. The dinghy is slung on davits aft or flopped upside down on top of the davits when at sea, the davits being a continuation of the cockpit coamings. For boarding, a pair of steps or boarding platforms are fitted on the ample transom.

A combined anchor roller and stowage chock is built into the bow and is served by a manual windlass with a chain anchor rode. A 25-lb. C.Q.R. plow anchor is carried in the chock with a 20-lb. Danforth for a spare, plus a pile of 5/16" anchor chain to match.

The appearance of a gaff-sloop rig of minimum complexity was requested, so a rig was sketched in with a heavy batten pocket and batten-cum-gaff. The main can be set with one halyard, and with the batten pocket of dark material she seems to carry a perfectly-setting topsail, whether reefed or with full sail. Lazy jacks gather in the main and the jib. A boom rather than roller furling was fitted on the jib, so that sheets don't have to be handed when tacking. The gaff jaws are formed by a heavy slide working on the sail track. You will note that the luff on the mainsail is relieved here to clear the throat, after which it swings back to the normal luff position. The jib is on snaps, with a jack line on the lower third to allow lowering without casting off the outhaul. The main above the gaff batten is fitted with a similar jack line to allow the gaff batten to lower when sail is stowed. Spars are solid spruce, varnished, and the boom is carried on standard jaws, with a sturdy gallows frame aft.

The hull form is reminiscent of a big sailing dinghy, with the keel continuing aft to pick up the rudder pintle and to carry the outside lead ballast of 2,500 lbs. The rudder is aft and outboard for maximum control. The stern boarding steps will help when swimming or accidentally overboard, and complement the full transom.

The wooden parts are mainly local. Hull planking is red cedar, one of the fragrant dugout-canoe woods of the West Coast Indian seafarers. Backbone and miscellaneous parts are of Douglas fir, the tough western forest tree. Spars are spruce, from the Queen Charlotte Islands. Worldwide sourcing is used for the rest of the bits and pieces: glue and resin from somebody's oil well via the petrochemical industry, bronze

Saanich Beagle*'s construction, cabin sections, and deck plan, will outline her structure of red-cedar planking on a backbone of Douglas fir.*

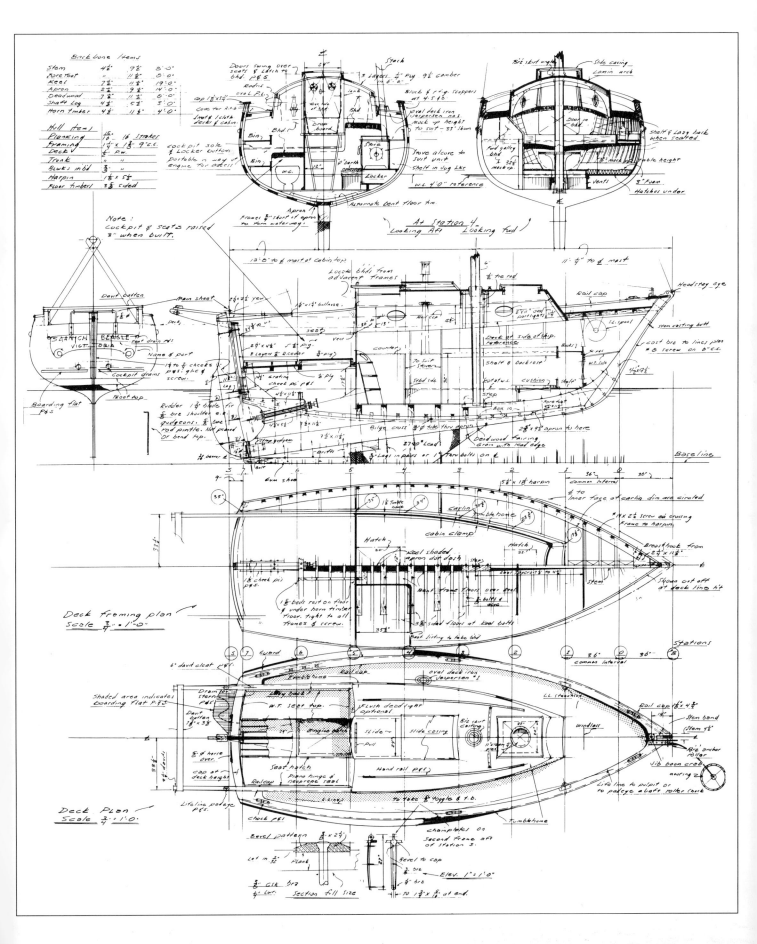

Saanich Beagle

15

Under sail, the Beagle's full-length mainsail batten appears to be a gaff with the white upper panel simulating a topsail.

fastenings and stainless steel from the U.S., engine from Europe, teak from Burma — the list is long and the invoices are endless.

In reviewing the rig, modern full-length batten hardware would be a vast improvement over the gear that was used. A modern fully-battened sail would do a much better job, and with luck she'll be retrofitted with this kind of mainsail one day.

I'll wind up the *Beagle* with the plan of No. 1, a larger boat and one that would make an equally interesting small yacht. This was the first preliminary sketch, or study, and is included here as a good source of something to ponder over and use to modify the standard thought — "If only it...", etc. A good chunky little cruiser for summers afloat.

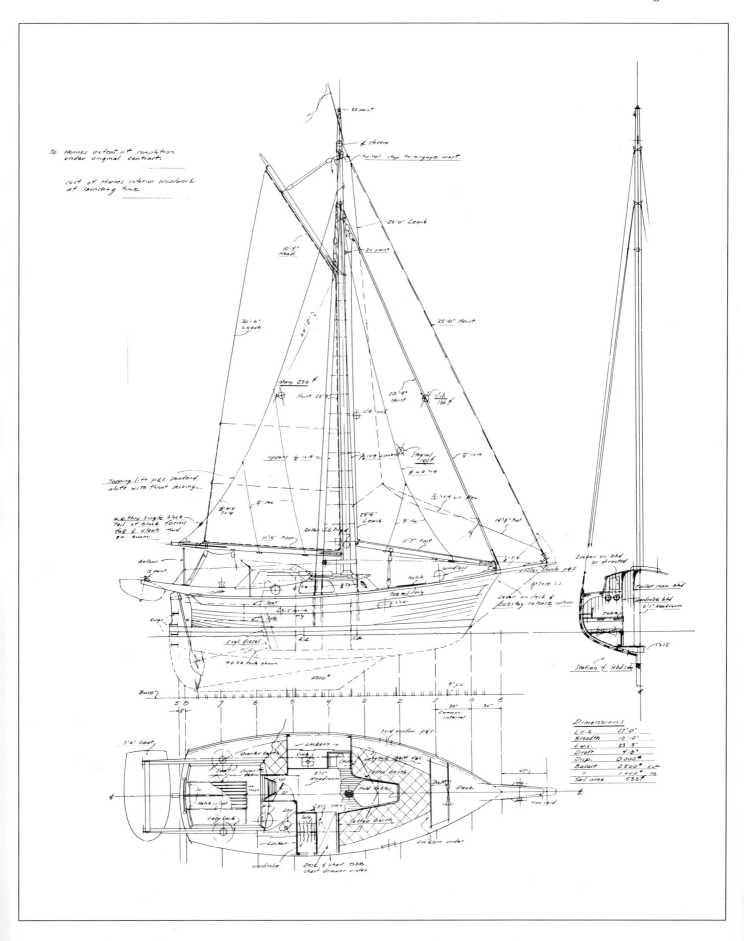

The lines plan of Saanich Beagle shows about the maximum boat that can be developed around a waterline length of 20'-9".

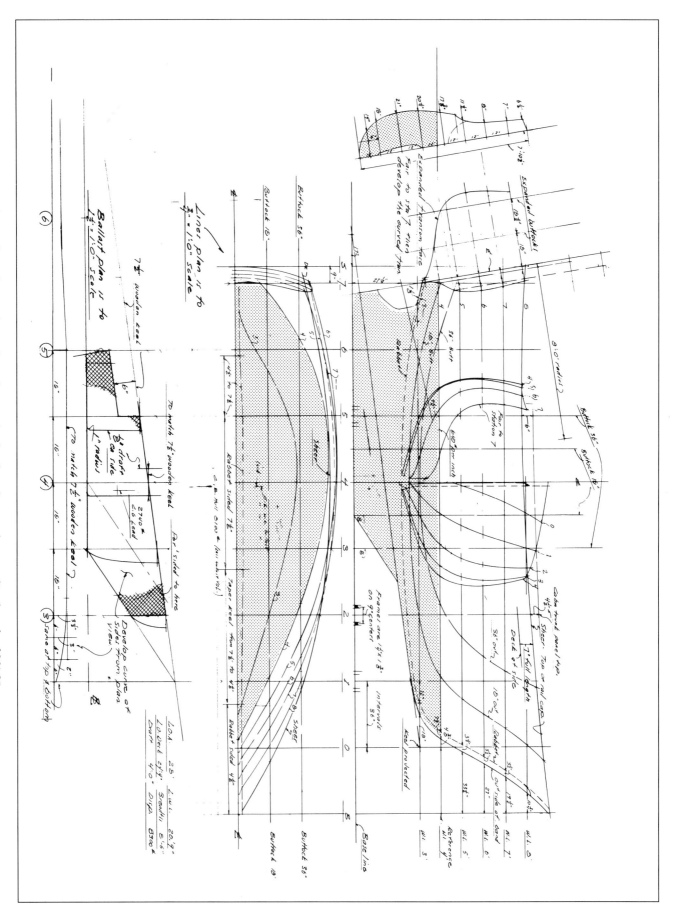

4

A Cruising Whale Boat

LOA:	30'6"
LWL:	24'6"
Breadth:	9'0"
Draft:	2'6" & 4'6"
Displacement:	9,800 lbs.
Ballast:	3,900 lbs.
Sail Area:	423 sq. ft.

I received a letter the other day from my old chum Last Gasp Jack. He said his legs were giving out like the worm-eaten shores under the boatyard's beach-hanging privy. This along with (as the note led me to imagine) rheumy eyes, some drooling, and mild palsy — all due to advancing age, fast women, and excessive use of rum as a shave lotion, the germ-killing follow-up swallow certainly adding to the pictured ruin.

All my chums are getting old, so further thought of boat-shaped coffins making a solemn course to the last mound came to mind's eye. Nothing would do but to pick up the phone and ring his bell across the world — a phenomenon, incidentally, that causes me endless wonder. Turn a dial a few times and one can ring a bell in Patagonia, England, Taiwan, or wherever. Hearing a familiar voice on the other end, though, never seems so impressive as getting a nobody-home, with the little bell jingling away in an empty house halfway round the world.

So, to shorten this up, I called Last Gasp to give him my condolences, only to be told that he was out in the garage workshop — she would call him. In the interval I again pictured him — he being an ingenious chap — methodically (due to his failing powers) involved in converting a grocery cart pinched from the local market into an inexpensive walker, the poor old legs periodically giving way as he carried on bravely into the sunset. By then my imagination had me close to tears.

Then I learned that the bugger had been in the garage tidying up his old Bentley Speeder, which he had discovered would bring a great bundle in the antique market. Greed always triumphs. The old legs were firmed up, the eyes bright. Last Gasp Jack was frantically working over the lovely old Bentley prior to flogging it off to some loaded Brit. Rejuvenation will undoubtedly mean another boat on the board, with the Box, happily, a few more gasps over the horizon.

Which brings us in a really roundabout way to all the delightful possibilities open to the distribution of such a bundle. Capital-gains tax will

For the sailor with a love of a lively little ship that will get out and go, something on this order will have a vast appeal. Shoal draft, room for two, and a boat of practical size to build and maintain.

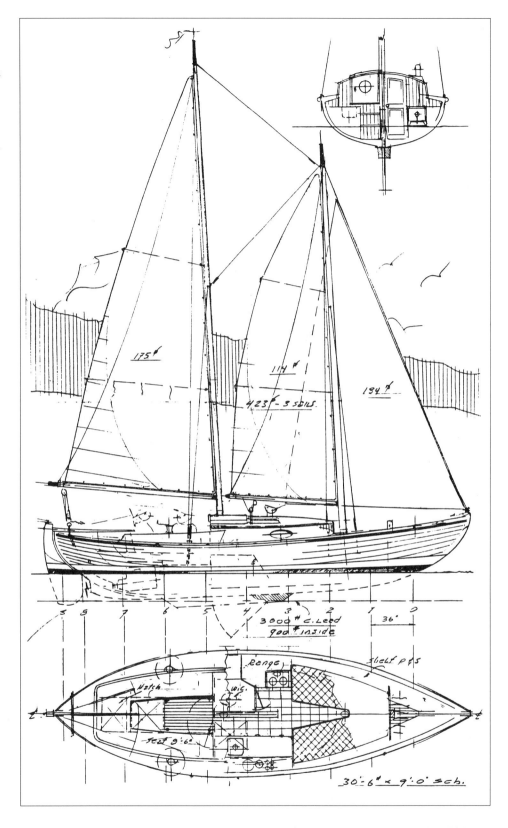

take the first bite, despite today's shrinking dollar having far less power than those that bought the Bentley new. Still, a nice chunk will be left over, and with fewer years left for its dispersal.

The decision about what sort of boat will make

one happy is a nice sort of problem. It should be a boat that will ensure optimum use, enjoyment and contentment, easy to say. The probability of realizing any of the above for very long is remote, but the anticipation of the good wooden boatshop sounds, the smells of freshly-cut yellow cedar and steamed oak frames, and the fascination of watching a little wooden ship slowly come to life from a pile of lumber is certainly worth a couple of Bentleys. So let's look into a possibility.

A small schooner would be a good choice. For a long time the rough sketch of a little two-sticker has slept in the office schooner bin. I have these things haphazardly marshaled in drawers — preliminary sketches and plans roughed out for long-gone clients. Most of the boats don't have lasting appeal and get nibbled away as morning fire-starters in the office stove, but occasionally one such as this retains some of its conceptual charm. So let's consider converting part of the newly-acquired bundle into this small, simple sailing boat. On an overall length of 30'-6" she draws just 30" with the board up. This is a handy depth for sneaking across shallow waters or anchoring well up the inlet, where she can sit on the sand and others can't follow.

For accommodations we'll need sitting headroom under the cabin, a nice cast-iron wood stove to break the off-season cruising chill and, above all, throughout the interior an element of simplicity, that long-gone feature we rarely see now in a time of complicated boats and lifestyles.

On deck she's rigged as a jib-headed schooner with fully battened sails and roller jib. The foremast we'll step on the keel and the mainmast on the centerboard trunk, both with shrouds, and one headstay plus a springstay. The jib is on a roller headstay and of two plys to split and wing out when running before the wind. Sails will be tanbark color, decks light gray, cabin sides white, and the sheer set off with a hardwood guard plus a good toe rail for safety.

The topsides we'll paint fish-blood red, or a mahogany reddish-brown simulating hardwood, which will be set off with a good wide white boottop stripe, and a bright half-oval wear strip of anodized aluminum on the face of the guard. The bottom will be red copper paint, with spars, tiller, and companionway doors varnished. The accommodation will get four coats of spar varnish, rubbed down for a nice mellow look in the lamp light.

Which brings us down below. Two berths in the saloon. The settee berths will be built with a slight hollow and a 1" fall outboard. This will do

wonders to keep the tired mariner off the cabin sole. The back rests will form proper seats for evenings below. Above all, the cabin is simple — just 10 minutes to clear out cushions, books, and miscellaneous gear prior to turning on the hose and giving her a good scrub. Think of doing that to one of the gold-plated and embroidered interiors of a modern tarted-up floating condo! One toilet overflow today and thousands of dollars' worth of custom carpet must be replaced, plus God knows what cost in floor-to-overhead silk wall covering.

So we'll keep her simple. In a burst of enthusiasm I almost threw the motor overboard just now, but we should keep it as extra insurance. A motor is a great thing to get us out of scrapes and to get her home on time when the wind is light or the current turns foul. It's an essential piece of equipment for a short-rigged boat. A 4-cylinder gasoline engine would be ideal for power — less thump than a high-compression diesel, and quieter.

On the negative side, greater care must be used with gasoline on board. A readily accessible fuel shut-off must be fitted at the tank and used at each shutdown. A gasoline engine of about 90-cubic-inch piston displacement, turning over at 1000 r.p.m., with direct drive and a 12"x10" 2-bladed propeller would be a good choice.

The engine could be electric-started or hand-crank started, and a simple 12-volt electrical system with two batteries might be fitted, one for the engine and one for the cabin lights and running lights. Plumbing would be minimal. The deck bucket might double as a toilet, the lack of a taffrail to hang over being one shortcoming of a double-ender.

The construction plan is worked up around a simple strip-built hull, planked upside-down over moulds. Some bent frames of steamed or laminated oak are fitted after she's right side-up and the hull has been smoothed up inside.

Ballast is a lead casting slotted for the centerboard, plus some pigs inside to experiment with trim when she's under sail. Decks are double-planked with one diagonal course, glued and fastened to the beams and sheer, plus a fore-and-aft run of decking set in glue. Tight if done well, and easy in upkeep if either oiled or painted. All this and money left over for a dinghy.

5

Bolero and Fast Passage 39

An interesting way to analyze accommodations and sailing potential is to compare boats that are generally similar. In reviewing these designs from the files this pair has been chosen, since design development of a new boat often begins as an overlay revision of an earlier model.

As we recall performance under some conditions, perhaps we'll decide to sharpen the entry, harden up the tuck for additional stability, or perhaps an adjustment of the centers is in order for another shot at nearer-right. When you think of the term "original design," and look at the fleet back to the mid-1800's, it becomes apparent that "original" is a design misnomer and "developed" or "refined" would be more accurate. Each well-thought-out boat is based on the input of thousands of present and past models. Outstanding developers in yacht design and changing techniques have gradually pushed performance ahead, along with thought, experimentation, new technology, and competition.

Applied technology has probably been the major force in improving performance since the 1930s. The development of synthetic fibers, better spars and rigging, and a vast improvement in sail-handling hardware and equipment have resulted in lighter, faster, and stronger sailing machines that are more than matched by the fierce, competitive drive of today's racing sailors.

One hundred highly skilled racing specialists are on the water now for every one that was around in the 1930s, so the state of the art has had unending pressure, particularly from inquiring minds unhampered by tradition. What we accept aesthetically today we would have questioned 50 years ago, for the sailor is basically conservative. Cruising experience and the measurement rules, like laws, only slowly influence a change in the form of things. Some changes are for the better, some are freakish features to win races under a particular rule, but all are of interest when propped up on the pinpoint of observation over time. Whether racer or cruiser, we're constantly getting an input of data to widen our knowledge.

Which brings me to *Bolero* and the Fast Passage 39. *Bolero* was developed from the smaller double-ended sloop called *Kayak*, built for George Wiley in the early 1950s by Martin Monson. The photo will give an idea of her form. Jimmy Hillman, an old boatbuilder friend, built *Bolero* just inside the Ballard Locks in the early 1960s for use as a sailing home. The newer Fast Passage 39, while about the same length as *Bolero*, is a theme development but of a different form, Fast Passage being a much greater change in shape than *Kayak* to *Bolero*.

Bolero

LOA:	40' 0"
LWL.	33' 0"
Breadth:	10' 6"
Draft:	5' 4"
Displacement:	26,400 lbs.
Lead ballast:	
Outside	8,150 lbs.
Inside	1,500 lbs.
Power:	
Chrysler Ace	70 h.p. @
	2,000 r.p.m.
	2:1 reduction
Sail Area:	
Main	390 sq. ft.
Foretriangle	356 sq. ft.

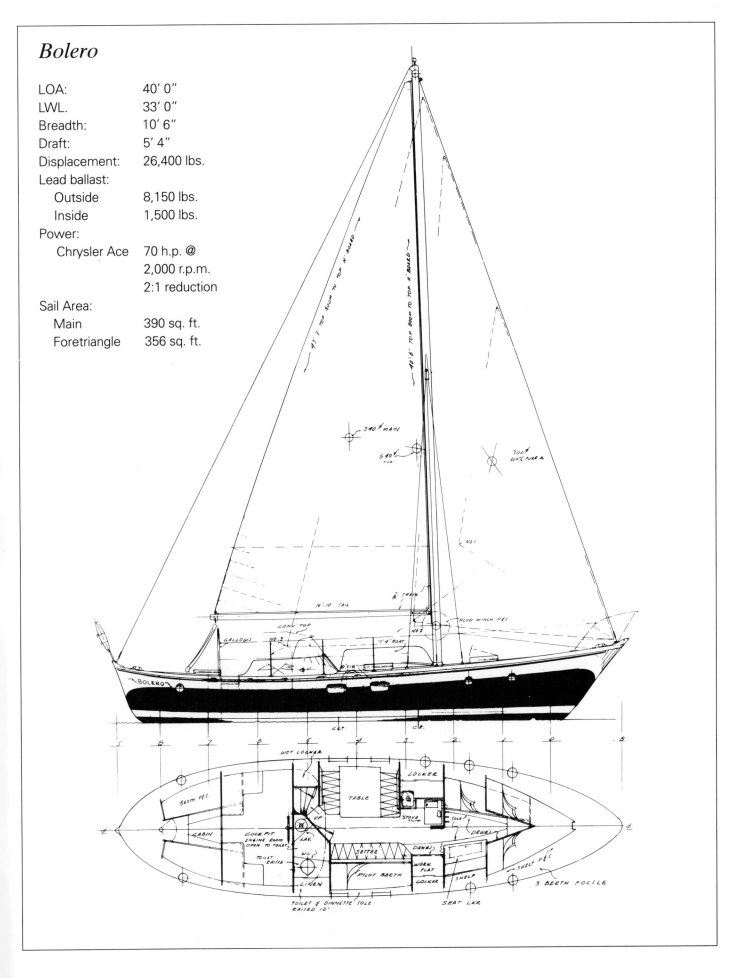

First let's look at *Bolero*, an ancestor of the Fast Passage 39 design. While not the most practical live-aboard, *Bolero* has always been a favorite, and she always seemed to have a nice shipshape look to her.

A flush deck is appealing, which in *Bolero*'s size puts the cabin sole well down in the hull, where width becomes a problem. For that reason, the seating area in *Bolero*'s dinette is raised to give seated visibility out of the hull windows. This in turn allows greater foot space higher up in the hull.

An aft cabin is a blessing for a live-aboard or for extended cruising. In *Bolero* the aft cabin can serve as a spot to put a snorer, or may be used as stowage space for all the items that accumulate over the years. If the aft cabin is used for sleeping, it gives *Bolero* two private cabins, with an admittedly rudimentary head in between.

Afloat, there is a nice jaunty air about her. The photo gives an impression of deck space, and of a deep cockpit that affords real shelter for a couple of tars standing at ease. A chain bin is fitted aft of the windlass, with a Babbit-model anchor in the roller chock forward. A small boat can be carried alongside the deck-stepped mast. The stern photo was taken when *Bolero* was new. She has since been shorn of Jim's aft-cabin booby hatch.

The perspective will give an idea of her hull form. She has a nice shapely underbody, easily driven, and comfortable in a seaway. The cost of her appealing stern lantern is made up somewhat by the ample and raking jack staff.

Framing is of bent oak, 1-7/16" x 1-3/4" on 10" centers. Planking is 1-3/8" red cedar, with the backbone and balance of the structure from Alaska yellow cedar. Decks are double 1/2" plywood glued together, with 2-3/4" moulded deck framing. Bilge stringers are 1-5/8" x 2-5/8", four per side, plus a clamp of 1-5/8" x 4-1/2".

Opposite, Kayak *running along at hull speed. Above,* Bolero's *flush deck is an appealing feature. The photo of* Bolero *from astern and the perspective drawing show her easily-driven hull form .*

Fast Passage 39

LOA:	39' 6"
LWL:	33' 6"
Breadth:	11' 2"
Draft:	5' 6"
Displacement:	22,000 lbs.
Ballast:	7,500 lbs.
Sail area:	
Main	356 sq. ft.
Staysail	227 sq. ft.
Yankee	379 sq. ft.

The Fast Passage 39, while about the same length as *Bolero*, is a theme development but of different form.

Denny Coverdale of Philbrook's Shipyards was the push behind the Fast Passage building project. The sloop *Bolero* and the Coverdale's 41' Taiwan ketch *Pacific Jade* cruised together for part of the 1975 summer holidays, and the double-ended *Bolero* caught Denny's fancy. During the fall of '75 Denny requested plans for an updated production version to build as a stock boat.

A review of *Bolero*'s plans resulted in a number of changes for the new boat. *Bolero*'s narrow sole ruled out a maximum utilization of room below in a boat of this length, so the sole was raised and a trunk added for light and ventilation. In hull form, the deadrise was reduced to the minimum required for non-pounding when powering into a head sea, the forefoot was cut away to reduce wetted surface, and the breadth was increased for initial stability and for sail-carrying power with proportionally less ballast and displacement. The lines faired in aft, somewhat like our old *Oceanus*, but with the form of the run terminating in a canoe-like bustle which faired into the rudder's skeg.

The accommodations of the two, you will notice, are equally far apart. With the Fast Passage 39 we simply started forward with a good two-berth coastal cabin, then we added lockers, a sit-around saloon, and a galley. With that done we moved aft and sketched the cockpit size we needed. Between these two developed ends was space for a stateroom, or, as an option, a sunken deckhouse. To starboard in the stateroom version a head and chart table plus a passage berth

or storage area would fit in. The aft stateroom layout as shown is a good place for privacy. With insulation and big vents, the engine adjacent to the stateroom seems to be a minor discomfort. The engine's weight is in the right place to match the hull's easy run, and it's tucked under the bureau and sink, with easy access panels all around. With the deckhouse option, the motor space is exceptional.

In profile, the Fast Passage 39 looks like a distant relative of *Bolero*, with the slightly hollow-profile canoe stern and raking bow. The sheer sweep is close, but from there on the development has been a departure, and, I think, a vast improvement in the use of a somewhat greater pile of material to encompass an interesting space.

For a study of form I've shown the lines of the Fast Passage 39 and perspective studies of the first two boats: *Kayak*, which Martin Monson built for George Wiley in the 1940s, Jim Hillman's *Bolero* built in the 1960s, and Denny Coverdale's Fast Passage 39 in the 1970s. You'll note that they along with *Kayak* are shallow-keel boats planned as handy cruising yachts, without the limiting factor of excessively deep draft. Many versions of each have been built over the years, and they have proven to be good performers.

About 40 Fast Passage 39s were built as a stock model in fiberglass, first by Philbrook's in Sidney, B.C., then by Tollycraft in Kelso, Washington. Tollycraft built Francis Stokes' *Mooneshine*, which Stokes sailed in the 1982 B.O.C. single-handed around-the-world race. A quote from a letter that Francis wrote about *Mooneshine*'s performance will be of interest, since it comes from a man of real seagoing experience:

"My best day's run doesn't compare with the larger boats. Mine was 190 miles on two occasions, once in the Indian Ocean and once coming home in the northeast trades. Both times there was some assist from ocean currents. Worst day's run was 25 miles, also with assist from current. No records here. I found that I did best relative to the larger boats in the lighter going. I could consistently keep up with boats like *Gypsy Moth V*, and she didn't pass me until well south of the equator on the first leg Newport to Capetown. I am sure that the 39 is very effective

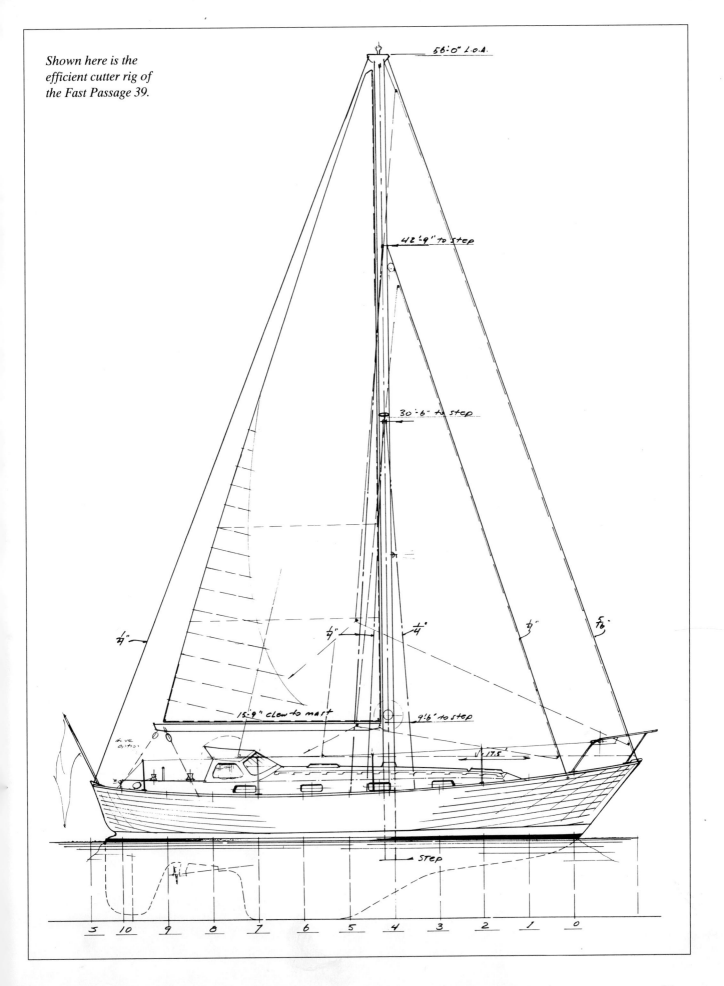

Shown here is the efficient cutter rig of the Fast Passage 39.

56'0" L.O.A.

42'9" to step

30'6" to step

15'9" clew to mast

9'6" to step

17.5

STEP

5 10   9   8   7   6   5   4   3   2   1   0

27

SAILBOATS

Francis Stokes and Mooneshine *at the start of the 1982 B.O.C. single-handed, around-the-world race. Stokes finished second in Class II, less than 36 hours behind Japanese single-hander Yukoh Tada, and rescued fellow competitor Tony Lush from his foundering boat in the Indian Ocean.*

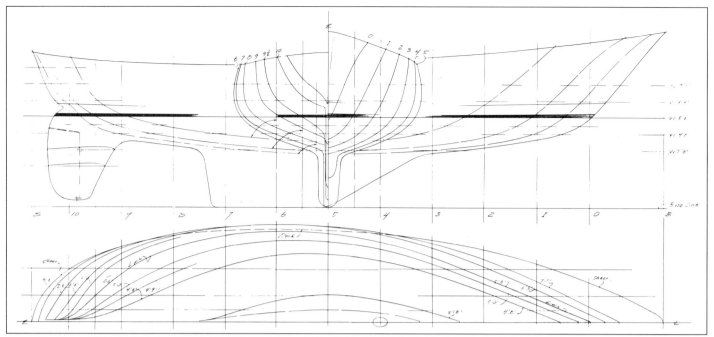

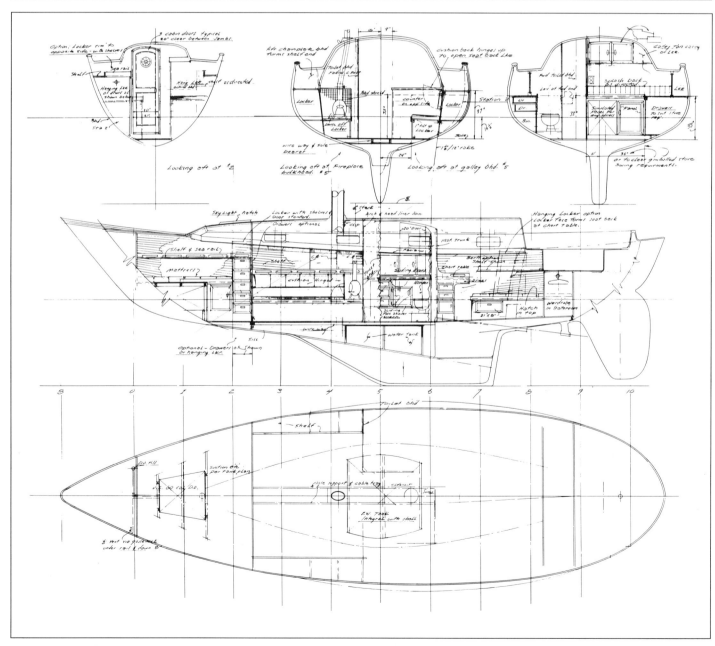

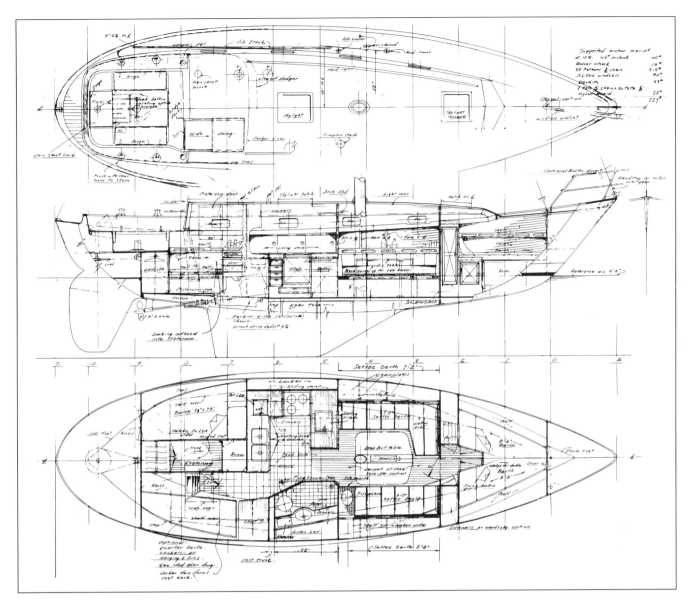

in the light going despite its being a true cruising design. My largest sail was a 140% genoa (besides spinnaker), and all sails were 1 oz. heavier than usual practice, e.g. the mainsail and staysail were 9 oz. dacron.

"The 5'6" draft seems to work well downwind in those more anxious times. I believe that I was knocked around less severely than most of the larger boats for a couple of reasons, besides luck. Moderate draft allows a boat to slew sideways if caught wrong by a wave instead of tripping. The other factor is the directional stability and quick response to the rudder to keep her square to steep waves coming up astern. I used an Aries vane which could spin the wheel over quite quickly when knocked off course. When that was broken the Alpha autopilot handled it quite well. That big rudder well aft worked well. The boat seemed directionally stable when surfing. There

was never any thought of towing anything to maintain control or slow her down.

"I couldn't go upwind in heavy air with the bigger boats. She makes a lot of leeway if the angle of heel is much greater than 20 degrees. For this reason I used small headsails going to weather, often using a 135 sq. ft. storm jib and the staysail with double-reefed main. She likes two small headsails working together. In sailing alongside a Valiant 40 I would tend to shorten down quicker but always went just as fast. I don't believe there is a better all-around sea boat than your 39. It's a happy combination of hull lines, beam, displacement, and all those other things that go into a boat."

The photos and drawings on these pages will outline *Bolero* and the Fast Passage 39, each quite different, but with an umbilical cord to others done a long time ago.

6

A 27' W. L. Schooner

LO Deck:	36' 0"
LWL:	27' 0"
Breadth:	9' 5"
Draft:	5' 7"
Sail Area:	753 sq. ft.
Ballast:	5,200 lbs.
Displacement:	14,300 lbs.

A little ship of this sort is a nice size either for day sailing or for extended voyaging. The schooner shown is based in Victoria, B.C., and was built as a backyard project to highly professional standards by her owner Byron Burns. The same boat, but with the cutter rig, was built in Finland and is based in Finnish waters. They are excellent boats under sail and handsome afloat.

The model is easy-lined, with a shallow rabbet depth, plus a high-efficiency lead fin keel for lateral plane and stability. The hull form also allows the engine to be placed well aft, clear of the accommodations, an appealing feature in a small cruiser.

Below decks the cabin plan is straightforward and practical, with a pleasant saloon, head and stateroom forward, and galley aft to starboard. A chart table with seat and a roomy quarterberth fill in the after port quarter area.

On deck is the security of a 6" bulwark, and lots of deck space gives her a good feel. A cock-

pit hood can also be fitted over the companionway, giving shelter for the roomy cockpit area.

Construction is of strip-planked cedar, with 1-1/4" bent-oak frames fitted after planking is completed and the hull interior sanded out. Decks are plywood, encapsulated with fiberglass from rail to rail, ensuring watertight integrity. Heavy hardwood floor timbers are fitted to transmit the keel's wringing strains to the hull. The structure is further supplemented with a galvanized steel channel that connects the floors to the mast partners above. A study of the construction plan will clarify some of the construction features employed.

Often, these backyard projects end up remarkably well. In Byron's case the workmanship is excellent, and seems worth all the late hours and costs involved. A nicely finished little schooner like this also makes one realize how many skilled workers there are who have opted for the professions rather than the shops. Byron Burns is a schoolteacher.

A family cruise up the northern Gulf of Georgia involves a swim call in an afternoon anchorage and an evening sail in light air.

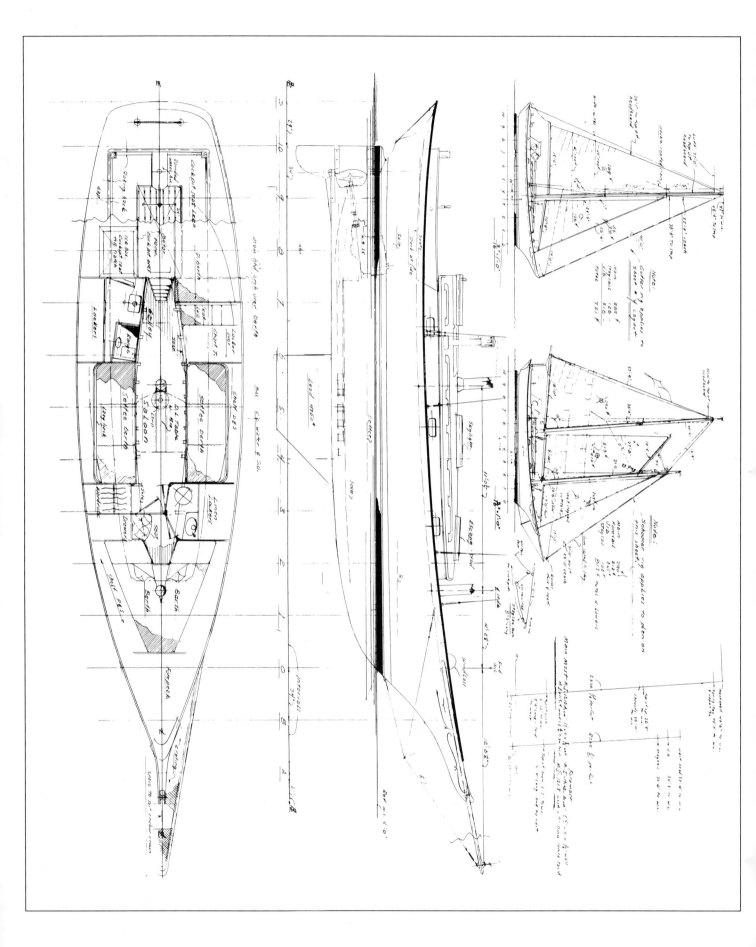

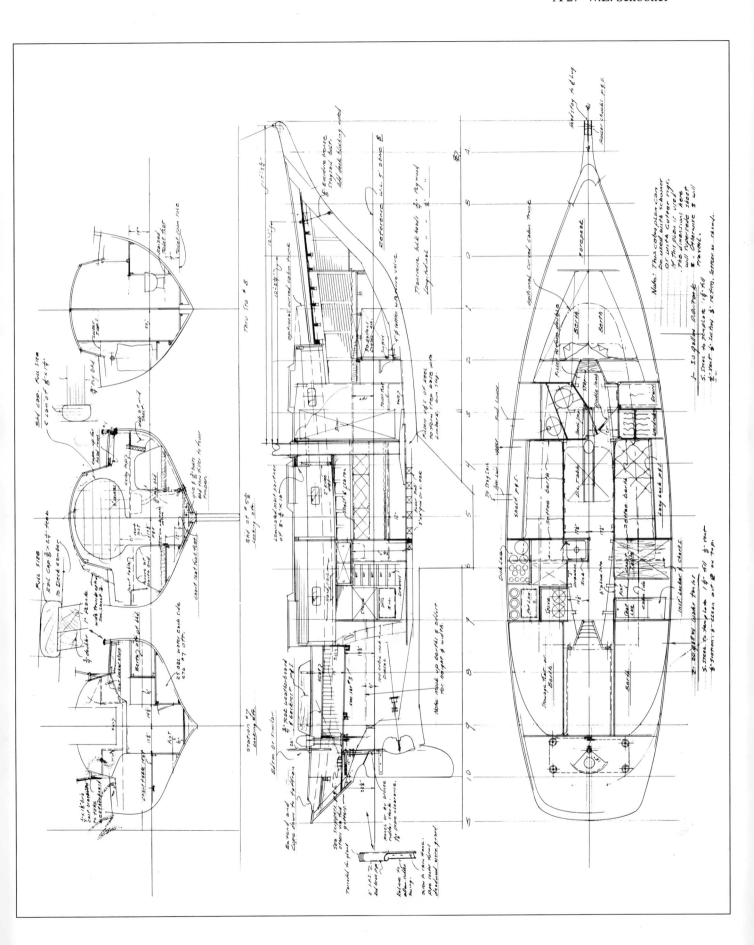

7

Commodore Trunion Class Dinghy

LOA: 14' 0"
Breadth: 6' 0"
Sail Area: 128 sq. ft.

These two studies for the Commodore Trunion class of sailing dinghies were done for Garrett Horder, who many will fondly remember as the skipper of *Mist of Lemolo*, the little twin-centerboard cat ketch in which he cruised both east and west coasts. Garry was a wonderfully warm-hearted mariner who made a host of friends wherever he dropped anchor.

Garry chose to have the prams built as the more practical of the two designs, for use as safe day-sailer trainers for kids. Room was needed for three small chaps and an instructor. Good stability, fair performance under sail, plus a little vessel of interesting appearance were specified, along with sufficient

buoyancy to float the crew if swamped. These features worked out very well, but we missed by a mile our nod toward reasonable cost of building, this due to the amount of detail work involved in these one-off wooden boats. If tooled up and built of fiberglass they would be a reasonable value.

Paul Gartside, a local boatbuilder and naval architect, built the first three as a fill-in, shortly after his arrival here from England and prior to re-establishing his naval-architecture practice. For the first three in wood and later a fourth in fiberglass, the multi-chine hull rather than the round-bilge model was chosen. The photos give an idea of the appearance of the boats afloat, nice shipshape lit-

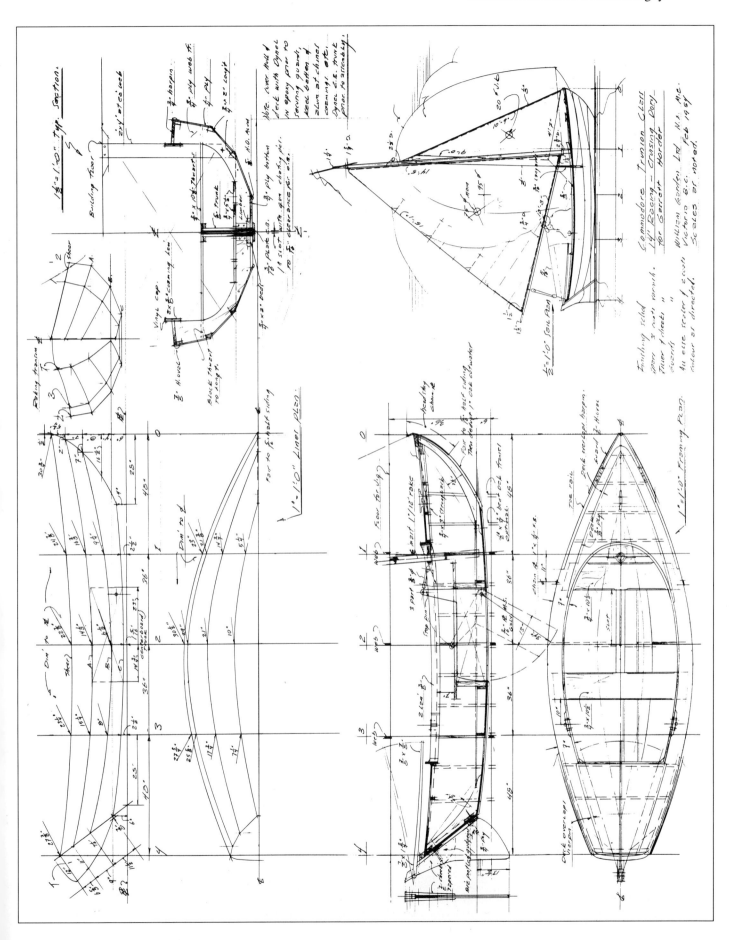

The roomy cockpit of the Commodore Trunion Class 14' x 6' sailing pram can accomodate half a dozen kids.

tle fellows with the warmth and charm — and the upkeep — of a wooden boat. *Red Rooster* is pictured. Numbers 2 & 3 were of different colors; their names have slipped my mind.

The round-bilge model would be my choice to build or own, but cost was important and Paul felt that he could build these first few in less time with the double-chine hulls. The difference in time between the two methods probably isn't that much when one considers that the actual hull shell, even in a dinghy, is a fairly minor element in the total effort required in building and outfitting.

Both the dory and the pram have about the same centerboard arrangement, and both are built on plywood web frames, the dory being skinned with 1/4" plywood. The pram, if round-bilged, is planked with 7/16" red cedar strips, edge-fastened and glued. As an alternate approach it could be cold-moulded. Dynel covering is fitted in either case.

The sponson on the pram is a round foam extrusion that Ruthie of Hill Sails sewed up in a canvas boot and laced to the gunwale. It is a great buffer for occasional training collisions, and a good way to supplement both buoyancy when swamped and ultimate stability under sail.

The gunter sloop rig allows a short mast to prevent capsizing at a mooring in heavy weather, but admittedly the long gaff or sprit is a complication. Spars are of varnished wood, Hill Sails did a nice job on the sails and canvas work, and Paul Gartside put it all together in his usual thoroughly shipshape manner.

A good powerful sailing dinghy such as this always seems to me to be a great way to explore a new harbor or a strange bit of coastline. It has room enough for two, with a hamper for sandwiches and a bottle or so, along with moderate draft, a good rig, and enough weight to feel right underfoot.

I trust that Garry has a good sailing dinghy in heaven. He's a long way over the horizon now, a real friend who is particularly missed, especially when a tanbark sail shows up across the bay, coming down toward the island before a fresh spring southeaster.

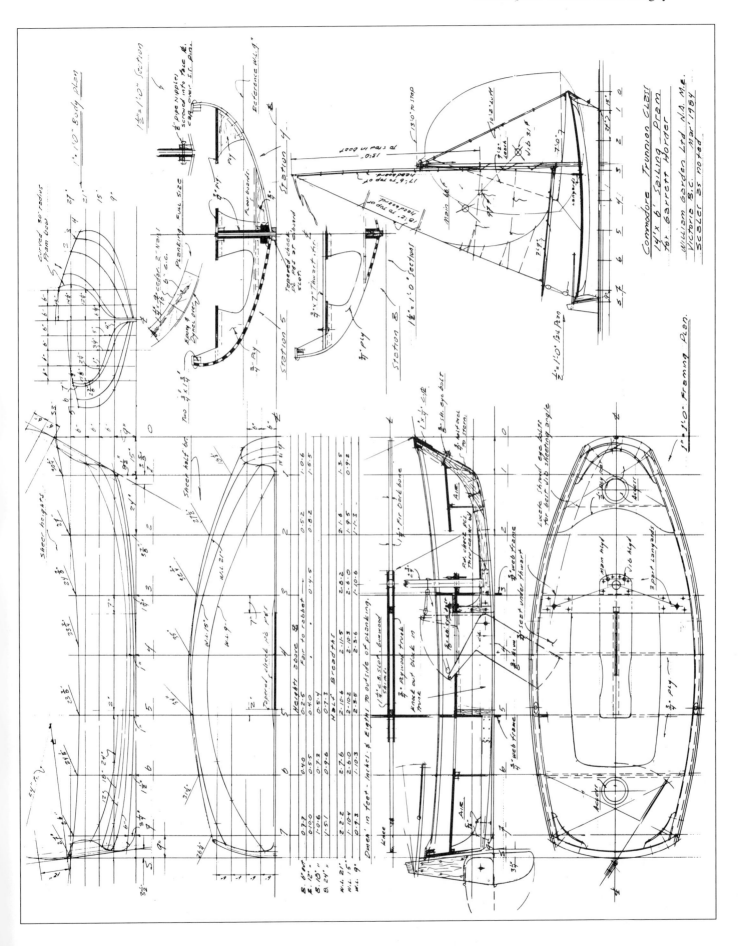

8

A Canoe Ketch

LOA:	24'6"
LWL:	18'4"
Breadth:	8'0"
Draft:	12" & 5'5"
Sail Area:	237 sq. ft.
Displacement:	2,114 lbs.

The chineboat development illustrated here was originally designed with a transom stern for a friend of many years. I almost said "an old friend," but it sounds wrong. One of the good things about old friends is that they still look 25 to each other.

Anyway, this friend, Bimbo Silchenstedt (a lot of my chums seem to have names like Bimbo, Blackie, Sharkeyes, Last Gasp, Moonface, or Snake), at one time built all sorts of boats on the Gulf Coast, but they were work boats, big serious things, not these toy boats that are so interesting. Every so often, Bimbo and I have teamed up on something, and a while back as a change of pace he wanted a little day sailer to put together as a family project. It was to be a powerful, or more specifically, a very stable boat, with a short, low rig — a boat to use around Rockport, Texas, where it seems to blow your hat off almost every day of the year. I've been told, for example, that

due to the headwind, jet aircraft there can land at 10 m.p.h.

There may be some exaggeration in that last statement, but the boat had to be a good sail carrier. So this hull was designed to stand up and go, with three members of the Rockport Happy Hour Club on the rail in about 20 knots of wind — a lot of force when the sheets are hardened in and she's close-hauled.

A wide afterbody was chosen for waterplane area and stability, with final lines a compromise on paper between Bimbo's oil-rig mud-boat buttock lines and the more delicate transom termination that I had in mind. He gracefully acquiesced at plan time, but from photos of the boat completed I see that he fudged some on the mud-boat side. Anyway, the reports were most enthusiastic, and she's supposed to balance nicely and go very well.

Some time later another fellow needed a trailerable family day boat for kids and grandkids to

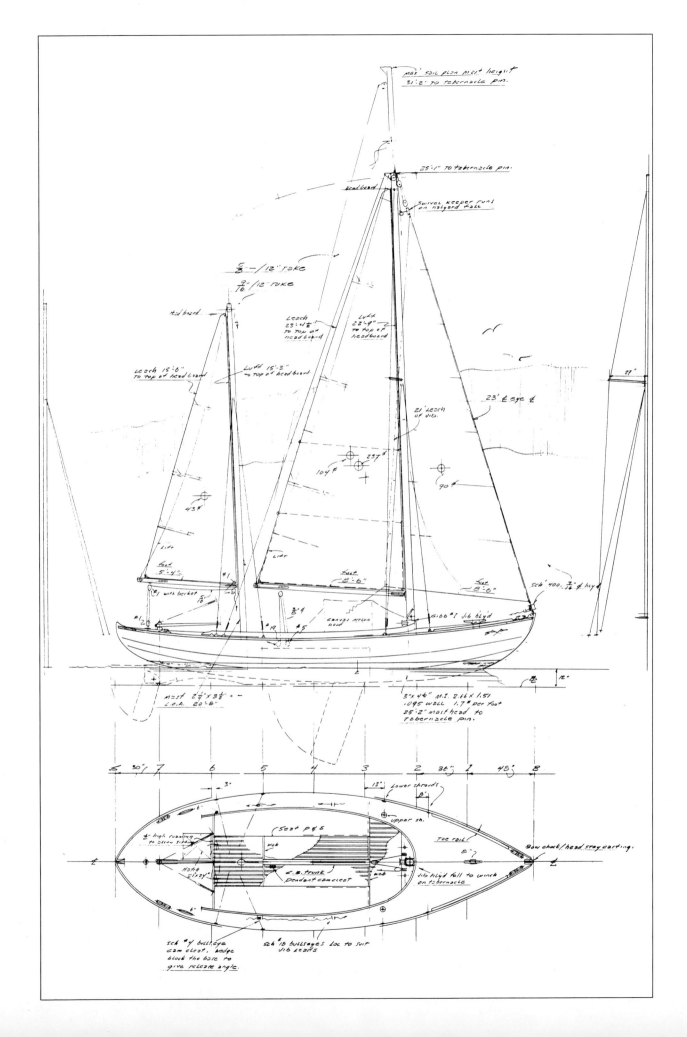

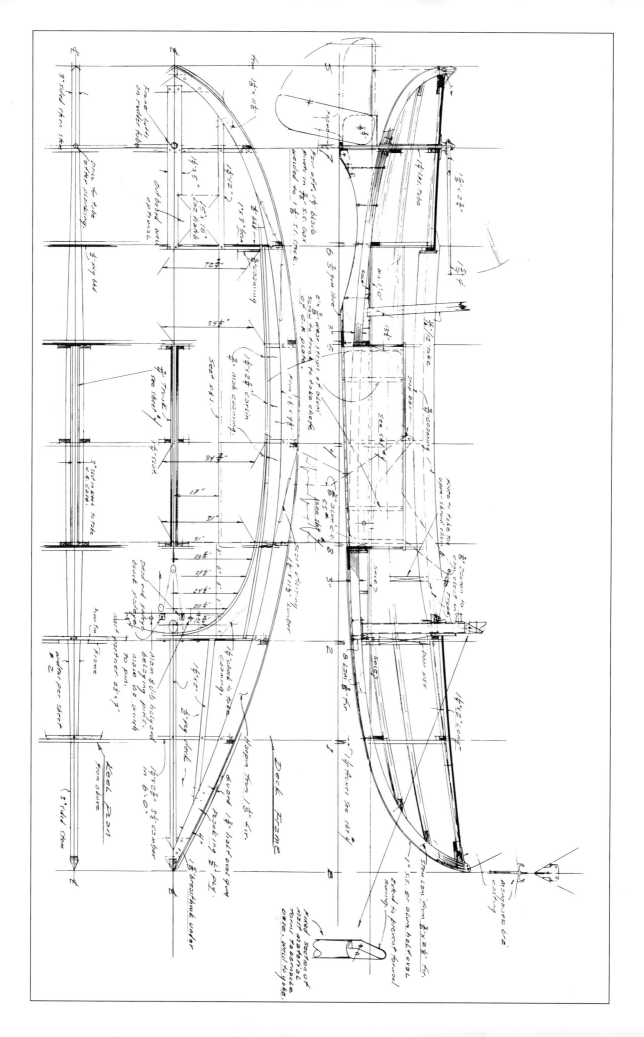

use along some great sandy beaches and interesting shoal inlets. In thinking about what would be best, I came across Bimbo's ketch in the files. A canoe stern was drawn as the proper termination of lines, and in essence we had a big, powerful sort of Swampscott-dory/canoe-yawl form.

Another chap who has the decent Christian name of John, and who lives in England, built one in his shed, which brings us up-to-date on background.

The boat is built on frames sawn to shape from 7/8" lumber, with butts secured by 1/4" plywood gussets and glued with urea or epoxy glue. The frame pieces can be sawn out without bothering with bevels, and then beveled off constant to the stringers after being set up at the indicated intervals on the simple jig. Lines are to the outside of planking, so the planking thickness deduction must be made prior to sawing out the frames.

With the frames and centerboard case erected, and with the stem and sternposts propped up at each end, the keel members are then sprung over as laminates and secured. Note that the centerboard trunk forms part of the backbone, so with the keel, stems and frames set up, the next step is to fit the chine strips. Next, bevel off the frames to take the planking. There is quite a twist to the lower panel forward and the mid-panel aft, so solid-core ply must be used.

The bottom planking is fitted first. The edges are dressed off and then the bilge plank goes on. Then the topsides are fitted. Upon completion of the shell she's ready for covering from sheer to sheer with a coat of Dynel and epoxy to seal the hull's exterior. Dynel is light and nice to work with for a good sealing membrane. The smoothing up is done with a hook scraper to fair off lumps, followed by rough sanding and glazing before painting.

Next comes the fitting of the stem and stern cutwaters and the keel grounding shoe. Stem and stern cutwaters are of 3/4" aluminum half-oval set in bedding compound. The keel shoe should be hardwood to take the ground and protect the hull. The shoe is also set in bedding compound and screwed on over the Dynel, then bullnosed at the edges and faired into the end pieces.

With the bottom work completed she's ready to turn over, a good job for about 12 friends plus a couple of mattresses to take any jolts. Block her up at good working height and proceed with the decks and finish, the deck covering being similar to the hull's epoxy/Dynel treatment.

For deck arrangement the simple cruising or day-sailing layout might be the most practical. Above all, don't try to put a large cabin on her. This is a low-freeboard boat with a correspondingly low center of gravity — a camping cruiser — so don't ruin her with a big deckhouse. A canvas cuddy cabin with sitting headroom as shown would be ideal. The same model but with another 10" of freeboard added, plus an old Star-boat keel for stability, could result in a greater depth and more cabin space. With the shallow trailerable configuration shown, however, a very minimal shelter house is the best choice.

Finish work can be the downfall of a home project. Little details of trim, proportions, and fairness will make all the difference in final appearance. I've noted the various guardrail, toe rail, coaming, and other sizes, which should be adhered to for a proper finished appearance.

Paintwork could be a soft gray, with white bootstripe, a red anti-fouling bottom if left afloat, and perhaps a lighter warm-gray deck, set off with varnished guards and trim.

Masts and booms can be built as simple box sections, or, if you're in the Northwest with access to small trees, they can be made from fir or red cedar saplings, similar to trolling poles. However, lighter-weight aluminum spars will be a blessing in upkeep, and will look very good onboard. Aluminum spars, in fact, would be my choice, purchased as a "deck-up" package from an aluminum mast builder. To lower the masts, a simple tabernacle can be fitted on the mainmast, while the mizzen can easily be lifted out of its step and stored onboard. The rig shown is short, and best for an area with lots of wind. For a light-weather area, a longer mizzen boom and a short bowsprit should be fitted — or the longer mainmast as sketched with full-length battens and lots of roach.

These little ships give such a lot for the investment of time and money that I often wonder about the big ones. A big yacht might be about 300 times the weight and a thousand times the price of the little canoe ketch, yet it's about the same value in pleasure and interest. I guess it all depends on your outlook and pocketbook.

9

A 106' Brigantine

LOA:	106'
LWL:	90'
Breadth:	25'
Draft:	12'
Sail Area:	
Fore & aft rig	3,838 sq. ft.
Square rig	2,250 sq. ft.
Total	6,088 sq. ft.

In the dreams of each of us is a painting or a property or a ship that was abandoned with regrets. Of the hundreds of preliminaries in the files, for me this little brigantine perhaps best qualifies. The browser should find her an ideal way to spend a few minutes of study. Unfortunately, the drawings are large, and when reduced to book size the lettering becomes illegible. But the general arrangement of rig and layout can still be followed.

The rig in particular will be of interest to the purist. Leads, etc. can be followed with a magnifying glass. You will notice that all the bunt lines, clew lines, braces, sheets, etc. lead to pinrails port and starboard, running through the well-deck area. I suppose I went up and down the masts mentally a couple of hundred times to get the leads in order, to avoid chafe and allow clear running.

This boat was designed in the 1950s, prior to today's proliferation of square-rigged school ships. At that time, despite the upgrading of gear,

it was decided that we were 30 years too late to get the people to man her. Today I suppose that reasonably competent people would stand in line for the privilege.

On completion of the drawings, the owner sent them off to Harold Underhill, then the world's authority on square rigs. Underhill's analysis of the rig was of great interest, particularly so since the owner had complained of so much time having been spent on the plans. From Underhill's letter:

"Of the rig in general, I think it is the most beautiful example of the brigantine rig I have seen in modern times, and I fail to see how it would be possible to improve on it. In detail, well I belong to the age of the fidded topmast and hoisting yards, and for me such arrangements will always have an appeal not to be found in the pole masts, but from the practical standpoint there is no doubt but that the rig shown on the drawing is by far the best and I doubt whether, even if the ship were being built for my own use,

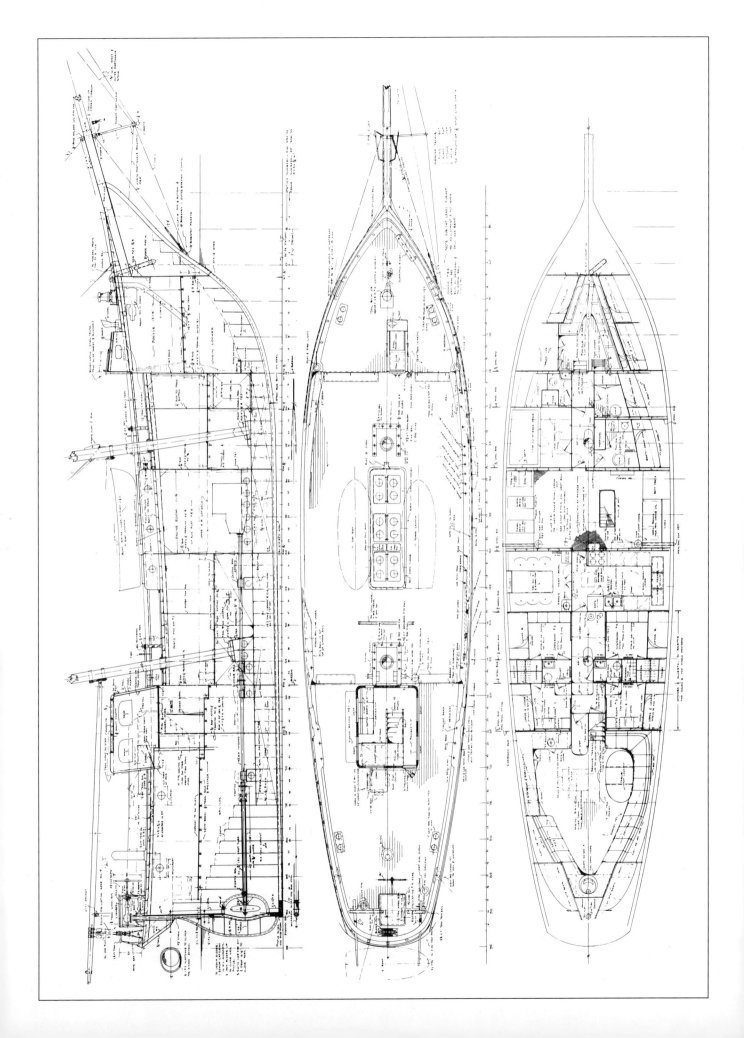

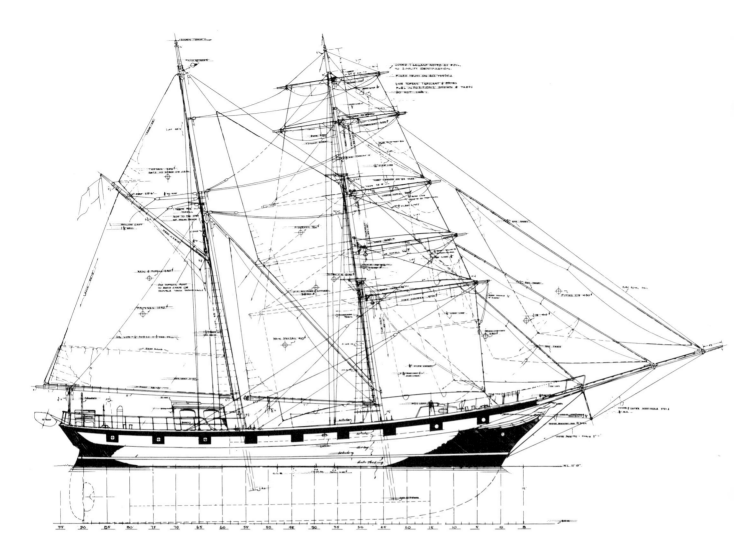

I would ask for any alteration from that shown. I am in fact amazed at how well the older tradition has been blended with modern ideas and fittings.

"This little ship is a true brigantine, and far ahead of many such yachts produced at the turn of the century, when one would have expected to find the true square-rigger much more pronounced.

"To sum up. The rig is one which more than pleases even an old-stager like myself and I am amazed that the true brigantine should have been followed so faithfully in these modern times, yet rigged in detail with an eye to saving both labour and gear. In fact a perfect blend of the two periods.

"One point, not concerned with the design, interests me. Will you be able to find a crew willing to work aloft and out on that long bowsprit?"

As to layout, she would be impractical by today's standards. Larger staterooms would be fitted, an unmanned engine room, and much loosening up throughout. As is, she's more of a miniature ship. Clear out the midships area for a hold, and a hundred years ago we probably could have made a living with her.

The layout as designed has a raised fo'c'sle head, then the long well deck amidships, and a raised poop from abaft the mainmast to the stern. A sunken deckhouse is arranged on the poop, and the steering gear aft is set up in a wheel box in the traditional manner. Going through the deckhouse, we find a chart table to port aft, and a settee, instrument racks, wet gear hooks, etc. A stairway leads down to a saloon of tremendous area, with fireplace, settees, drop-leaf gimballed table, sideboard, bookshelf, bar, etc. Directly below the saloon is a large hatch, and you will notice in the inboard profile an

A fore-and-aft view of the rig showing the pole masts and sails furled to quarters on the fixed yards.

extremely roomy sail locker under the sole.

Forward of the main saloon are four staterooms — two doubles and two singles, each with adjoining toilets. Amidships to port is the crew's mess; to starboard is the galley, with electric range, refrigeration, stainless-steel counters, and a 35-cubic-foot deep freeze. The hatch in the sole opens up for additional galley stowage.

The door from the galley passage opens up onto a grating in the engine room, the engine room being deep enough that a grating covers the entire main engine, with canvas runners underfoot to mark the walkways. A railed stairway to starboard leads down alongside the upper engine room into the lower engine room, which has full headroom and contains the main engine, pumps, and components. The upper engine room has a work bench, battery trays, diesel generators and compressors, etc.

Moving forward, on the port side is a roomy area for additional galley stores and a walk-in freezer compartment. (As an alternative arrangement, it was planned to fit the regular mess into another double stateroom for the owner's party, and to move the crew's mess into this area.)

To starboard of the foremast is the captain's stateroom, the cook directly forward of this, a toilet room to port, and a six-man fo'c'sle to supplement the owner's sailing party. Oiled teak joinerwork was specified throughout below, and fixtures were keyed to the 1870s era.

Construction is of steel on transverse framing, with steel deckhouse and booby hatches. A motor launch and a whale boat were to be stowed on skids over the engine room fidley, plus the boat on davits aft.

You will note that the vessel has sufficient area in her fore-and-aft sails to give her fair short-handed operation on the wind, especially when supplemented by the main engine. The square rig consists of the course, upper and lower topsails, topgallant, and royal. The sailplan shows the square sails furled to quarters. The yards are all on fixed cranes, and you will also note the pole masts in lieu of the usual fiddled topmasts and doublers, as mentioned earlier.

The inboard profile and deck frame plan shows the general structural members, tank tops, etc. Fuel capacity is 9,600 gallons, and water capacity 3,000 gallons. Under power alone she can make any normal passage; under sail and power her range is unlimited.

Her replacement was the purchase of the motorsailer *Nereus* from my friend Clarence Postley. *Nereus* was an 85-footer, illustrated in the first volume of *Yacht Designs*. Not as interesting a rig, but a more practical boat for the contemplated world cruise.

Two Small Brigantines

LOA (hull):	75'0"
LWL:	67'6
Breadth:	19'9"
Draft:	8'4"
Displacement:	102 tons
Ballast:	24 tons
Power:	250 b.h.p.
Reduction:	2:1
Sail Area:	4525 sq. ft.
Fore & aft portion:	2,845 sq. ft.

Here is something on a couple of little brigantines, somewhat similar in proportions, although much reduced in size, to the small British naval-training brigs of the 1880s. A lot of boat for the length — heavily built, great fuel and water capacity and fair space below decks. Two of these were built at the Ingalls Shipyards in Taiwan in the mid-1950s when H.P. McLaughlin was involved in the yard. One was built for his own use and the second for Laris Craig.

I had long since lost track of the boats when, in a conversation with Krist Martinsen, the Orcas Island boatbuilder, mention was made of a friend of his who he thought had owned a square-rigger that I had designed.

Sure enough the friend proved to be Laris Craig, the owner of *Laura*, brigantine number two, who mentioned he still had a photo of her underway, unfortunately too dim to reproduce here, all else having been lost when she was wrecked outside Hong Kong harbour during a typhoon. By a second coincidence, I last saw Craig's boat moored to a navy sea buoy with about 200 feet of chain, stripped down in preparation for a rising typhoon. A vivid picture comes to mind of the little old-timer, drenched in driving rain and spray, riding to the big mooring buoy, and all but the buoy and a freighter visible off in the murk destroyed the image of an 1860 typhoon seascape.

As we ran past, *Laura*'s name was indistinguishable through the spray. But about a cable length to windward on another buoy was the stern of a handsome motorship whose name I recall was *Tarn of Goteborg*. I must have had about the last look at *Laura* since Laris said she was run down, in the same typhoon, by a ship that was adrift. During the collision she broke loose and was carried off and lost on the rocks of an island outside the harbour entrance with the loss of one crew member. *Wan Fu*, ex Harry McLaughlin's *Mei Ling,* I'm told, nearly suffered the same fate but was lucky enough to have blown down on an area of sand, where she stuck and was salvaged.

The memory of the little brigantine showing up through the rain and spray, with the crests blowing off the top of the seas, comes easily to mind while today I seem to have trouble remembering what happened last week.

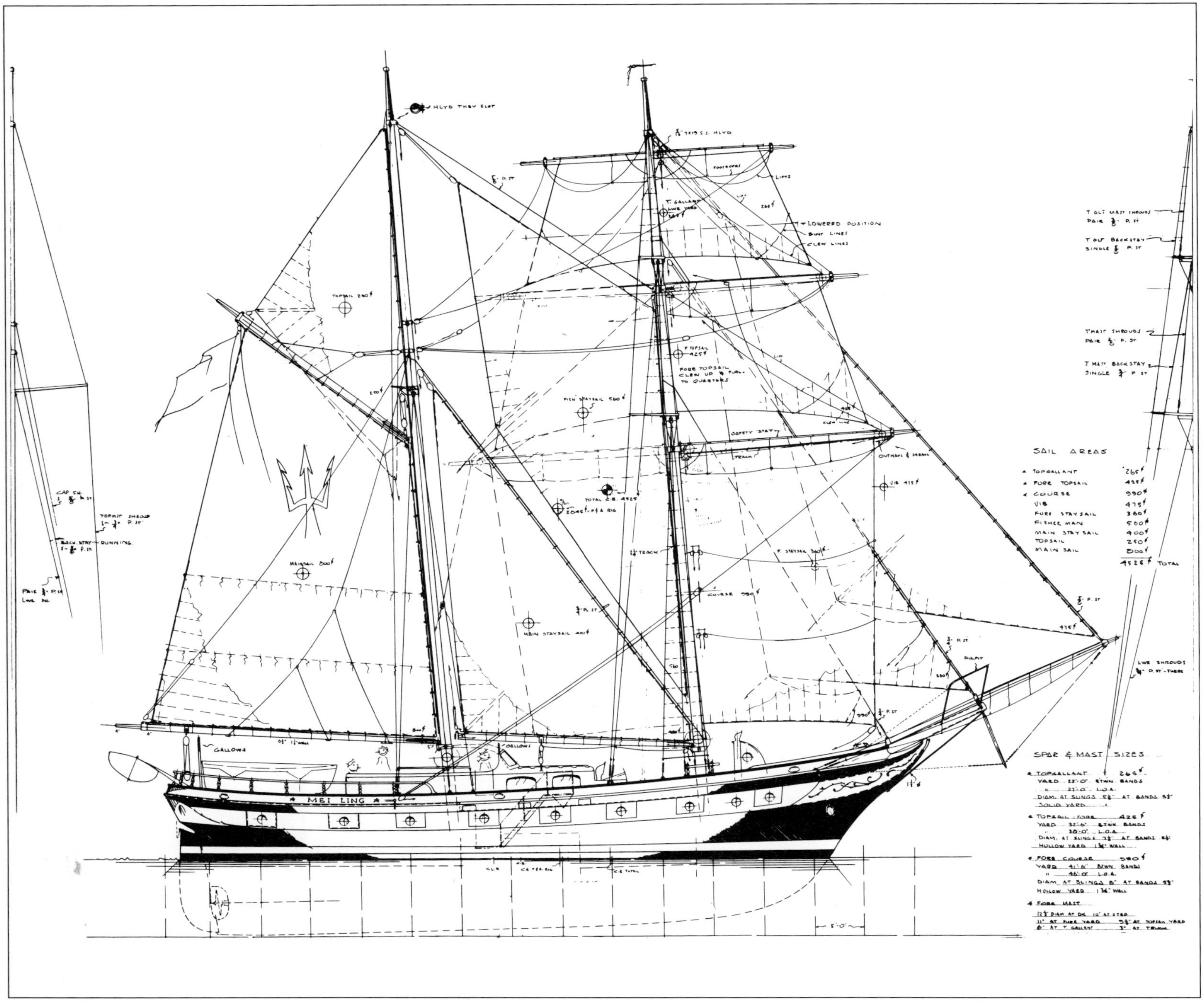

Both Mei Ling and Laura carried big rigs to match their burdensome hulls. A fair area in fore-and-afters gave reasonable performance on the wind.

SAIL AREAS

TOPGALLANT	266 f
FORE TOPSAIL	41 f
COURSE	590 f
JIB	415 f
FORE STAYSAIL	360 f
FISHERMAN	500 f
MAIN STAYSAIL	400 f
TOPSAIL	210 f
MAIN SAIL	800 f
TOTAL	**4118 f**

SPAR & MAST SIZES

Several layouts can be fitted within a hull of the proportions of these small brigantines.

10

A Shoal-Draft Cruising Ketch

LOA:	50' 10"
LWL:	40' 0"
Breadth:	14' 0"
Draft:	6' 2"
Displacement:	56,000 lbs.
Power:	350-cubic-inch diesel, 2:1 reduction gear
Speed:	7.6 knots cruising
Sail Area:	1,280 sq. ft.

China Clippers," some folks call them. We've had many of these types built — hundreds, actually — plus many bastardized versions we sometimes get blamed for. Some of them come from pirated moulds reworked from bankrupt builders' stock, with the Taiwan builders' quality varying from very bad to good.

Quality control has always been a problem with small boats built overseas. The value involved usually can't carry the cost of a number-one man to oversee the project, and the sort of man needed on the job usually is too well-employed at home to bother with overseas living.

The result is a wide range of quality. The best advice for a prospective buyer seems to be to buy through a reputable (read solvent) dealer who can outfit the boat on arrival, and who can handle warranty. On top of this, one must allow for an additional 20-percent contingency to cover the many additions required to make a complete yacht of it, and another 10-15 percent of the initial cost available annually for moorage, insurance, hauling, maintenance, and repair.

On the subject of quality, some sad calls have come in over the years. Some are due to a builder's inexperience, but some are due to sharp practice, cost saving, or lack of experienced supervision. Last month I got a call from a wobe-gone man whose boat had run aground. When they hauled her off she floated about a foot too high, like a boat without a keel.

At drydock it was found that loose ball mill scrap had been substituted for the ballast speci-

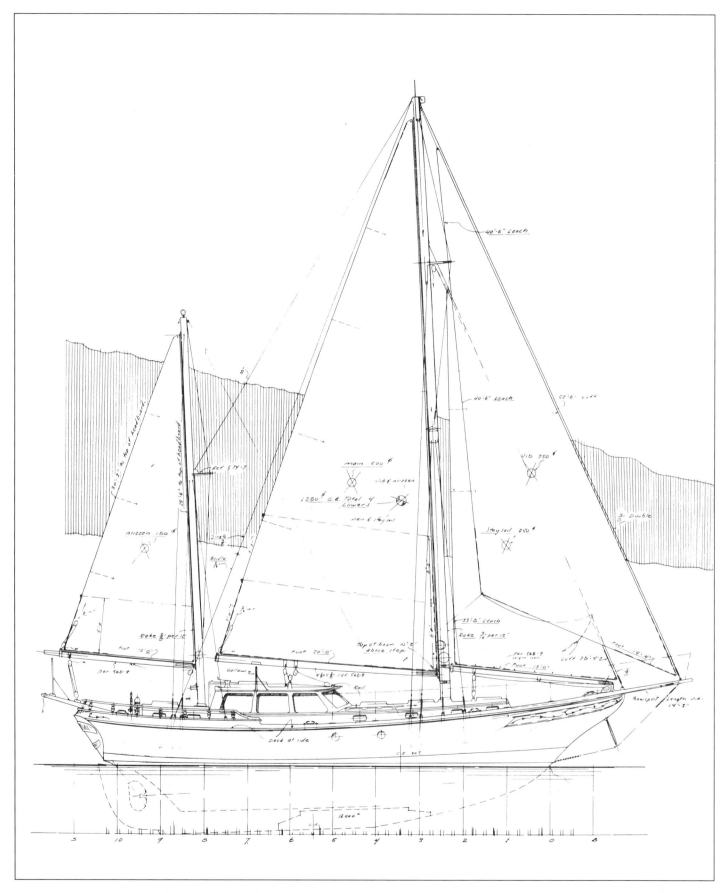

Several of the originals of this design were built of wood prior to the Taiwan fiberglass versions.

fied, which was five cast-iron moulded ballast blocks bedded in resin, then overlaid with fiberglass to form the bilge area. The loose ball mill scrap had fallen out when the encapsulating keel shell was ruptured. A few dollars saved by the builder, a major job to correct. In fact, the repair job affords some interesting speculation as to time and method.

So, shipmates, buy foreign with extreme caution, and through a reputable broker. Payment should be through a Letter of Credit, payable to the broker upon your acceptance of the boat, after she is completed to the contract requirements. A 100-percent L.C. takes all the "ifs" out of the transaction; the broker is assured of payment when delivery is made, and the L.C. can be used by the broker at his risk for bank financing to back up progress payments from broker to builder if required.

On major work in North America, we use performance bonds issued by a bonding company. Performance bonds assure the buyer that the work as contracted will be completed, in which case progress payments may be made with relative safety. To assure the safety of progress payments in Europe, we've used bank guarantees by both parties.

In all cases, either you will pay up front for a good lawyer to set up a workable building agreement, or you may pay the lawyer much more later to help unscramble a bad situation. Many of the hardest business heads seem to go through a softening process when involved in business around saltwater, so in all cases get some experienced professional help as protection for both sides of a transaction.

Finally we get to the ketch illustrated. She was originally designed in the late 1940s as a wooden boat capable of being built as a backyard project by a skilled amateur. This is about the upper size limit for such work, and not to be undertaken without ample funds and several years for the building. Unfortunately, divorce papers really should be part of the design package for home-built boats.

The original model of this ketch was somewhat shorter-ended, and carried a different layout. Over the years and through many boats the plans have been revised, until by the 1960s they ended up about as shown — a wooden ketch of strong seagoing construction, with a practical liveaboard or extended-cruising layout. Dozens of this model have been built in Taiwan under various trade names and with varying quality.

Looking at things above deck, for my own seagoing use the rig would have about four feet taken off the main boom, and the jib fitted with roller furling. I've noticed that in the interests of handling, many deep-sea cruisers come back from leisurely circumnavigations with reduced sail area. Headsails remain normal, but mainsails on sloops or cutters seem happiest with a fair reduction, and the boats go just about as well.

With our ketch, the best arrangement for short-handed sailing could be roller gear on all four sails, although the added complexity and cost is something to consider. In any case, the roller jib would be mandatory. With the jib rolled up, maybe a scrap of mizzen, the main deep-reefed, and a full staysail, she would be about as bullet-proof and snug as possible for going to windward in ultimate sailing conditions.

The big deckhouse will disturb the purist who dreams of lashing his backside to a ring bolt on the flush deck, but the house makes a great shelter from tropical sun or northern cold. You will notice the alternate inside steering for long runs under power. The major instruments are inside, dry and easily tended.

The decks are roomy, although nothing to compare with a flush-decker's great expanse. The trunk cabin permits admirable light and ventilation, however, and makes a handy seat for contemplating a happy voyage. On an overlong voyage it can be used while contemplating ways to do in the bastard on the helm. Above all, it allows a high cabin sole for ample width of accommodations.

The cockpit aft can be fitted with a canvas weather cloth or hood. The taffrail, with its strong, high stanchions, can carry a weather cloth around the poop. And some good seat backs can be fitted for comfort under sail.

Below decks the plan outlines a liveable arrangement. Today, in the 1990s, people seem set on double beds, which also can be fitted. The power plant is under the deckhouse sole, with ample access hatches. The lower saloon can be arranged as shown, or made up as another stateroom. A hull of this size has ample space for a

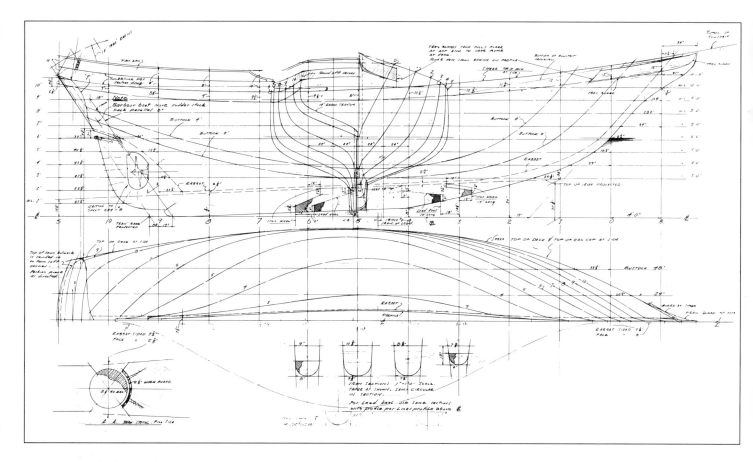

The lines indicate a powerful model with good initial stability. The wooden version with outside ballast is shown.

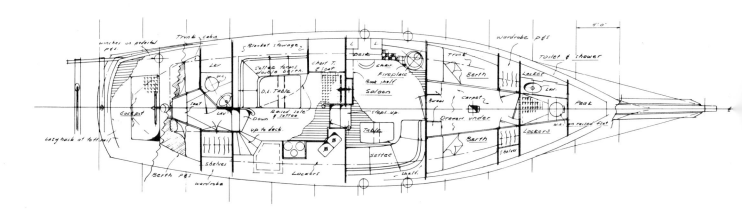

number of layouts, from midships cockpit to great cabin aft. It is a most practical size in this respect.

The hull form is burdensome but easy-lined, docile on the helm, with well-extended lateral plane, easy to drydock or put on a tidal grid, and always a good, stable, sail-on-its-bottom model for seagoing comfort. For my own use I would be inclined to pull out the ends for deck space, retaining about the same underbody. As to layout, this would have to develop to suit my needs

at the moment, but as age and creakiness continue, a cleaned-up deckhouse model with longer ends might do the job.

Dozens of these boats have been built in fiberglass. In wood, construction is straightforward bent-frame carvel. It is simple, rugged, and about a standoff in building time with strip or diagonal planking. One-off time required for such a ship is about 12,000 man-hours in North America. This is with yacht finish. It translates into six to eight man-years — a big job to contemplate.

11

Teal

LOA:	30'5"
LWL:	22'10"
Breadth:	8'8"
Draft:	4'9"
Displacement:	11,300 lbs.
Ballast:	4,900 lbs
Sail Area:	
Main & Fore	426 sq. ft.
Main & Genoa	592 sq. ft.

The year 1953 saw the first of this general model under construction in Ed Gove's barn in Portland, Oregon, the aperture of the barn door dictating a maximum breadth of 7'-10". Coming out of the shop door always seems to be a symbolic hatching, and in this case the clearance generally dictated the slimmer form of Ed's boat. The first three boats to the earlier model were built by Ed and his friends Peterson and Nichols. A half-dozen more of Ed's model were built around the country.

In 1964 she was redesigned, with another strake of topside planking plus greater breadth, and a generally loosened-up interior to the basic configuration of the original *Teal* design. Several more have been built to this more current plan, both as sloops and as yawls, and have proven to be good little ships. Es and Maureen Horne's

Fax (short for Es's wartime frigate *Halifax*) is the one shown in the photo, and will give an idea of the boat's appearance afloat. She has replaced the Hornes' cutter *Swoop*, which was illustrated in the earlier book of yacht designs.

Peter Donahoe built *Fax* (ex *Lore Lei*) to his usual meticulous standards. She still looks good, after several years of cruising under other good owners prior to the Hornes' purchase. Peter Donahoe sailed her for the first few years, then replaced her with one of the *Diane*-model cutters, and lately with one of the little *Eel* yawls. Both the *Diane* and the little *Eel* were illustrated in the first volume of *Yacht Designs*.

The job of building a wooden boat of this sort is about as straightforward as possible. With backbone and ballast set up, moulds are erected at 3' centers, tied together at deck height with the laminated clamps, plus a couple of bilge battens.

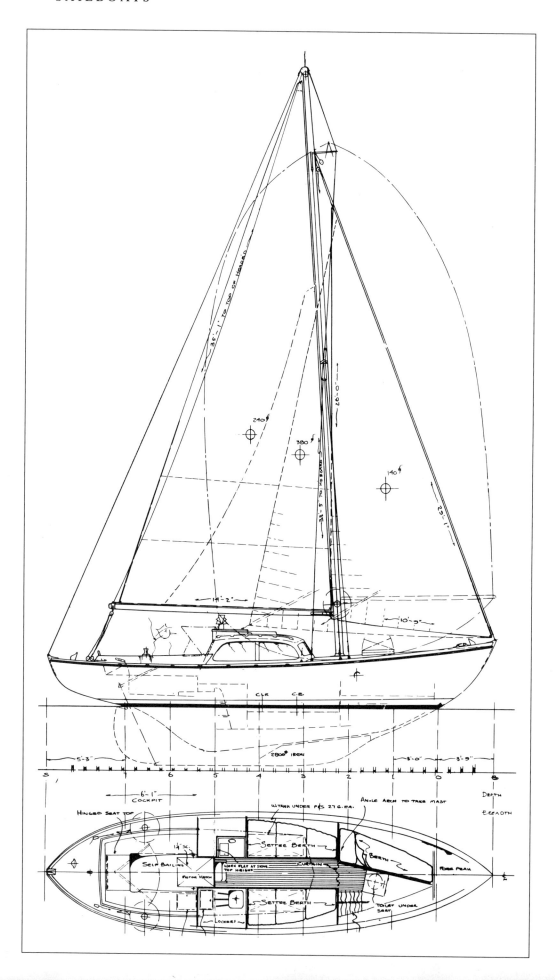

Shown here is the profile and plan of Ed Gove's earlier model of this series — the development basis for Teal's design.

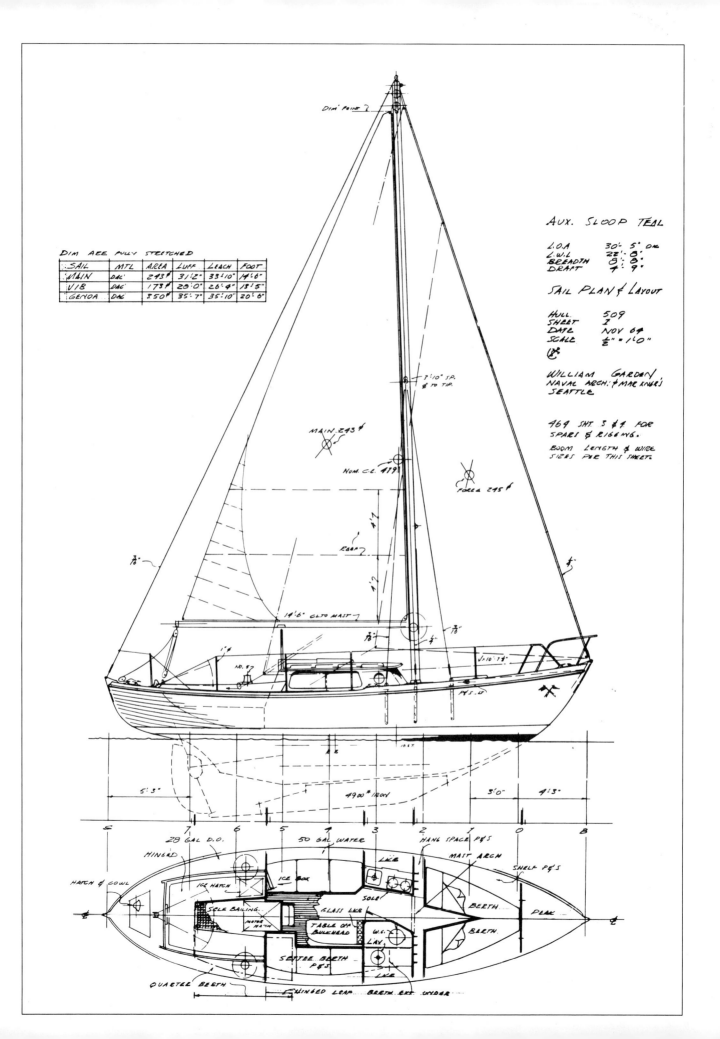

DIM ARE FULLY STRETCHED

SAIL	MTL	AREA	LUFF	LEACH	FOOT
MAIN	DAC	243ʸ	31'2"	33'10"	14'6"
JIB	DAC	173ʸ	29'0"	26'4"	18'5"
GENOA	DAC	350ʸ	35'7"	35'10"	20'6"

DIM' POINT ?

AUX. SLOOP TEAL

L.O.A   30'-5' O.A
L.W.L   22'-0'
BREADTH   9'-8'
DRAFT   4'-9'

SAIL PLAN & LAYOUT

HULL   509
SHEET   2
DATE   NOV 64
SCALE   ½" = 1'-0"

WILLIAM GARDEN
NAVAL ARCH. & MAR. ENGR'S
SEATTLE

469 SHT 3 & 4 FOR
SPARS & RIGGING.

BOOM LENGTH & WIRE
SIZES PER THIS SHEET.

3'-10" SP.
& TO TIP.

MAIN 243ʸ

NOM. C.L. 479ʸ

FORE 245ʸ

14'6" C.L. TO MAST

28 GAL D.O.   50 GAL WATER   HANG SPACE P&S
HINGED   MAST ARCH
HATCH & COWL   LKR   SHELF P&S
                ICE HATCH   ICE BOX
                             SELF BAILING   SOLE   BERTH   PEAK
                             GLASS LKR
                MOTOR HATCH   TABLE ON   BERTH
                             BULKHEAD   W.C.
                                             LAV.
                SETTEE BERTH
                P&S   LKR
QUARTER BERTH
HINGED LEAF   BERTH EXT. UNDER

Outward bound on the starboard tack, Peter Donahoe's Lore Lei *is shown in the Gulf islands.*

Then she's ready for the 1-1/4" x 2-1/8" edge-nailed strip planking. After planking, the bulkheads and deck beams are fitted. Then the balance of the moulds are removed, and interior work, decks, and outfitting can proceed.

This sounds quick, but it will take about 800 man-hours if the work is done by a skilled boatbuilder, with another 400 to 600 hours needed to get her out the door.

Of the boats built to date the layout shown has generally been followed, although a galley-aft arrangement has been fitted about as shown on Ed's boat, and on the yawl version. For limited cruising and day sailing a small galley forward is out of the way, but for more extended voyaging a galley aft in the more usual position is the better choice. This would keep the companionway wetness away from the berths, and if a bridge deck is fitted the galley counter can extend under it and across the ship.

Fax has proven to be a nice size for general cruising. She is docile under sail, with enough room to enjoy the cabin during periods below. In the summertime it's always nice to have *Fax* poke her nose into the pass for a visit on her way to the islands up the Gulf.

No. 3 on page 62 is the latest revision of Ed's earlier boat. Here the layout has been drawn with the galley aft, but at the expense of cockpit length. The longer deckhouse also allows us to work in a toilet room and hanging locker opposite.

The main cabin has been altered with an appealing horseshoe-shaped arrangement of settee berths. The middle section can be removable, with two berths located in the bow, or a double can be fitted with access by climbing in over the end. Masts are on deck, supported by a heavy bulkhead and a steel arch.

The hull is basically the same, but with a 7" longer bow. The rudder stock is shifted aft. Lifelines are similar to that of the sloop.

The yawl rig appeals to me. A boat with two masts seems to look right — more of a ship somehow.

Like the old Ford Thunderbird cars that grew from being two-seater sports cars to become real gunboats, Ed's little sloop seems to keep growing.

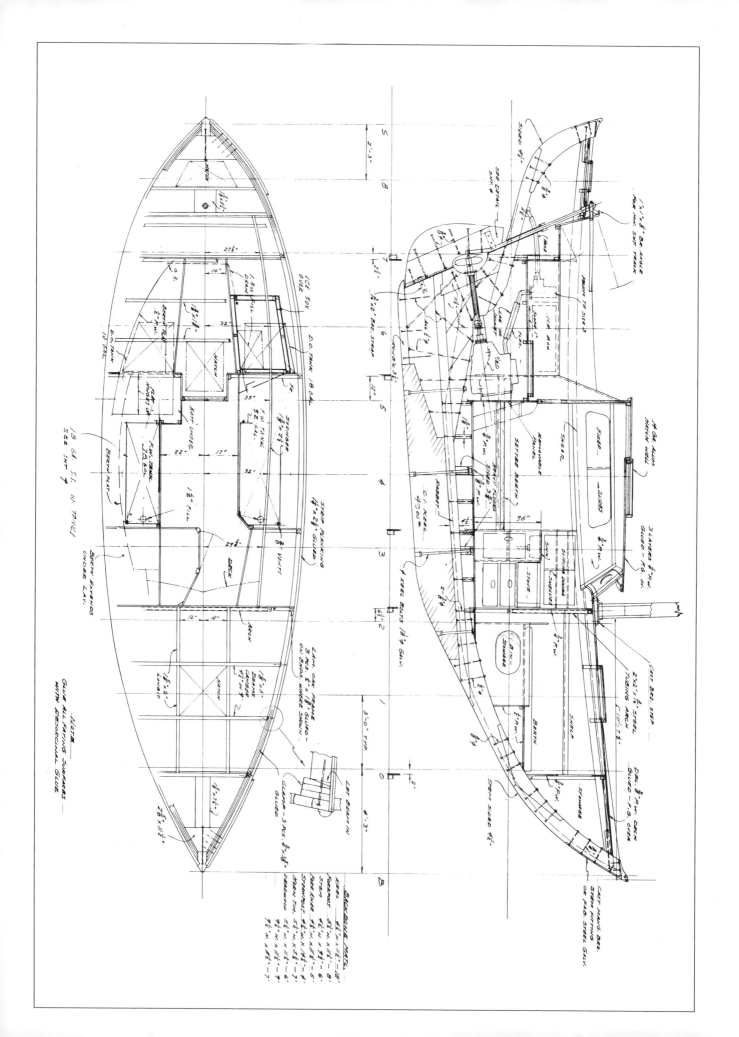

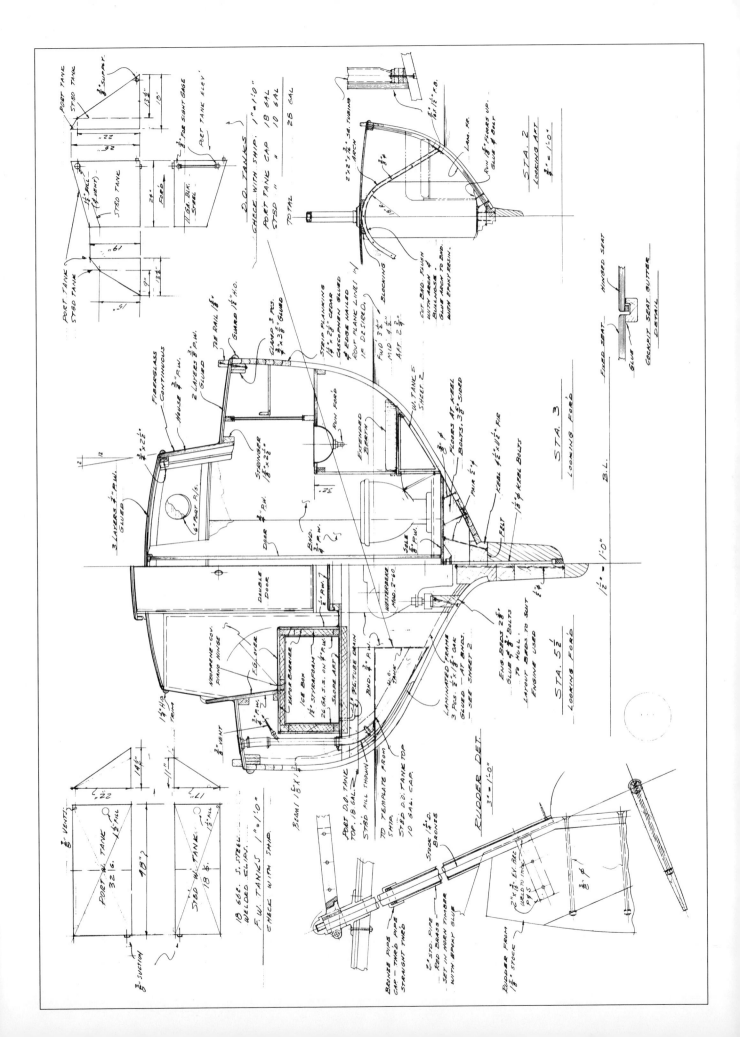

*Shown here is a yawl-
rigged revision of the
Teal/Fax model.*

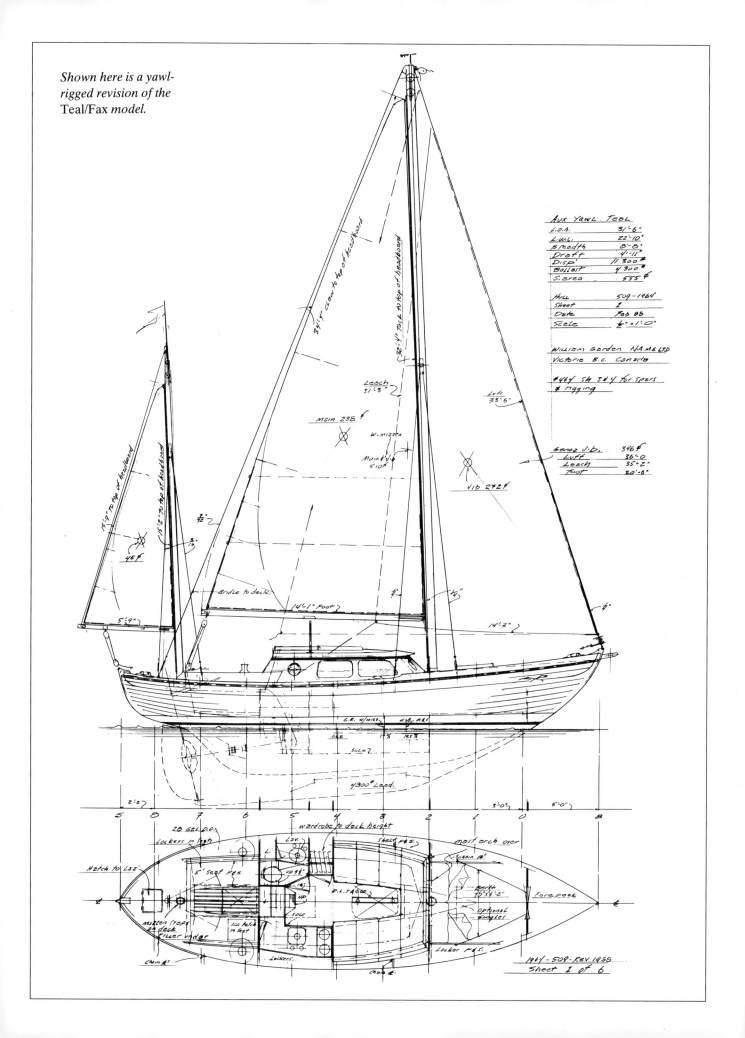

Aux. Yawl Teal
L.O.A.	31'-6"
L.W.L.	22'-10"
Breadth	8'-8"
Draft	4'-11"
Disp	11,300#
Ballast	4300#
S.area	555 ¢

Hull	509-1964
Sheet	I
Date	Feb 88
Scale	⅜"=1'0"

William Garden N.A.M.E.LTD
Victoria B.C. Canada

#464 Sh 3 & 4 for spars
& rigging

Genoa Jib.	346 ¢
Luff	36'-0
Leech	35'-2"
foot	20'-0"

1964-509-Rev 1955
Sheet I of 6

12

Knockabout Schooners

The tales of hard-driving ships in books such as J.B. Connolly's *Out of Gloucester* and Rudyard Kipling's *Captains Courageous* filled a past generation with deep regard for the beautiful Grand Banks fishing schooner.

From memory of Connolly's writings, the schooner, which usually was referred to as an "able vessel," or an "able dog," always seemed to be carrying too much sail. The man at the wheel often was described as standing to weather of the wheel box, well braced, ". . . in swash up to his armpits but solid water only to his waist." Great days they were, with the schooner in half a gale of wind, a good trip of fish in the hold, the 78' main boom bending like a fishing pole, and the well deck buried in foam to the hatch coamings.

So a lot of us ended up as schooner freaks. Lots of us must still be around, but not so many surface in these efficient days. Nevertheless, for those in love with the way of going rather than in the fastest way of getting there, the schooner rig and type still have disciples hooked on their charm and nostalgic appeal.

On the West Coast in the early 1900s there were two big knockabouts, the *Victor and Ethan* and the *Commonwealth*. Both were fishing for halibut as dory boats with complete schooner rigs. They had been sent around the Horn from the East Coast prior to the development of the motor schooners. *La Paloma*, another knockabout, but short-rigged and leaning to power, was built in Seattle from a McManus model in 1909. She had a nice underbody for a power schooner, although as a sailing boat she was over-full in the forebody to increase her carrying capacity. *La Paloma* was 71' overall, 17'-7" breadth, and 7'-8" depth of hold. Power was originally an 80-horse-power Frisco Standard gasoline engine. *Commonwealth*, noted above, was about the size of the *Helen B. Thomas*, whose photo is shown here. *Commonwealth* was still to be seen in Seattle during the 1930s, but with her rig cut down to that of a power schooner.

Harvey Rogers' *America* and A.W. Thomas' *Margaret* were another pair of generally similar early West Coast power knockabouts, but all the schooners, after trying the Pacific fisheries under sail, resorted to power. Unfortunately, the West Coast is windward/leeward country, with calm or light-air summer weather not conducive to commercial sail. The gasoline engine, and later the oil and diesel engines, rapidly replaced the full schooner rig. *Dragon-Fly* is an example of a smaller West Coast power schooner design of the early 1950s designed for tuna trolling.

All yachts during the period of working sail seem to have been influenced in some way by their working counterparts. The fishing schooner was widely imitated in the yachting fleets, but the knockabout schooner rig never achieved the popularity of the usual bowsprit model. However, the knockabouts shown in the following chapters will appeal to the schooner fraternity.

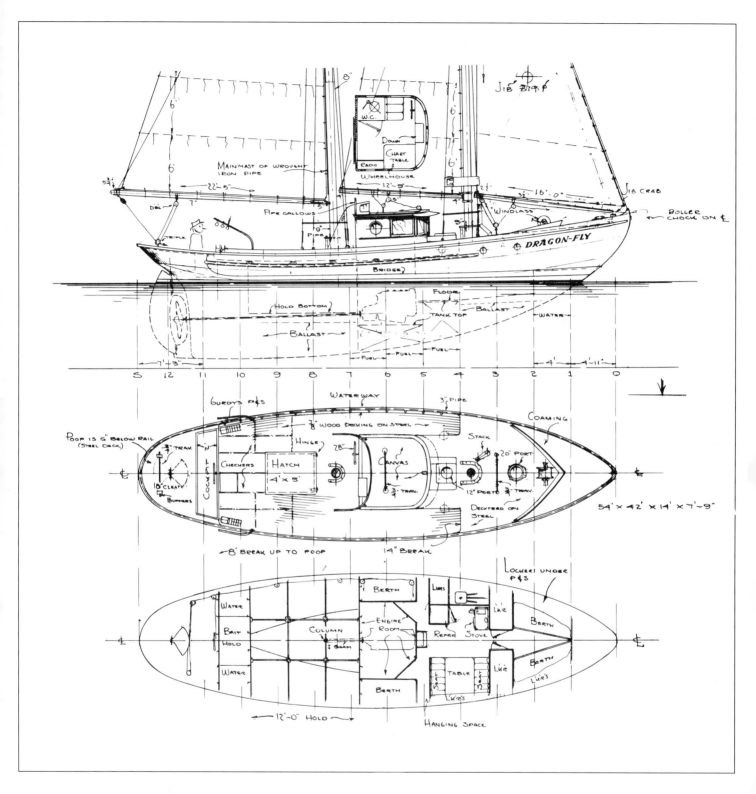

Dragon-Fly, *above, was
designed in steel for
Noble and Earl Goodwin.
At right is the handsome
Helen B. Thomas,
designed by Tom
McManus. Mystic*

*Seaport Museum has
many McManus drawings.
Autocrat, a McManus
ketch built for C. W. H.
Foster of Marblehead, is
another all-time favorite
knockabout.*

13

Rain Bird

LOA:	40′ 0″
LWL:	28′ 0″
Breadth:	10′ 0″
Draft:	6′ 0″
Displacement:	22,000 lbs.
Ballast:	9,000 lbs.
Sail Area:	756 sq. ft.

For a few years in the fifties, my old schooner *Rain Bird* gave us some good times. Hailing now from Friday Harbor in the San Juan Islands, she's a much-loved and well-used possession of Lee Brewer.

From the lines plan you will see that she was designed to be a good performer. Under sail she went along very well, a lively schooner with enough area to move well in Puget Sound's light weather, and still a small enough rig for one man to handle easily.

The late Joe Patton, an old friend and *Gleam* shipmate, referred to *Rain Bird* as a "larger edition of the mistakes made" on *Gleam*, my previous schooner which is shown in Chapter 15. Compared with the comfort and sailing ability of *Oceanus* that followed *Rain Bird*, he was dead right. But for a lover of the Grand Banks fishing schooners and their yacht modifications that were so popular in the 1920s and 1930s, a small schooner with knockabout bow has vast appeal.

Something on *Rain Bird*'s background: From the end of the war through 1949 I had an office in Seattle, hanging out over the bay about 40 feet up on the face of an ex-sawmill. This was on the third level, in an annex off the old gang-saw area. On the next level, another 20 feet up, was the old saw-filing room. It was a great area for a shop, with a view all over the world, but inaccessible except by switchback stairs or by a trap door where the saw hoist had been.

Rain Bird's lines were laid out there, in the loft high above the office. With the help of sailing friends, the backbone, transom, and heavier pieces I had roughed out were hoisted up through the trap by tackle, while the lighter moulds, clamps, stringers, beams, and floor timbers were put together up in the loft. The adze tailings, sawdust, chips, and rubbish went out the southeast window to go flying down into the bay in those days (or rather nights) before pollution was invented.

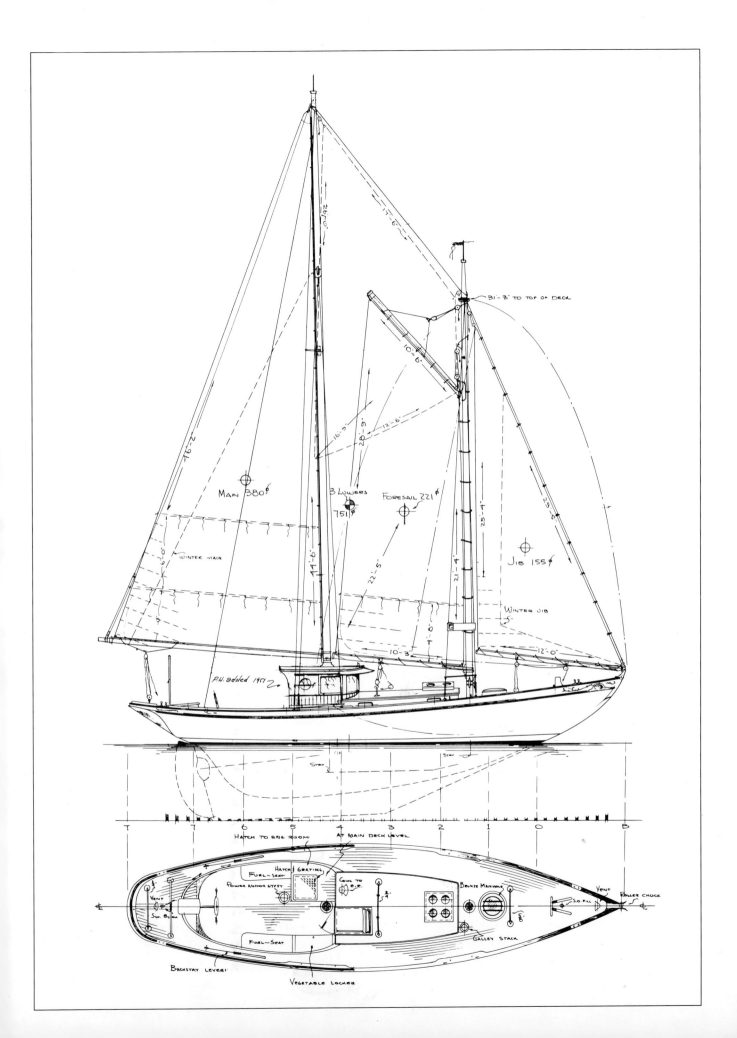

As time passed I had the keel assembly set up on blocking to the right declivity, the moulds erected, and the floor timbers and transom put in place. Before long, high up in the loft, we had a 40' schooner set up, with a couple of ribbands sprung around for a preview of her form, while we waited for a suitable space to assemble her.

Marty Monson, a No.1 boatbuilder chum, and

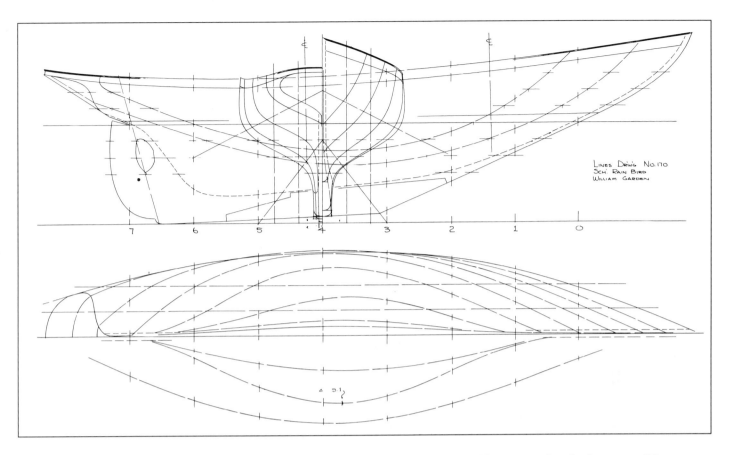

his right-hand man Jim Goldade worked out of a floating shop at the end of Seattle's Lake Union at that time, and there we planned to put the bits together. When all the parts were completed, down from the loft they came by tackle and grunts, some to be trucked and some to be sailed on the deck of *Gleam*, down the canal and up Lake Union to Marty's shop.

With all the parts made, we pitched in and had *Rain Bird* launched in about six weeks, with beams, bulwarks, covering boards, etc. completed. The hull money was gone, but my first schooner, *Gleam*, was lying alongside with a "For Sale" sign on her. Meanwhile, working at the office at night was keeping a few dollars ahead, and when *Gleam* was sold the job was given another spurt.

Using nights and weekends, as the funds became available, the new schooner finally was finished to minimum sailing trim, utilizing the recut sails and a foremast that came out of the old gaff-rigged Q-boat *Virginia*. I bought all of *Virginia*'s gear and sails from the deck up for a couple of hundred dollars, and figured that her gaff mainmast would make a perfect foremast for the schooner.

When we put *Virginia* under the boom to lift the mast out, we were surprised that her bow came up about a foot. *Virginia* was a beautiful piece of work and it was hard to believe that the mast would be solid rather than hollow. To get rid of weight, the mast was split end-to-end on the band saw and troughed out to leave a 1" wall. Then the inside surface was shellacked and the two sections were glued back together as *Rain Bird*'s foremast.

Upon completion, *Rain Bird* was finished bright inside, to show off the 30 or so natural-crook knees worked into her cabin, including one great pointer knee that extended from the stem, four feet diagonally back and up to the forward chainplates, port and starboard. This knee was worked up from a slab off a huge hanging knee that we liberated from the old office sawmill's building frame.

With everything varnished, and fitted with standby oil lamps, and a friendly black-iron wood-burning cook stove chocked off forward, it was a great cabin.

I haven't sailed *Rain Bird* for many years, but I hope to try her out again in a breeze one day, to see if she is as I remember.

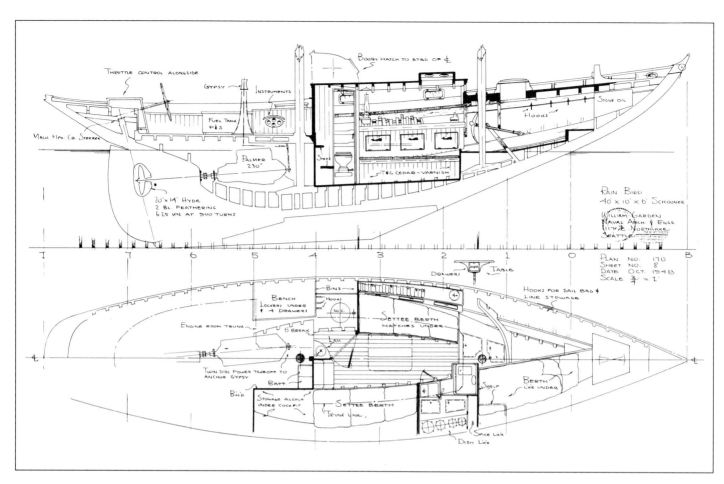

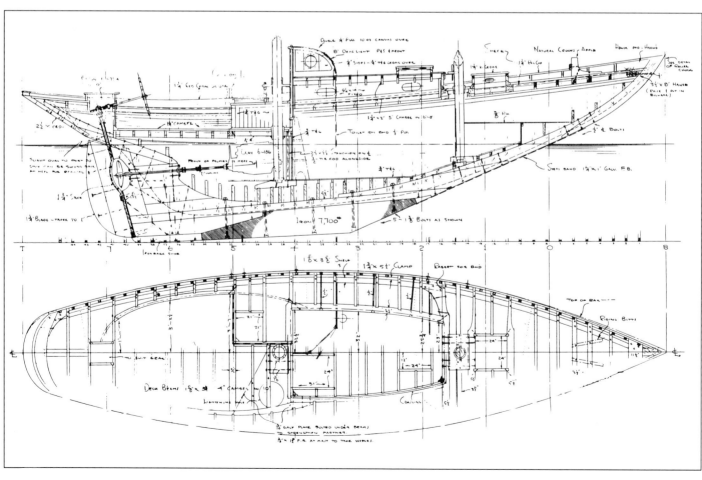

70

14

Union Jack

LOA:	49′ 0″
LWL:	35′ 0″
Breadth:	12′ 0″
Breadth of deck:	11′ 1″
Draft:	6′ 8″
Ballast:	14,000 lbs.
Sail Area:	1189 sq. ft.

Next we come to *Union Jack*, a larger version of the knockabout fishing schooner theme, with a short, powerful transom stern and the long bow of the knockabout. *Union Jack* was named after the second gasoline-engined codfish schooner on the Pacific coast. The basis for *Union Jack* was a schooner that I had sailing around on paper as a larger follow-up to *Rain Bird*, but the schooner never jelled and the sloop *Oceanus* was built instead.

Oceanus was a far more practical boat for our needs at the time, and kept us happy for the next 12 years. *Oceanus* was, in turn, developed from a 48' double-ender of somewhat similar form — one that I had worked out on a foot locker during the war years as an ideal liveaboard northern cruising boat. So, before I am branded as a total schooner nut, you must remember that for more than 50 years the drawing board has sailed off in all directions, with lots of interesting themes and rigs — sloops, cutters, yawls, square-riggers, and

cats. A nice impractical schooner, however, has always had a second look.

Union Jack is a real chunk of a ship, powerful, heavily-ballasted, and with a big rig to let her get out and move. The bulwarks are deep, fastened to timber heads as in *Rain Bird*, and topped off with the same white-painted rail cap and chock rail around the poop. Waterways here would be a soft gray, and the wood decks given hot tar and oil for a nut-brown finish. Trunk sides, coamings, cabin top, wheel box, and masts up to the booms are the same soft gray — almost white — and the cockpit color would be fish-blood red with a slat grating of raw teak. Bulwarks outboard are painted flat black. These are all typical schooner colors, traditional and hard to improve on. Bone cream-white enamel would prevail inside, with teak trim, lots of brass, wine-colored corduroy cushions, and a scrubbed fir sole.

The layout, although not the decor, is on the theme of a big fo'c'sle with emphasis on elbow room. Galley and dining area are in the deck-

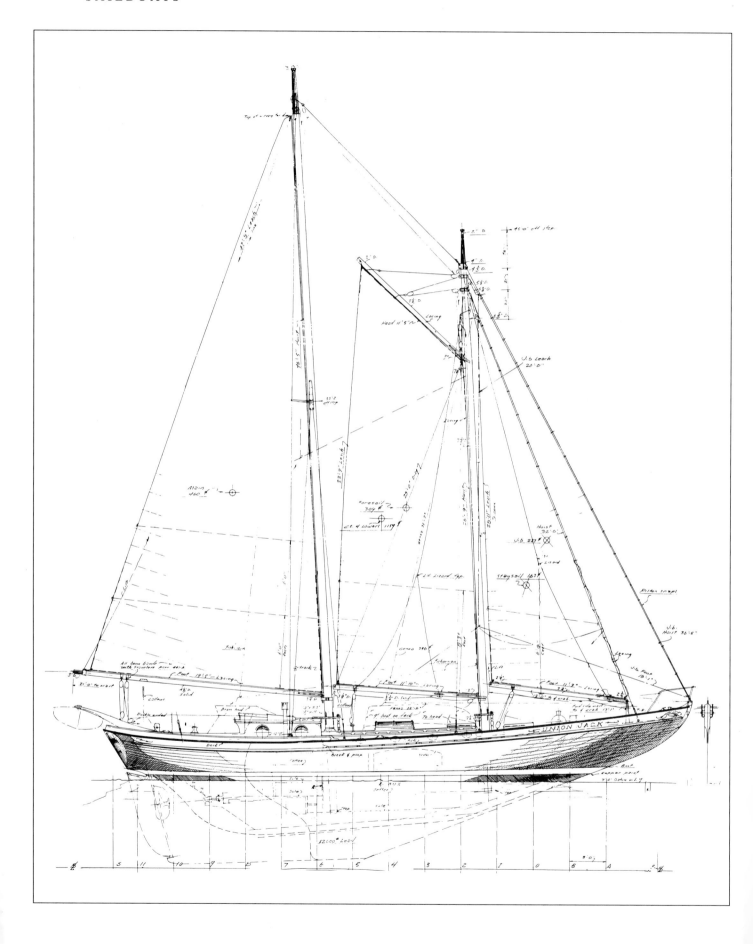

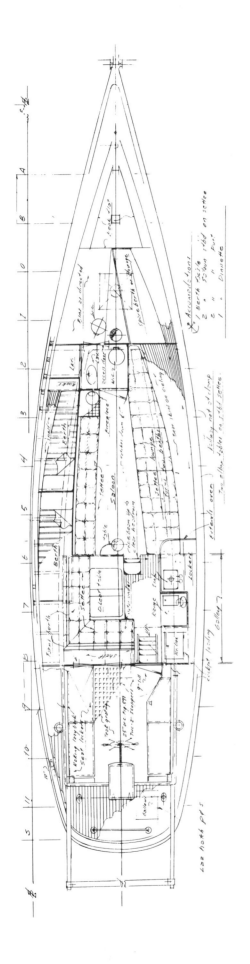

house. It's a nice place to sit and look out, with eye level over sill height. The saloon has two berths to port, and to starboard is a long settee which can form two berths. A toilet room is forward to port, and forward again of this bulkhead is a single-berth fo'c'sle, with head plus stowage for warps, sails, and gear.

The hull is of bent-frame construction, 1-3/4" x 2-1/4" oak on 12" centers. Planking is double red cedar, with one 3/8" diagonal inner and 1-1/8" outer skins. Decks are diagonal red cedar glued to the deck framing, and fitted with a light vee edge showing below, with a normal fore-and-aft teak layer over, the teak to be layed in and payed with Thiokol rubber. Backbone, floor timbers, clamps, and deck frame are all of yellow cedar.

Scantlings are thinned down forward to help minimize weight in the ends and resultant pitching, along with a fairly full U-shaped forebody to help counteract the inertia of the spars and long forward overhang when working to windward in a seaway.

As to sailing, a knockabout schooner is relatively quick on the helm, due to the short keel and the cutaway forefoot required for balance without a bowsprit. The configuration of the knockabout schooner rig puts the center of effort well aft along its base, and consequently the center of lateral resistance also has to move aft to retain balance. With ballast of lead or iron concentrated well aft, the long bow of the knockabout can be balanced and the short-sterned model held in sailing trim.

By contrast, many of the inside-ballasted knockabout fishing schooners of the *Helen B. Thomas* era ended up trimmed by the head, requiring them to have a bowsprit added in later years for improved balance.

So *Union Jack* is what J.B. Connolly would have called an "able dog." About now you should read his *Gloucestermen*. I'll have to fish it off the top shelf and catch up once more on all that schooner sail-carrying.

The sunken deckhouse with galley and dinette is above the engine with a roomy saloon forward. This affords minimun privacy, but a good open feeling of space.

15

Gleam

LOA:	33′ 0″
LWL:	23′ 0″
Breadth:	8′ 6″
Draft:	4′ 0″
Ballast:	7,500 lbs.
Sail Area:	450 sq. ft

Gleam was the first schooner that I built for my own use in 1939. Originally built as a replacement for the yawl *Pelican*, *Gleam* was built as a centerboarder with a spoon bow, short counter stern, and a gaff main with fidded topmast, main topsail, and fisherman staysail. Later I lengthened her with a clipper bow and overhang aft to the appearance in the photo. Prior to the rebuild and after a couple of knockdowns, I removed the centerboard and put all the ballast on the keel. Mainly in the trim shown in the photo we sailed her for many interesting miles.

She was hauled out during the war when Uncle Sam got me. The period from 1946 to 1949 saw her sailing again, but changed to carry a more efficient jib-headed main. We had some great times on board.

Gleam was carvel-planked of red cedar on Indiana red-oak frames, with a yellow-cedar backbone. Decks were narrow strakes of caulked fir, finished with pine tar, linseed oil, litharge, and turpentine applied hot. As I remember, they were always tight, but my memory isn't all that good.

Original power was a rebuilt 2-cylinder Kermath of 6-8 h.p. that came out of *Gray Gull*, a Hippocampus-model yawl that must still be sailing down in Puget Sound. The Kermath was replaced in 1947 by a neat little Palmer magneto-ignition, hand-starting, 4-cylinder LLH engine. At 600 r.p.m. it was one of the best of shipmates.

As to her ability, *Gleam* sailed reasonably well for our needs, but lacked the draft to really hang on to windward in a fresh breeze and seaway. Perhaps the moderate draft was a good match for the schooner rig's basic lack of windward ability. Certainly the 4′ draft was handy for the cruising she did in those years.

Cost of materials was $675. Bigger dollars then, the savings from the preceding year's boat-building, happily dumped into the new boat, plus about 1,200 man-hours of construction time. Transportation to the shop then was by foot or by the 18′ double-chine dory *Omar K*, powered

Gleam *in about 1947, and in a fresh breeze. Burke Williamson in the cockpit with the author, and John Cook in the companionway.*

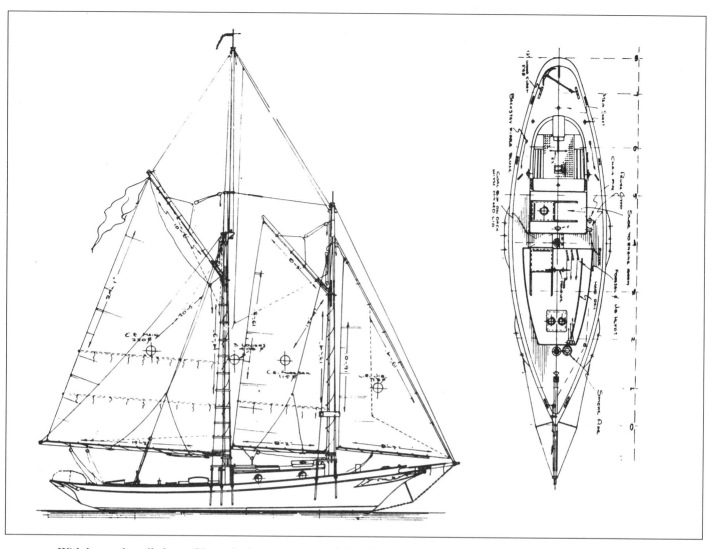

With her ends pulled out, Gleam *had a more practical deck layout and a nicer appearance afloat.*

by a single-cylinder 6-h.p. 4-cycle Hallin engine.

The photo of *Gleam* on page 75 shows her in about 1947, on port tack in a nice breeze, with a reef tucked in the main. Shipmate John Cook is in the companionway, Burke Williamson and I are in the cockpit.

It's interesting the way recollections of how things were or seemed to be sometimes come in a rush, with the particular drift of the air, a smell, the noise of a block, or perhaps the quality of light on a particular morning. When *Gleam* was launched a long time ago, like any kid I couldn't wait to sail her. She was empty inside but quickly rigged, with a suit of creamy cotton sails fitted with tarred Italian-hemp bolt ropes made up by McLellan of Fall River, Massachusetts. Without interior joinerwork, but with outside ballast of 1,000 lbs. and some 500 lbs. of bricks inside and no tanks, equipment, or engine weight, I sailed her around the lakes whenever a breeze came

up. With conditions right, how she seemed to go.

The recollection of one such sail came back to me recently on a raw November morning. With that same sort of fresh, cold westerly, I could feel little *Gleam* take off again on a reach in her empty big-dinghy condition — all hollow-sounding below and smelling of fresh wet red cedar.

The first postwar cruise on *Gleam* was with my old and honored sailing partner, John Adams. We spent eight weeks aboard in 1946, cruising north and around Vancouver Island. In 1948 Joe Patton, another good shipmate, joined me for a month's cruise to the Goose Islands. The following year it was just three weeks north.

Then the urge for a larger schooner, *Rain Bird*, became too strong, and 1949 was devoted to putting her together. Forty years after parting with *Gleam*, I saw a photo of her being rebuilt again in California, and with luck she's sailing again.

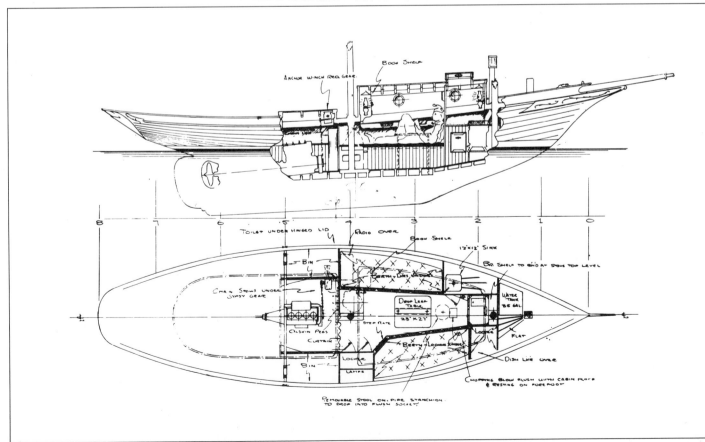

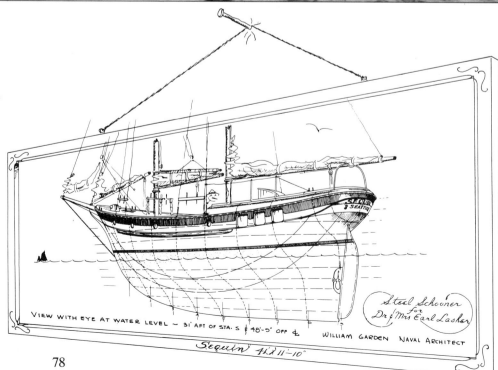

Above, Sequin *in a good breeze and off for the weekend on a nice Puget Sound sunny morning. The perspective view gives a good impression of* Sequin's *hull form.*

VIEW WITH EYE AT WATER LEVEL ~ 31' AFT OF STA. 5 & 48'-5" OFF ℄

Steel Schooner
for
Dr & Mrs Earl Lasher

WILLIAM GARDEN NAVAL ARCHITECT

Sequin 41.8 11'-10"

16

Sequin

LOA:	43′ 6″
LWL:	34′ 8″
Breadth:	11′ 10″
Draft:	6′ 4″
Displacement:	47,000 lbs.
Ballast:	14,000 lbs.
Sail Area:	933 sq. ft

In our wanderings through these pages we've looked over a couple of yacht-model schooners and a couple on the theme of knockabout fishing-boat types. *Sequin* is another approach. *Sequin* is a little steel schooner, somewhat on the British coaster model of the last century, and with the appealing rolled-home poop of the British ships. One of *Sequin*'s sisters shown was built with a square course and a foretopsail, but *Sequin* carried a simple fore-and-aft schooner sail plan. The photo shows her sailing outward-bound on a nice Puget Sound morning, under the command of a late and honored shipmate, Dr. Earl Lasher, one of my crew of *Oceanus* stalwarts.

Earl — "Taloose," to us fellow painters while in the *Oceanus* afterguard — had *Sequin*'s steel work done in Seattle at a little yard on the Duwamish River, and he finished her over the next two or three years as the part-time therapy of a busy surgeon. Losing a finger end in the building process was part of the price, although we always intimat-ed that the loss actually was due to some rather freewheeling knife work in surgery.

The Lashers had some good cruises with *Sequin*. Then she was sold and she sailed away a long time ago, and I trust she is back again in hands that will get the best out of her.

The shell is 3/16″ mild steel, with the round-bilge shell plating run diagonally in about 30″ widths to follow easily the rounded sides and deep "S" sections. We framed her transversely with tee-bar and flatbar. For ballast she has a great inside lump of cut-up war-surplus cannon barrels embedded in concrete.

Charley Boatsmith has another *Sequin* model going together west of Port Angeles for a long-planned voyage to the South Seas.

The topsail-schooner version shown was built for Chadwick Baertschy and has done some ambitious cruising. Those with a long memory may recall a photo of her taken in the Straits of Gibraltar which *Rudder* magazine once ran on the cover.

Sequin's cabin plan would be more sociable with a passage below decks joining the aft cabin and the forward accommodations. The engine would be on the centerline and the mainmast on an arch.

Perhaps the nicest thing about rethinking these boats is the recollections of the close friends who had a part in them — friends such as yacht builder Norm Blanchard, who once gave me the teak leaf from his dining room table to use as a half-model backboard; Martin Monson, with gray whiskers now, but as full of steam as ever, although long retired; and Jimmy Goldade, recently retired from marine surveying after years of boatbuilding; Ted Godel was another of the finest kind, who wound it up in an auto accident.

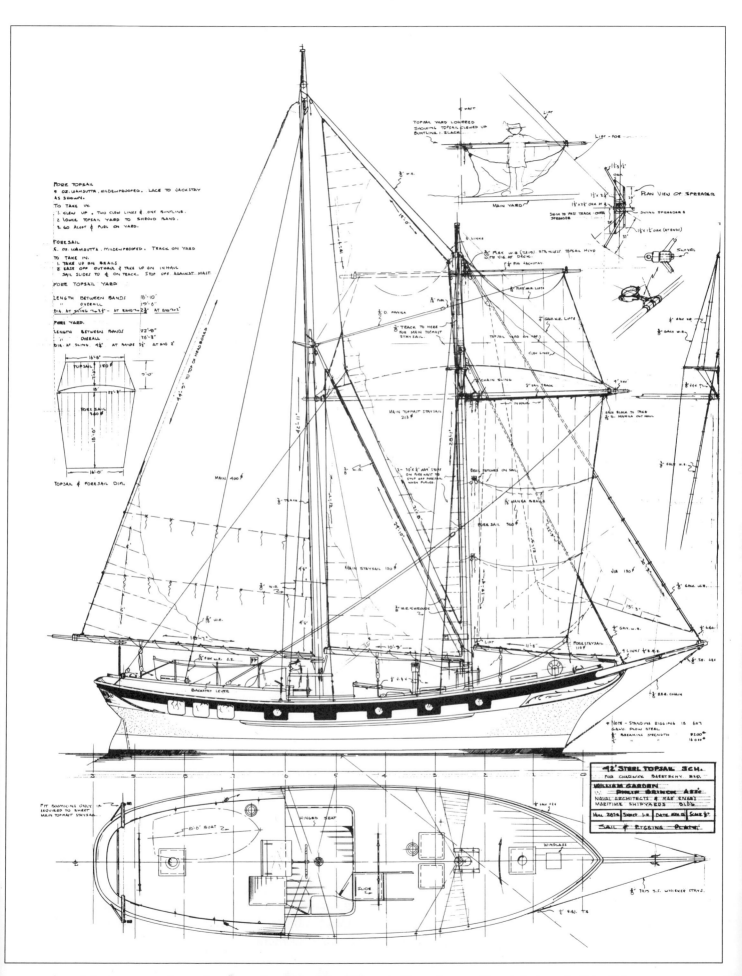

A fore course and topsail seems to fit a little ship of this sort. Shown is one of Sequin's sisters built in Chicago.

17

The 36' Yawl *Querida*

LOA:	35' 9"
LWL:	24' 0"
Breadth:	8' 5"
Draft:	5' 9"
Displacement:	13,100 lbs.
Ballast:	6,100 lbs.
Sail Area:	554 sq. ft. with 100% foretriangle

The mid-1940s saw Seattle as home to quite a fleet of aging Six Meter boats, among them the lovely *Saga*, all somewhat tired after the neglect of the war years, and all in need of recertification. At the time I had the pleasure of being employed as measurer for the fleet, so you will note that some of the feel of a big husky Six has worked its way into the 1947 design of the little yawl *Querida*.

Querida was built for Jim Francis by Emerson Doble, for use in the San Francisco Bay area. This boat has always appealed to me. She had the go of a Six, along with reasonable accommodations, and, to my eye, a more interesting rig to play with.

Flying the Cruising Club of America burgee, Jim and his family raced and cruised *Querida* in the Bay area for years, with many miles passing

under the keel. When she was new we had many good comments on her, both from her competitors and her admirers, since she seemed a nice combination of looks and performance.

Balance under sail is always a fascinating study and search. *Querida* seemed to hit the elements spot-on. Without mizzen but with the main and jib, she had neutral helm in 12-15 knots of wind, developing into a slight lee helm when the wind made up. This was with a used main and jib, smaller than those shown on the sail plan, their areas being 235 sq. ft. and 190 sq. ft. respectively.

With the mizzen finally added and the sail area up to specifications, *Querida* was reported to be light on the helm and a real galloper to windward when it blew, being able to take anything in her class under those conditions in rough water. Jim mentioned once that his eight-year-old

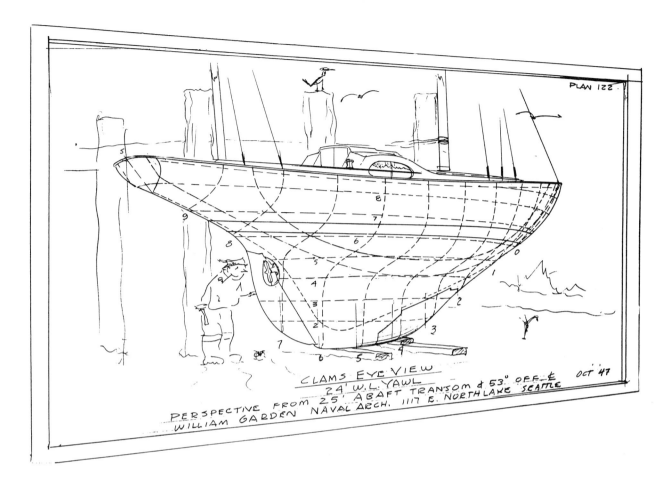

CLAMS EYE VIEW
24' W.L. YAWL
PERSPECTIVE FROM 25' ABAFT TRANSOM & 53° OFF &
WILLIAM GARDEN NAVAL ARCH. 1117 E. NORTH LAKE SEATTLE   OCT '47

PLAN 122.

boy could sail her easily in any normal San Francisco Bay breeze. When it blew really hard the jib and mizzen alone formed a good cruising rig. Under power her speed was 5.5 knots at 1200 r.p.m. with a 15" x 15" 2-bladed propeller on a 2:1 gear.

Today most of the yachts are plastic. From a practical standpoint the well-thought-out simplicity and low maintenance of the many fiberglass production boats makes a custom boat of interest mainly to the purist or die-hard who can afford to have a special boat built, but to my eye nothing can compare with a well-turned-out wooden boat.

Querida's simple and well-proportioned structure will be worth study. The simple bent-frame carvel hull was built to a tight budget, but it was good for many years of hard driving. In building her today, we probably would fit a couple of diagonal skins with a nicely lined off fore-and-aft skin over all, glued and given a final overlay of Dynel and epoxy. For decks, there would be two layers of plywood, glued together and to the deck framing. And the entire superstructure, rail-to-

rail, would be fiberglassed for low upkeep.

Going below, what a world of difference the warmth and interest of a wooden boat's interior can have, compared with many of the glass boats' refrigerator-style surfaces and shapes. Here, the wooden boat's varnished inner diagonal skin, set off in turn by the satin gold color of bent-oak framing, plus the pattern of beams overhead and of nicely-finished joinerwork, all create an ambience that is lacking in any other material.

As I recall, Jim, being a foundry man, once considered a stainless-steel ballast casting — another puzzle for archaeologists ten thousand years from now. My files don't indicate Jim's final selection, but lead as shown would be the better choice.

A few years ago *Querida*, with Jim and Winkie on board, sailed away to Valhalla a couple thousand feet deep off Monterey. *Querida* was a lovely carriage for the last voyage. Jim and Winkie were terminally ill and *Querida* was aging. After long deliberation and with peace of mind, the final sail and the quiet descent to the ocean floor.

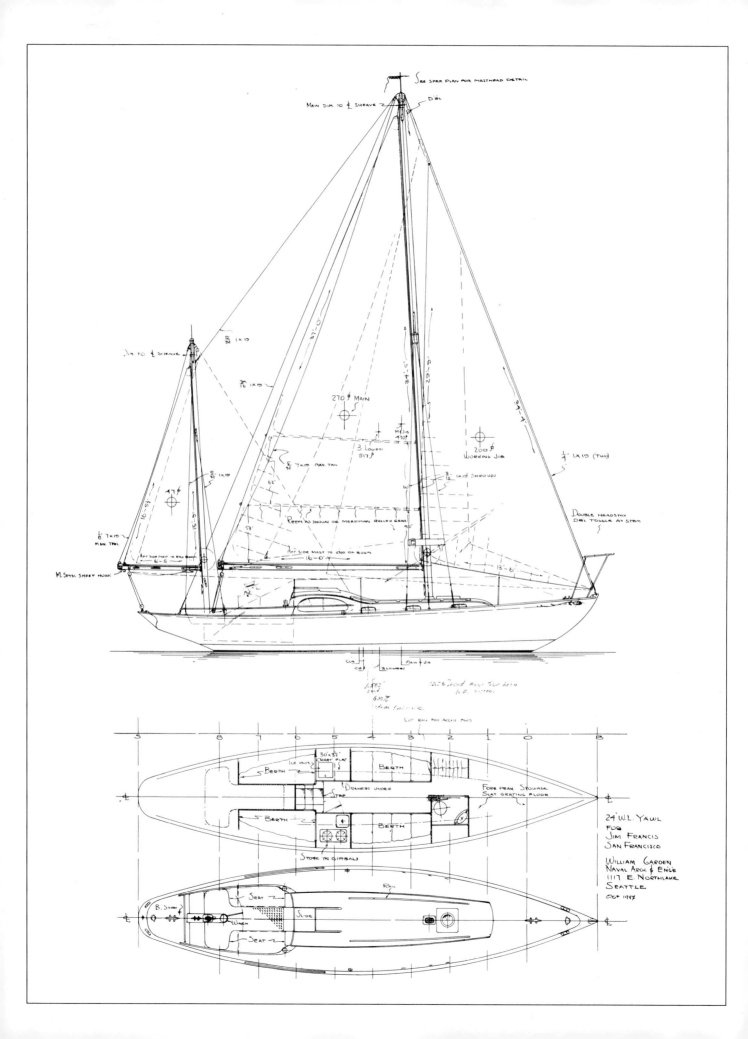

24' W.L. Yawl
for
Jim Francis
San Francisco

William Garden
Naval Arch. & Eng'r
1117 E. Northlake
Seattle
Oct 1947

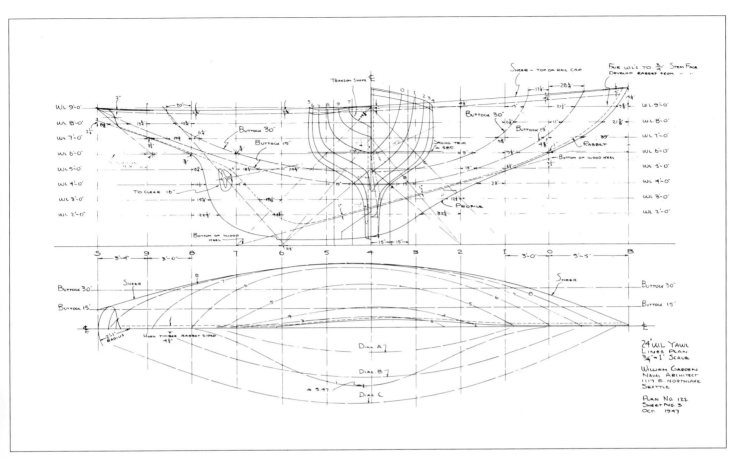

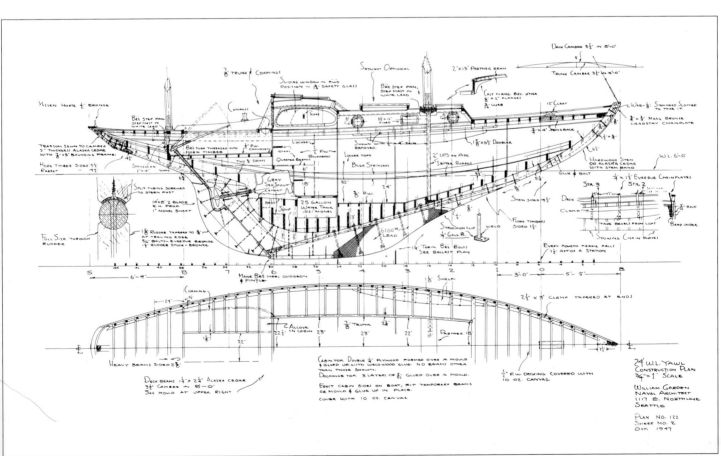

18
Oyster

LO Deck:	24' 6"
LWL:	20' 0"
Breadth:	8' 0"
Draft of hull:	1' 4"
Draft w/ board:	2' 6"
Displacement:	3,600 lbs.
Sail Area:	400 sq. ft.

Oyster's sail plan and
profile are shown here. A
liveboard scow for
inshore cruising.

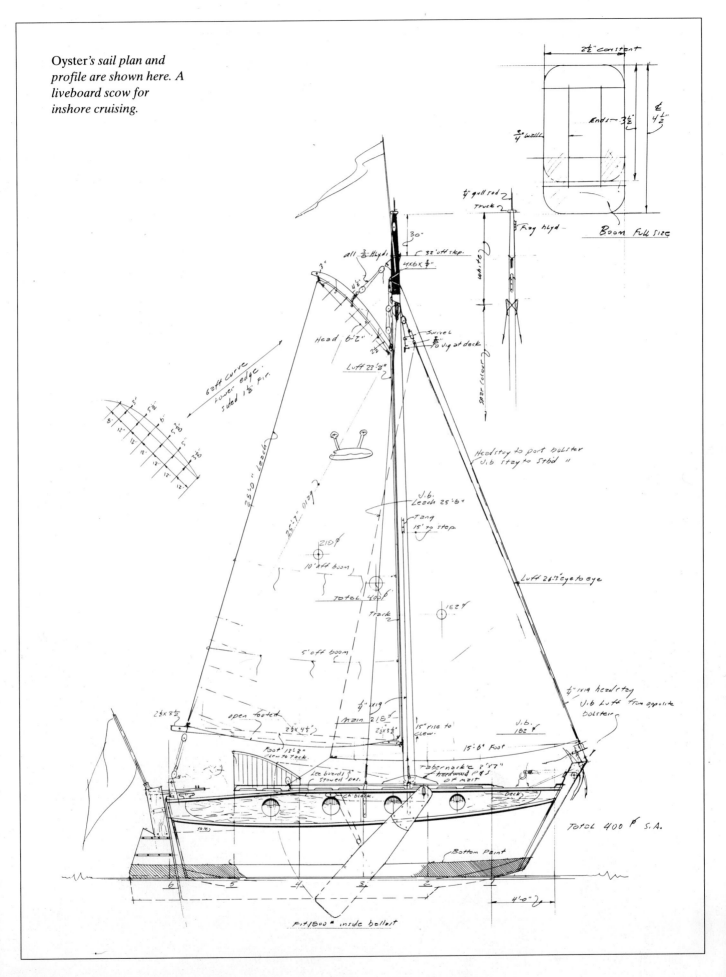

Oyster started life as a pile of 4' x 8' plywood, three of the 8' panels dictating her length of 24'. The 4' panel width plus highway restrictions hold breadth to 8'. Hull height suits a 4' panel width, and the tumblehome topsides come from a ripped 4' panel. Frames can be lumber-yard 2x4's, but strangely, in this land of big timber, we found hard mahogany easier to come by than the stuff that grows all around us here in the Northwest.

Export is the enemy of the wooden boat. With shiploads of beautiful Douglas-fir and cedar cants leaving for the Orient every day, the big mills are set up and happy only with orders far beyond the small amount required by the wooden-boat builder. Today, for instance, we're buying the timbers for a 50' wooden schooner, and find that for 20 percent more than the cost of non-available fir, we can get beautiful timbers of gum hauled in from halfway around the world. Meanwhile, I suppose our fir, yellow cedar, and spruce is outward-bound on the return voyage.

Oyster was designed for Connie Horder as a liveaboard, tied-up, go-to-school home afloat for a girl then of 20. It's a neat little hideaway, self-contained and fitted with the basic amenities of a tiny houseboat. The layout affords headroom, fair elbow room, and lots of stowage space — even a long locker for skis.

Leeboards were fitted for lateral plane while under sail. The boards and big rudder give reasonable performance, with an appearance reminiscent of a little Chinese junk or a Dutch boat.

Peter London built Oyster in his Sidney, B.C. shop, to his usual sturdy, workmanlike standards. About 3-1/2 months with two men was required for the project.

Oyster has proven to be a neat little mud-thumping home afloat for one or two. She will float in less than 18 inches of water, and at low tide she will sit on the bottom like a duck. For the shore-bound season, city water can be connected, electric power and phone plugged in, and the owner will be set up with a snug roost during the winter gales.

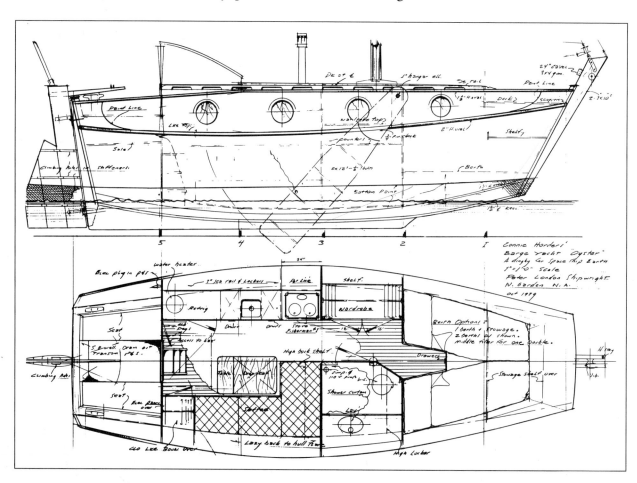

Oyster is a sort of dinghy for Space Ship Earth.

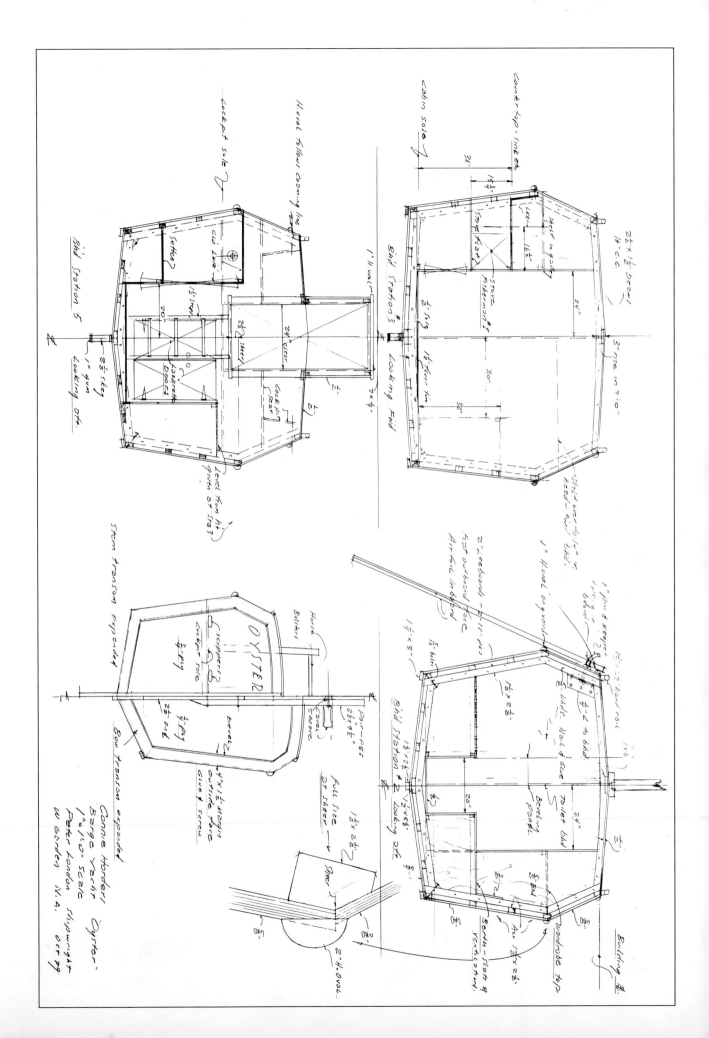

Connie Harden,
Barge Yacht "Oyster"
1":1'0" Scale
Peter London Shipwright
W Barden N.A.   Oct 79

19

Day Sailers

No. 1

LOA:	24' 6"
LWL:	21' 0"
Breadth:	7' 7"
Draft:	4' 0"
Displacement:	1,300 lbs.
Ballast:	800 lbs.
Sail Area:	250 sq. ft.

I once planned to build this little fellow, but put it aside when a nice International 110 came on the market. The 110 currently hoists out on davits alongside the shop, ready for day sailing when the weather holds promise. A great little boat for the service. The sketch shown here was planned around an old Star boat keel that still sits in a corner of the shop, although a simple welded-up fin of 3/16" plate as shown could easily serve as an alternate keel.

Such a keel is easy to fabricate, with a wide top flange and a lower endplate extended out as a winglet to increase the apparent-aspect ratio. The shell for the ballast cavity is rolled and welded up, then propped up plumb athwartships, but tilted forward. Molten lead is poured into the

forward half of the cavity, over some lead pigs that have been positioned before the pour. The pigs are encapsulated as they cool the molten lead. Prior to pouring, a half-dozen vertical angles are tacked to the outside of the shell. These angles plus the interior web will prevent heat distortion of the mild steel. The angles will be knocked off once the lead has cooled.

The ballast, fin, and rig are in general proportion for balance under sail, but you will notice them to be as far aft as possible. I once had a sloop with the rig well aft, and in a real breeze she would go off on a reach like a motorboat. Her normally excessive helm would go slack, she'd seem to stiffen up, and the feeling was great. Later, we moved the rig forward substantially. The helm was perfect, but she never again had that wonderful feeling of *Go*. The rig here is adjustable, so some interesting experiments can be made with balance and trim.

In a keel of this sort, both stability and lateral plane are encompassed in the same fin. To accommodate the weight this far aft, the hull form takes on a long, outreaching bow, with a wide, buoyant, flat run.

As to sailplan, a modern 7/8 bendy rig similar to that on the 110 would be ideal, but for the day sailing I do, a masthead foretriangle and a simple oval wooden spar provide the minimum number of strings to pull and seem best.

The hull is of two skins of red cedar on longitudinal framing, with hull and decks encapsulated in fiberglass. All considered, a great way to utilize the shop's wood pile.

The 110 is a great little boat, but with luck the urge to build the new one probably will surface before I run out of gas.

This slim 24'6" day sailer combines a simple cold-moulded hull with a short, efficient rig.

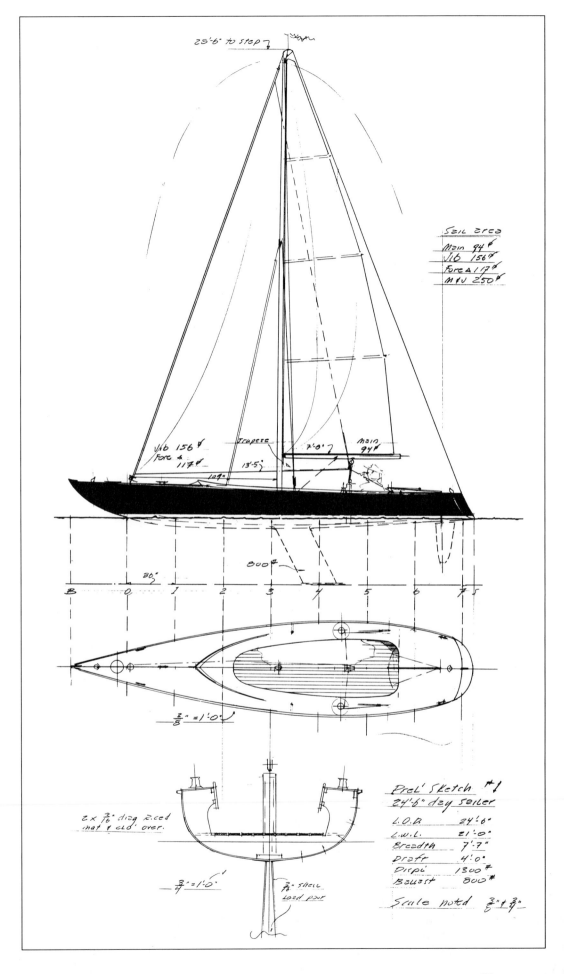

28'6" to step

Sail area
Main 94▯
Jib 156▯
Fore A 117▯
M+V 250▯

Jib 156▯
Fore &
117▯

Trapeze

7'0"

main
94▯

13'5"

104"

36°

800▯

B   0   1   2   3   4   5   6   7 5

$\frac{3}{8}$" = 1'0"

2 x $\frac{3}{16}$" diag. R.ced
mat + cld. over.

$\frac{3}{4}$" = 1'0'

$\frac{3}{16}$" shell
Lead pour

Prel' Sketch #1
24'6" day sailer

L.O.A.   24'6"
L.W.L.   21'0"
Breadth   7'7"
Draft   4'0"
Displ.   1300▯
Ballast   800▯

Scale noted $\frac{3}{8}$" + $\frac{3}{4}$"

Study number two,
Tadpole *is an opposite*
extreme. She's a big
sailing dinghy with
limited accommodations.

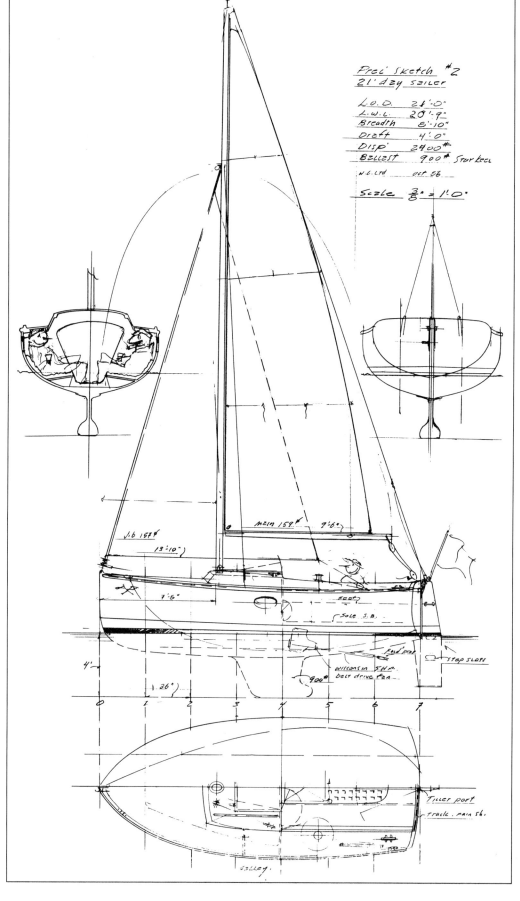

No. 2, *Tadpole*

LOA:	21' 0"
LWL:	20' 9"
Breadth:	8' 10"
Draft:	4'0"
Displacement:	2,400 lbs.
Ballast:	900 lbs.
Sail area:	316 sq. ft.
Power:	3 h.p.

No. 3, Star Boat Conversions

This little fellow was approach No.2, prior to acquiring the International 110. The all-out day-boat sketch of No. 1 led in turn to thoughts of a minimum cuddy boat with a couple of settee berths affording sitting headroom, space for a portable head and a small galley, plus a return to the recycled Star-boat keel theme.

Such thoughts turned the day-boat idea upside-down. Sitting headroom means freeboard, and light weight dictates a short boat of inflated dinghy form. We end up at the other extreme of proportions, with a better all-around boat that an old chap won't be so apt to fall off of.

Thus exploratory sketch No. 2 became a contender to the all-around use and affection bestowed on my schooner *Toadstool*. Utilization was too close to that of *Toadstool* to make construction practical, so the 110 filled the bill. I like this No. 2 boat. It's a nice size to keep at the marina if the island ever sinks.

The power noted is a little air-cooled Wisconsin fitted with clutch and reverse gear. For cooling, a blower can be run off the flywheel vee-belt pulley, with ducts fitted for intake and discharge. When run at a reasonable speed the sound level is acceptable, and for our summertime light weather (read *often glassy calm*), the little engine would be a real help in getting home to dinner.

Construction would be a toss-up between cold moulded (similar to Day Sailer No.1's method), or strip-built over a few moulds. Either way would take about the same glue pot and result in a good little ship.

I can see myself sitting in these boats, in colour, a nice breeze making up off the point, the bow wave starting to gurgle, and in the mind's eye every detail there to inspect and adjust. So many nice boats to build, and so short a voyage.

Scattered around our coastal backyards and storage sheds we have a wealth of potentially exciting day and overnight racing/cruising boats that often can be picked up for about the cost of the material. These sleepers are disguised as old Star boats. They are past their time of competitive performance, often tired, neglected, and badly in need of care, but with enough life left in them for more generations of sailors to enjoy.

About 35 years ago I made conversion plans for Star boats that were old even then, and I've often wondered why, despite our affluent times, more boats of this class weren't rebuilt into minimum yachts.

The old hulls usually are ruggedly built, and repairs or replacements where needed are not beyond the skills of the average handyman. This source of high-performance hull and fin sparks the imagination. All sorts of adaptations start sailing around the table, for here is a real minimum-cost yacht that will go like a thoroughbred, and a hull that offers a half-dozen interesting conversion possibilities to the sailor with time and imagination.

This spring, an oddly familiar, well-worn, and obviously much-used little sloop sailed by. On closing it proved to be one of the old boats we rejuvenated in the late 1940s. She's been sailing around for the past 40 years, giving her people a lot of pleasure, and at a cost per mile that would please even Silas Marner.

The old ones that we did with deck raised and a small house added had some 250 lbs. of additional lead ballast cast and saddled on each side of the fin, and faired into the bulb. As an option, the extra lead was cast in a half-oval and secured up under the existing casting with stainless-steel cap screws. A good shot of epoxy tar will insulate the lead and iron from each other and prevent corrosion.

Accommodations were simple, with a couple of folding pipe berths, a Primus stove, bucket toilet, and peanut outboard for power.

For my own ship, doing it again, I would raise the sheer about 8" with a 3/8" plywood wale strake. The new strake would be installed outside of and overlapping the original sheer strake by about 2-1/2" for a glued and screwed land. Stub frames alongside the original frames would continue the topside flare, and terminate in a new sheer clamp to fasten the deck and new wale strake together. About 3" of deck camber would do. The cockpit would be extended forward to encompass a shelter area with a strong canvas pram hood cabin.

The rig could utilize the existing gear, with the boom well-raised for clearance. A better choice would be a simple shorter masthead rig with a good genoa and spinnaker. A lower center of effort would be the result, with nearly equal drive.

The new mast could be wood, or an aluminum stock section could be fitted. The sail plan could be a sloop, a cat ketch, or even a yawl with a little overcoat-sized mizzen to give the elegance of a two-sticker. So the possibilities are endless.

My ship, with her light-blue underbody, white boot-top, dark-blue topsides, and black wale strake would be set off with sand beige decks and spars. A khaki pram hood cabin snapped over a teak coaming would finish off the deck. A high rail with a nice teak cap would keep us on board. Sails would be soft weave red-brown Dacron.

Sailing along in a fresh breeze she would make an attractive picture. The sight of a varied fleet of the little conversions coming up on a mark on a sparkling blue sea would make the Star boat's designers, old Billy Gardner and Francis Sweisguth, do the Hornpipe.

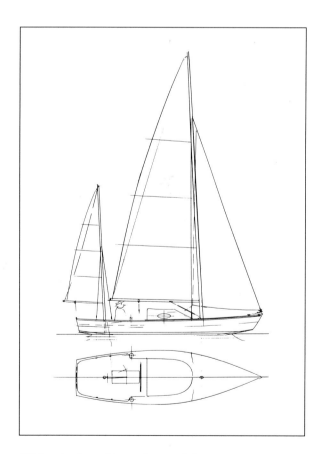

With raised topsides and a yawl rig . . .

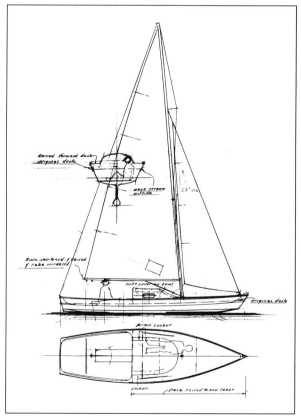

Or rigged as a sloop.

PART TWO

Motor Sailers

20

Motor Sailers

For today's few authentic 22-gong Taicoons who can afford the ultimate, one of the major motor sailers seems to be the real way to go, far surpassing the usual motor yacht. With a large motor sailer we have the pleasure of sailing, combined with good accommodations and speed under power, and a cruising range limited only by the owner's available time.

For a given length, the accommodations of a motor sailer suffer when compared with a three-tiered condominium. But for the knowledgeable boatman who has been on the water and sailing for years, the floating prune dryer won't do, however lavish the interior decor.

Along this line there are perhaps two ways to look at boats: either from the inside out, or the outside in. The experienced man who plans on extended cruising must have, first of all, a seaworthy boat. For him the outside-in model is the prerequisite. The "inside-out" buyer, by contrast, is the interior decorator's meat, for essentially this buyer needs a floating place, reasonably mobile, for entertaining and for marina functions. The boat need only have sufficient range and seaworthiness for short, along-shore hops. Any sort of off-the-shelf thing that can be deco-

rated and colored to suit will do. But for the go-places experienced yachtsman, the long-range seagoing motor sailer that combines beauty of line, fine accommodations, and true sailing ability has really come into its own.

The major development that popularized the larger motor sailer was the introduction and refinement of roller-reefing and furling gear for large sails. With such equipment the crew can be reduced to about half of what once was needed for a major sailing yacht.

I had the change vividly illustrated recently while watching a crew bend a new mainsail on a 90' traditional-model cutter. Nine men, two of them with stepladders, were doing the job. The simple harbor task of putting on a sail cover required six men, with stepladders still in evidence — a genuine muscle-job that makes a large boat with a conventional rig a white elephant without a beefsteak crew. Such a collection of Burt Reynolds moustaches in their yellow boots will be great company around the buoys, but the no-talk-back buttons of a roller rig can make sail-handling a simple pleasure, cut crew problems, and allow really comfortable quarters for the reduced number of hands required.

For this apparent simplicity, however, we need

a good mechanic and an electrician to keep the increased mechanical complexity in working order. The train of systems required to make a three-man, 120-footer practical requires in turn a far more technically-oriented captain and mate compared with the sailormen of the past.

Along with the smaller but more technically qualified crew or management team, the complexity of the systems requires a highly sophisticated design effort. Many, many more detail drawings — sheets covering, among other things, electrical, structural, mechanical and hydraulic complexities, piping, acoustics, rigging, accommodations, and security — are called for, plus dozens of other miscellaneous sheets of details. This design package is supplemented by a phonebook-size set of Specifications and Bid Conditions, covering the contractual details. So the design, technical liason, and development time generally matches the yacht's complexity. A vast amount of specialized reference data is collected for these major sailing-yacht projects, all of great interest as the systems and design are integrated.

During the past few years we've been active in developing some of the new breed of motor sailers. They have afforded us a most interesting study of this type and its potential for really pleasant voyaging.

For illustration I've chosen some of the boats in the 90'-to 160' range that we have been involved with — boats that appeal to me, and I trust will give you some of the pleasure in their review that they have given us in their design and development.

The 165-footer is a good one to put us in the mood for motor sailers. At 165' x 34', she's a nice size to maintain an easy 14-knot cruising speed under power, while an array of buttons will replace the bully boys before the mast. All rollaway furling sails; the mizzen boom tops up; and the boats swing out to clear the helicopter landing pad. The headsail arrangement has been revised from what the drawing shows to a single jib on a boom to avoid the problem of handling an overlapping sail of this size.

Our crew of nine includes an all-around engineer/electrician with his helper, and a seafaring captain whose skills include diplomacy and hotel management, plus chef, steward, housekeepers, and two others in the complement. There is end-less work for them on a yacht of this size and complexity when she is in commission, and time during layup keeps them busy with the inevitable maintenance and repairs.

Let's fly on board: rendezvous is in a sheltered bight down the coast. As we descend in our Jet Ranger, the mizzen is topped up and the pad target cleared. From the air she looks tiny, but as we hop down from the chopper the area of boat deck is really impressive, and there to meet us are the skipper and the steward with a tray of pick-me-ups. A couple of the crew whisk off with our bags, and we move forward and into the pilothouse. Here is the main control station, with wheels port and starboard as required for visibility due to the yacht's breadth. Behind us is the deeply upholstered leather settee, a good spot to sort out drinks and introductions before the steward leads us down through the saloon to show us our staterooms #4 and #5 amidships.

Lots of room in the staterooms, and beautiful decor, with queen-sized beds, endless closets and drawers, plus a marble bath with whirlpool tub. But let's go up on the flying bridge, since sounds of getting under way can be heard.

From our vantage point the skipper can be seen on the sailing bridge forward as the splayed-out anchors come on board, starboard first slacked off until the rode of the port anchor is up and down, then broken out and automatically hosed down as the starboard hook takes a strain. Then while both anchors are swinging inboard over the bow, a nudge from the twin 1000-h.p. diesels gets her slowly under way. The quiet electric windlass disappears under its casing, and she's all clear forward. Meanwhile, the sails are rolled out, two crewmen with walkie-talkies and the skipper being the only people visible on deck. while one of the three 120-kw generators supplies the muscle for the sailing equipment's hydraulic power packs.

Outside the headland the engines are stopped and she settles down on the wind, port tack, 25 knots apparent, 10 degrees of heel, doing an easy 12 knots. The good sound of the steward's lunch chime calls us to a buffet on the flying bridge — a private island of snowy linen and impeccable service — with an assortment of treats to sample in the sheltered lee of the bridge glass.

Life on the ocean wave. I've sent my brig to the knackers.

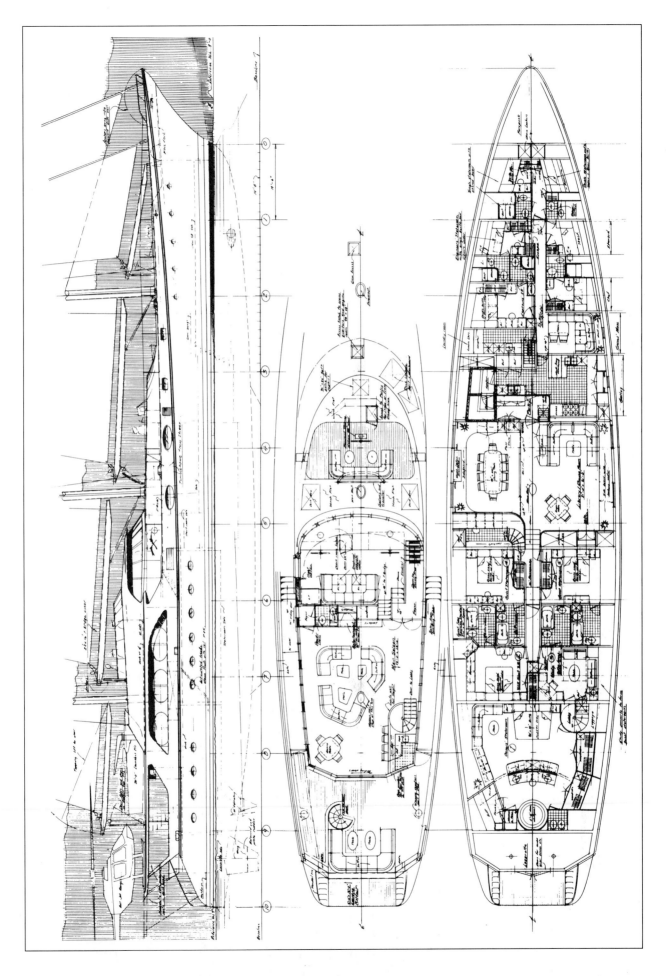

99

21

Saucy Bess

LOA:	24′ 0″
LWL:	21′ 0″
Breadth:	7′ 6″
Speed:	4.5 knots
Draft:	3'9"

The little *Saucy Bess* will be a refreshing start before continuing with some of today's highly technical models. About a hundred years ago the firm of Simpson & Denisons, of Dartmouth, England, designed this 24' steam auxiliary yawl — a boat totally impractical by today's standards, but a true motor sailer since she carries sail and is powered by a compound condensing engine of about four indicated horsepower. Steam is developed by a simple vertical, natural-draft boiler with condensing pipes under the hull, similar to today's keel-pipe heat exchangers.

The indicated horsepower (I.H.P.) as noted is used mainly as a measure for steam reciprocating engines, and is determined by the mean effective pressure in pounds per square inch on the pistons x piston area x the stroke length x rpm, divided by 33,000. I.H.P., less the engine's friction losses (about 15%, depending upon design), equals Brake Horsepower — the figure normally given for internal-combustion engines.

In looking over the plans it's apparent that *Saucy Bess* must have had a real crew problem, although the combination engineer/stoker could sit out of the way facing forward while the skipper took his ease in the stern sheets as he dodged the smoke.

The lack of a boomkin to take the mizzen sheet was an oversight on the plan, easily corrected on launching day. All in all a sturdy, full-bodied launch, with the always-appealing fantail stern. So, having established the beginning of things with this little yawl, we'll move on to some far larger and more complex models more in keeping with today's needs.

An early version of the motor sailer, Saucy Bess *was powered like the steam launches of her time by a small compound condensing engine amidships.*

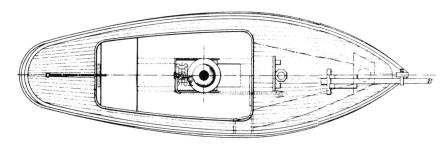

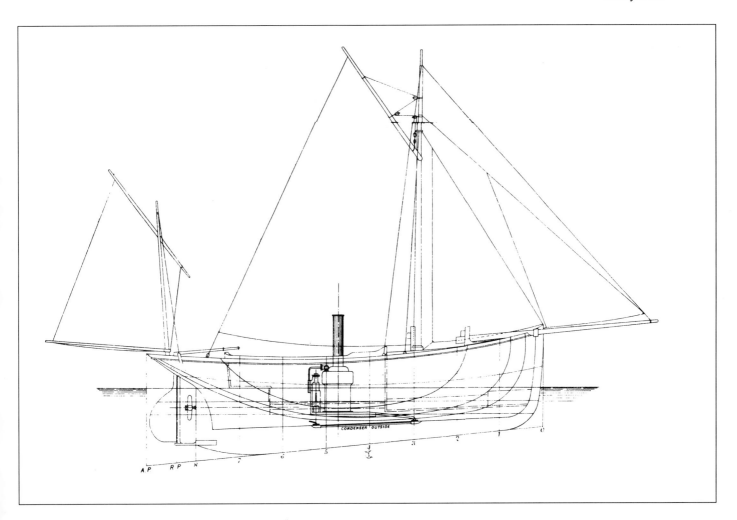

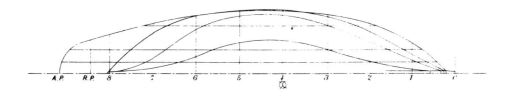

Lines of Saucy Bess *show a nicely formed body plan of ample displacement.*

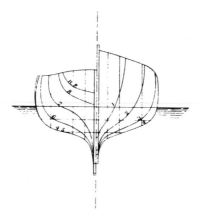

22

Mandalay ex *Shalimar*

LOA:	89' 8"
LWL:	82' 2"
Breadth:	21' 0"
Draft:	9'6"
Displacement:	195,000 lbs.
Ballast:	55,000 lbs.
WL to Masthead:	102'
Sail Area:	3,566 sq. ft. working sail area

At 90' x 21', *Mandalay* ex *Scotch Mist II* ex *Shalimar* is the smallest of this motor sailer group, and about the minimum size that justifies her classification as a major vessel of the type. Her other leading dimensions of 82' L.W.L. and draft of only 9' 6" result in a relatively shoal-draft keel boat.

For a passage-making motor sailer, a shoal-draft boat makes good sense, since a yacht of this caliber invariably ends up turning on the power and motor sailing when the wind is ahead or turns light. With twin screws, the leeward engine can be turning over at reduced speed and the windward propeller feathered. Any breeze at all will supplement the engine for economical performance. In hard conditions at sea, when deep draft or a board is needed to really get a grip, the relatively shoal draft can again be helped out with power, to more than equal the windward

performance of a maxi. For normal cruising operation, even the best centerboard seems to be a questionable complication.

When *Shalimar* was built in 1978, her rig was the first of the large Hood systems to be installed. The sail-handling has worked out well, although the mast section as furnished by Hood had a much larger moment of inertia than specified. The increased size was due to the vendor's concerns that on this first of the big-boat rollaway rigs the cavity wouldn't completely contain the rolled sail. As it turned out, the sail has room to spare, so the boat has sailed all these years with a mast well in excess of her needs. I've always hoped that one day a lighter mast section would be fitted. Many thousands of dollars have been spent on decor, but still this telephone pole aloft.

On the subject of rig, we learned from *Shalimar* how widely a boat of this form and windage

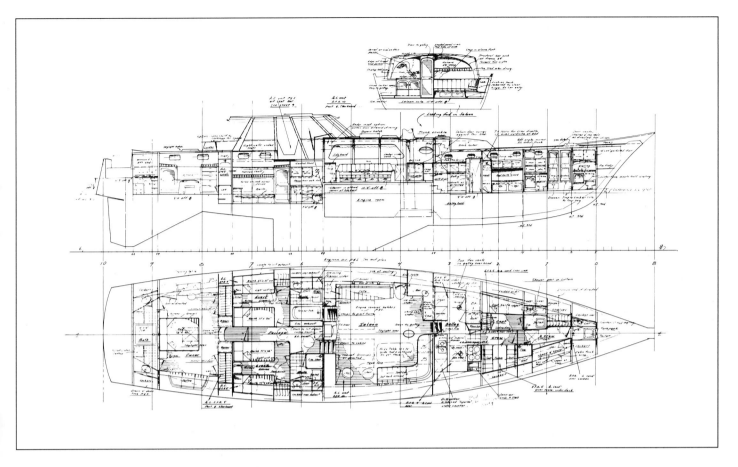

will wander while at anchor in a gale. When anchored in shallow water with lots of scope out, a large-section mast so far forward causes the boat to sheer violently in the squalls. A ketch seems to be a more practical rig, since a reefed mizzen can be set as a riding sail to settle her down and weathercock her while at anchor. For a cutter, a vestigial after mast could carry a riding sail and double as a radar and communications tower.

As to accommodation, the years have proven *Shalimar* to be a good little ship, with a practical arrangement for the owner, plus twin guest staterooms. On the negative side, the space forward is laid out for a minimum crew, an arrangement that usually results in the skipper and mate moving aft during owner-absent long delivery passages. Another 10' of length seems indicated for a three-stateroom boat, and to properly loosen up the crew's area. The crew, we must remember, lives on board year-round. To get and keep top people, their quarters are important.

The layout can be followed on the plans — tight in the crew area, but otherwise a practical cabin plan for comfortable cruising.

Shalimar was built of aluminum in 1978 for Sam Hashman to the good standards and economy of the former Stephens yard in Stockton, California. Dick and Theo Stephens were a good team to work with. It was a most pleasant association, with a knowledgeable owner and a good yard.

Over the years *Shalimar*, (later named *Mandalay* and *Scotch Mist)* has cruised from the North Atlantic to Australia while under the command of John Clyde-Smith, who has sailed under the house flags of both the Packer and Doubleday families.

This brings me to a larger version of *Shalimar*, her "when and if" replacement that was developed in sketch form with John's input during the early 1980s. Unfortunately, when they were ready to go ahead with building plans we had too heavy a work load to take them on.

The replacement was of a practical size and model that catches the fancy, so I'll add the preliminary drawings to our collection of "if only's."

The layout required 119' on deck to loosen things up with an additional stateroom aft and a far roomier crew area. Basically, the larger boat is a stretched-out *Shalimar*, with ketch rig and

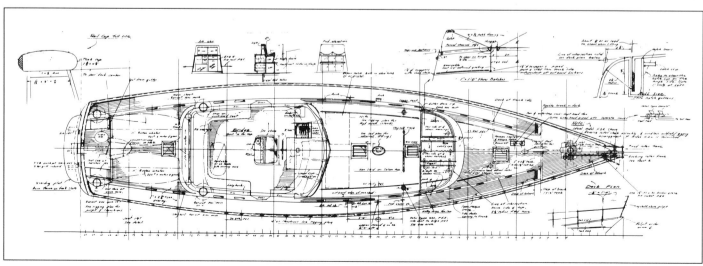

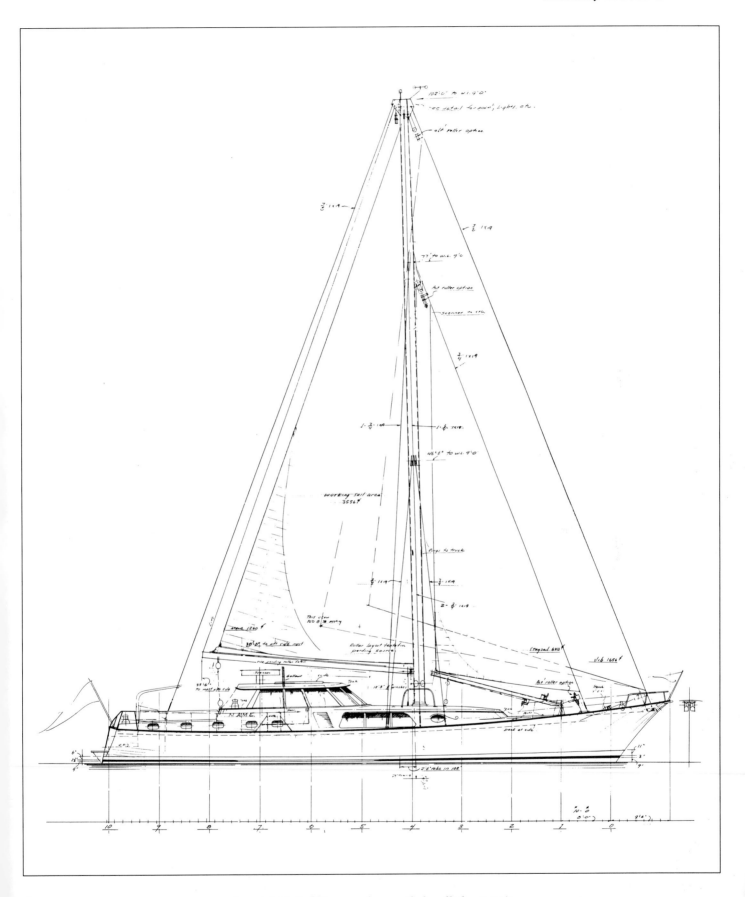

A practical deckhouse and an easily handled cutter rig.

flying bridge added. This is a nice size, but in looking her over today I see she could use another 10 feet of length to improve the galley, work in a proper laundry, and give the saloon some additional room, all of which undoubtedly would have come to light as the sketch was developed. And on this subject, a discussion of the development of plans should be of interest.

Normally, the owner or his captain might make the initial contact. Often it is an exploratory call, along the lines of, "We enjoyed seeing your boat at Cannes, (or maybe Mud Bay), and wondered about her, or about other boats of interest you might have under construction."

· Preliminary discussions might take a couple of months or a year or two, during which time some existing plans or preliminary sketches are roughed out. I should add that first we ascertain whether the client is qualified to handle the project. Lots of dreamers out there — the "We'll build three and I'll get mine as the profit" kind. Generally they are sorted out in the first phone call. A simple question about the construction budget often avoids wasted time for both parties. A minute or so on the phone usually is sufficient to discover if they are real, and a visit or two usually will tell whether they would be pleasant to work with.

At this stage the client's needs are sorted out, and advice given as to which way they should go. The first and logical choice is to buy an existing boat and avoid the decisions, delays, and frustrations of building. If nothing on the market is suitable, and a rough estimate of initial cost and its duplication in upkeep every six or seven years isn't a deterrence, then some preliminary work can proceed.

Of the several large-yacht projects that for

Shalimar *is shown on her first sail in San Francisco Bay. Lots of sail adjustment yet to be made but moving along in a nice breeze.*

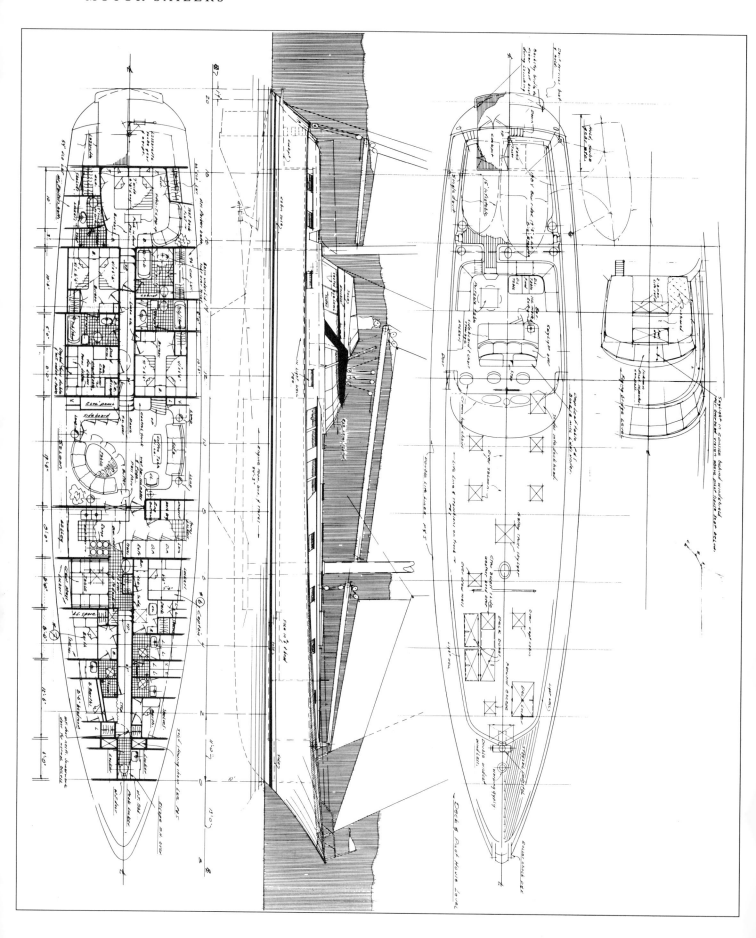

various reasons we have dropped over the years, it would be interesting (and, I'm sure, both enlightening and embarrassing) to have access to comments from those substantial nibbles that have gone elsewhere. On our side would be comments such as, "Abrasive bastard will be difficult to work with"; "Family obviously against a new yacht"; and "Captain more interested than owner." Should any of these pcople happen to read this they can write a margin-note rebuttal in their copy, but not bother to send it.

So some we've gone through with and wished we hadn't, but to even up the score are recollections of many wonderful clients and eventual friends, who have made the profession more than worthwhile.

Back to the nuts and bolts. We've covered the first, so in the bolts area the sketches of a proposal are developed and revised many times to get the general theme in order, then revised again in minor ways as the detailed bid plans are finalized. Simultaneously the specifications are developed, incorporating the equipment and structure to be utilized, all to be brought together and dovetailed into a working entity.

Usually, in a small office, the naval architect establishes the design through sketches and preliminary plans that pin the work down. In my case these first four drawings are profile and plan, construction plan, lines plan, and construction sections. In the case of small boats these are usually in sufficient detail to cover the project. With larger boats the work ends up as more of a team effort, with the designer doing the above conceptual work and then orchestrating the engineers, draftsmen and subcontractors. An involved process, time-consuming but of great

At left, deck plan, profile plan, and interior plan for Mandalay's *proposed replacement. Her basic dimensions will be 119'x 24'x 8'6".*

interest, although not the fun of a one-man design effort that might take one or two weeks.

For the larger boats that we've done over the years, I've had some good people involved. Brinton Sprague and Phil Brinck come to mind as two of the top-notch engineers and naval architects that I've had the good fortune to work with, plus many excellent craftsmen and technicians who have contributed through the years. I should also mention Greg Marshall as an outstanding design talent.

Brin did many of the detail drawings in *Yacht Designs #1.* Both Brin and Phil Brinck would consistently turn out the work of three draftsmen — fast, accurate design work, either structural or mechanical. Work that was always a pleasure to utilize.

On completion of the bid plans and specifications, the documents are sent out to qualified builders for cost estimates. The resulting prices are evaluated, the contract conditions developed, and the builder selected. Then we come to financial guarantees by both parties, delivery, payment schedules, insurance, and the hundred details required to ensure a complete understanding of what each party contributes to the final product. With the resulting contract then reviewed by pessimistic lawyers, the chances of a relatively friction-free program are fairly good.

During construction an owner's captain or representative should be on hand, with his duties carefully spelled out. He will be a watchdog without teeth, who reports to the owner and is empowered to make change orders only with prior authorization and cost agreement by the owner and builder. Tight chains of command, responsibility, and authority are all-important.

The architect's supervision of the work isn't possible without special staff, since each of these big yachts requires nearly a full-time representative at the site. The word "supervision" is full of fishhooks, too, and can be interpreted to mean an all-inclusive check on every nut and bolt. "Technical liason" works better, and consists of periodic visits to the work for general guidance.

So we get her built, she sheds some costly parts (hopefully all under warranty), and after a few thousand miles she's about shaken down. The bad times are well back in the foaming wake, and at last we're off to coconut land.

23

Ora

LOA:	118' 0"
LWL:	96' 6"
Breadth:	24' 0"
Draft:	7'6" & 17'6"
Displacement:	125 tons
Sail Area:	4,456 sq. ft.
D/L ratio:	158
Power:	twin Caterpillar 3406 diesels (370 h.p. each)

Interest and activity in the design and construction of major sailing yachts have greatly accelerated during the past few years. Today there are several large boats building on this continent and in Europe, sparked in most cases by today's state of the art in sail-handling equipment and advanced electronics. As mentioned earlier, the self-stowing sail systems have greatly reduced the crew needed to sail a major yacht. Reducing the size of the crew certainly has reduced the number of problems that go with a big fo'c'sle.

Twenty years ago a ketch the size of *Ora* would have carried four to six men in the fo'c'sle, plus the normal guests'-service crew. Today, in the 1990s, automated sail-handling makes it practical to carry fewer hands, and put the added space into better crew cabins and into the owner's living area. The only negative side to the smaller crew is the greater amount of electrical and mechanical knowledge required to service the complex systems.

With power winches and furling gear, *Ora* can be handled in moderate conditions by two men. Loads go up rapidly on a rig of this size, so some of the parts will seem gigantic next to those on the average boat. Jib sheets have a calculated load of 13,600 lbs., and require 7/8" diameter polyester braid. When *Ora* is shortened down to staysail and half mizzen, the staysail could put a total load on the four-part staysail sheet of some 23,000 lbs. Blocks, swivels, shackles, pins, bales, and all other sail-handling hardware require careful load analysis. The jib-sheet turning block,

however, was the only one that had to be manufactured when *Ora* was rigged, the balance of the large blocks being stock items. For *Ora*, the toggles also had to be designed and manufactured so they would marry up with the rigging screws and fit the stainless steel-bushed aluminum chainplates. These toggles were cast in 17 P-H stainless steel of 70,000 p.s.i. yield strength. Today, all that hardware is available out of catalogs. For rigging loads in the design stage we supplemented the calculations with a loaded scale model and relative-size strain-gauge measurement.

The mainmast section measures 24" x 11", with the tube alone weighing 3,360 lbs. The top portion is tapered. The main mast is 120' and mizzen mast is 74'. The main boom is 32' long. The two whisker poles are 38' long. The standing rigging was made up by Spencer's at Cowes on the Isle of Wight. The gear not custom-made was supplied by Sparcraft, Lewmar, Ronstan, and Schaefer.

The Hood Stoway main and mizzen mast are electrically operated from the flying bridge, as are the yankee and jib furling systems. All sails on the boat can be set in five minutes. The sails were supplied by North's loft in Vancouver.

Under sail a boat of this size lacks a feeling of speed, due to the crew's distance from the water. You realize how fast you're going when, in a moderate breeze, you sail through a fishing fleet that can't keep up, despite lots of exhaust smoke and heavy bow waves. In fresh conditions and despite her short rig, to sail alongside something like *Ora* in a smaller, off-the-shelf boat is discouraging.

In hull form *Ora* might be classed as a huge keel/centerboard sailing dinghy with moderate deadrise, round bilge, and minimum wetted surface. Seventy thousand pounds of lead are encapsulated in the keel, which also serves as the base for the centerboard trunk. A centerboarder seems to be the most practical model for sailing performace in shoal areas such as the Bahamas, but having moveable gear under water is a mixed blessing even in the best of times.

The centerboard is interesting in that it is of hollow aluminum construction. The water within the shell can be expelled by compressed air, reducing the board's underwater weight and easing removal by divers should repairs be necessary in a remote area. The centerboard is guided within the trunk by large lignum vitae rollers in removable cartridge housings. Raising and lowering is accomplished electrically.

The hydraulically-powered bow thruster is located in the forefoot, and the boat's main propulsion is by twin 3406 Caterpillar diesels, turbocharged and aftercooled, each developing 370 h.p. In speed trials *Ora* ran at 12.4 knots over the measured mile.

The engine room contains three 30-k.w. Onan generators, a watermaker, two air-conditioning compressors, and miles of wiring.

The air-conditioning is a chilled-water J.D.

Ora sliding along with a nice breeze in the English Channel.

Nall heating and cooling system, feeding 14 units throughout the ship. Fire control is a Halon flooding system.

The most obvious electronic installation is the satellite communication radome, a ball with a diameter of seven feet, perched on a gallows frame above the flying bridge. The radome houses an L-band satellite dish that constantly monitors satellites over the Pacific, Atlantic, and Indian oceans. At the push of a button, private voice or telex communications can be made from the middle of the ocean to any major city in the world. Business can be discussed in confidence 24 hours a day.

Ora was completely outfitted with all the state-of-the-art electronics. But state of the art changes so fast that they were nearly obsolete when they were installed. The electronics inventory included a single-sideband radio with auto-

matic coupler and full remote control. The VHF phone was a multi-remote system with an antenna on top of the 120' mainmast and remote stations in the navigation room, flying bridge, owner's cabin, and captain's cabin. Another VHF phone, independent of the first, was mounted in the wheelhouse. A ham radio was installed, and a CB radio on the flying bridge, plus an intercom.

The navigation equipment included a radar of 80-mile range, with antenna mounted 35 feet above the flying bridge on the mizzen mast. Another radar, with color display, has a 6' antenna under the satcom dome, ensuring full radar capability in case the mizzen mast is lost.

The satellite navigation system provides fixes updated accurately to within 30 meters, anywhere in the world.

Additional navigation equipment included loran-C; automatic digital direction finder with

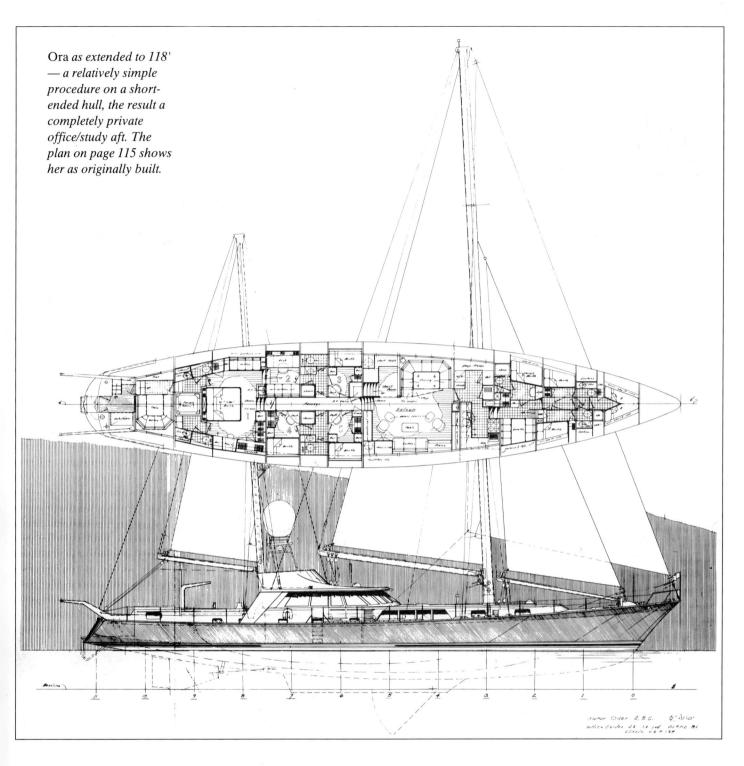

Ora as extended to 118'
— a relatively simple
procedure on a short-
ended hull, the result a
completely private
office/study aft. The
plan on page 115 shows
her as originally built.

beacon, broadcast and marine bands; marine weather facsimile; echosounder, and sonar.

An omnidirectional television antenna was installed to feed multi-standard television sets in the owner's stateroom, owner's saloon, and crew's mess.

Scantlings were in excess of Lloyds or the American Bureau of Shipping, with mechanical and electrical systems to Canadian Steamship inspection standards.

Ora was built in the early 1980s by Shore Boats of Vancouver to their usual high standards, with seagoing commercial-quality mechanical components designed for long life and low maintenance. *Ora* hails from London, a good rugged ship for my friends the Mettlers.

The photo shows her off a glacier during her shakedown cruise to Alaska. The cover shot was taken while in the English Channel. Home base is Mallorca.

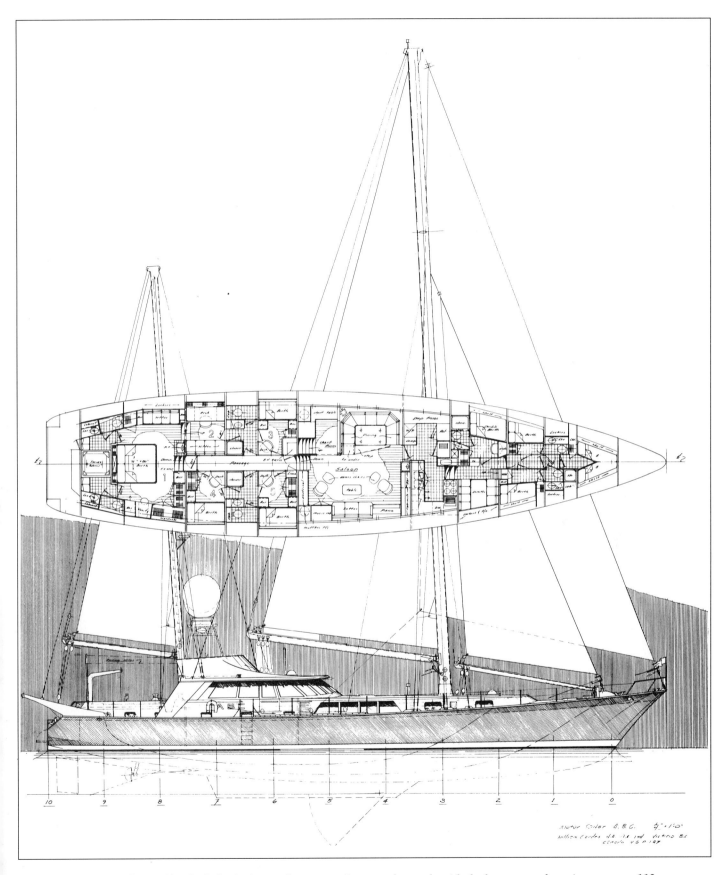

Ora as built was 104' L.O.A. An interesting comparison can be made with the long-sterned version on page 113.

24

Quest

LOA:	58' 0"
LWL:	53' 6"
Breadth:	16' 2"
Draft:	6"8"
Displacement:	93,000 lbs.
Power:	Cat D-334
Speed:	8.5 knots

About a cable length to the west of my island office window floats another of the lovely islands of this charmed corner of the Gulf of Georgia. Around the back of this neighboring island is the mooring of *Quest*, featured in this chapter. This is the area called Canoe Cove on the charts. Locally it's known as Freeloader's Cove, a well-sheltered harbor at the base of the Gulf Islands, and nearly at the end of the Saanich Peninsula.

Quest's island mooring is in a good lee from the worst southeasters. The island is home for Dave and Irene Myers, *Quest*'s owners, who find it an ideal base for coastal cruising, whale watching, or general exploring along the vast British Columbia coastline. The mooring has good water, close proximity to a shore base at the nearby marina, and for daily interest the endless tidal movement and boat traffic, and birds and sea life of all sorts.

The name Freeloader's Cove isn't meant to be disparaging, since it also harbors a steadily-changing fleet of regular and transient boats, liveaboards, and cruisers, who use the bay for a sheltered mooring or anchorage.

Bill Tellier of *Black Dog II* is a frequent visitor. Bill is in his 80's now, and has had his home afloat here and in the Caribbean for the past 40 years. A well-done version of Slocum's *Spray* has been moored in the cove near *Quest* during the past months, and the Farrells' imaginative and colorful junk has been in, plus a steady movement of cruising boats that slip in, stay for awhile, and move on — all affording an interest lacking in the usual marina fleet.

This activity floats by under the binoculars of Dave Myers, who is a social man — probably an eight on a scale of 10. I am about a three. So my island is happily out of view of much of the cove. My windows look up and down channel, through the islands to the north, and toward the Strait of Juan de Fuca and the Olympic mountain range to the south. From my boat shop side I look over a lovely clam bed and drying passage toward Fernie Island, which forms my breakwater from winter southeasters and which is the home of my other near neighbor, Capt. Walrus. All in all, a great place for boating.

But back to something on *Quest*. Dave and Irene Myers had her built in the 1970s by

Philbrook's Shipyards, in Sidney, B.C. Since then she has given them many hours of cruising, and has proven to be a good little ship for coastal exploring.

The design began as a motorsailer or heavy powerboat, the hull form being adaptable to ballasting if sail were to be carried. As built she has been outfitted as a motor yacht with minimum top hamper, although the paravane stabilizer gear admittedly forms a fairly complex bird cage of rigging. In size she is close to ideal for long-distance cruising with a limited crew on board.

The accommodations are straightforward, but give a much greater feeling of space than the plan would indicate. The Myers have done a beautiful job of detailing the interior and in the outfitting, which has further enhanced the spacious feeling below.

You will notice that the accommodations take up about three-fourths of the boat's length, with the other section holding the engine — a Caterpillar D-334, which gives an easy cruising speed of 8.5 knots through an 8-vee-belt-driven vee-drive. With the piggyback engine over the tail-shaft, the engine room space is very well utilized, allowing room for a good work bench, batteries, pumps, and a 15-k.w. auxiliary generator.

On this ship, unlike the big motor sailers illustrated, the owner is his own engineer and captain. Dave Myers is well-qualified, having a commercial pilot's license and a long background in general engineering. Every system was installed under his eye, which makes for peace of mind when cruising.

Construction is based on a simple strip-planked hull. The hull was planked up over moulds when upside-down, then given a heavy overlay of fiberglass, so essentially she is a glass boat with a built-in red-cedar liner. The liner doubles as insulation and as a sympathetic shell to take the joinerwork. Decks and superstructure are of wood with a heavy glass overlay, so she might be classified as a one-off glass boat.

The flush deck forward gives a world of workspace. Aft of the pilothouse is a snug flying bridge with dual controls and access from the afterdeck.

So *Quest* is an interesting member of the fleet in these islands, well-loved and cared for, in good trim and on hand for voyaging when the spirit moves.

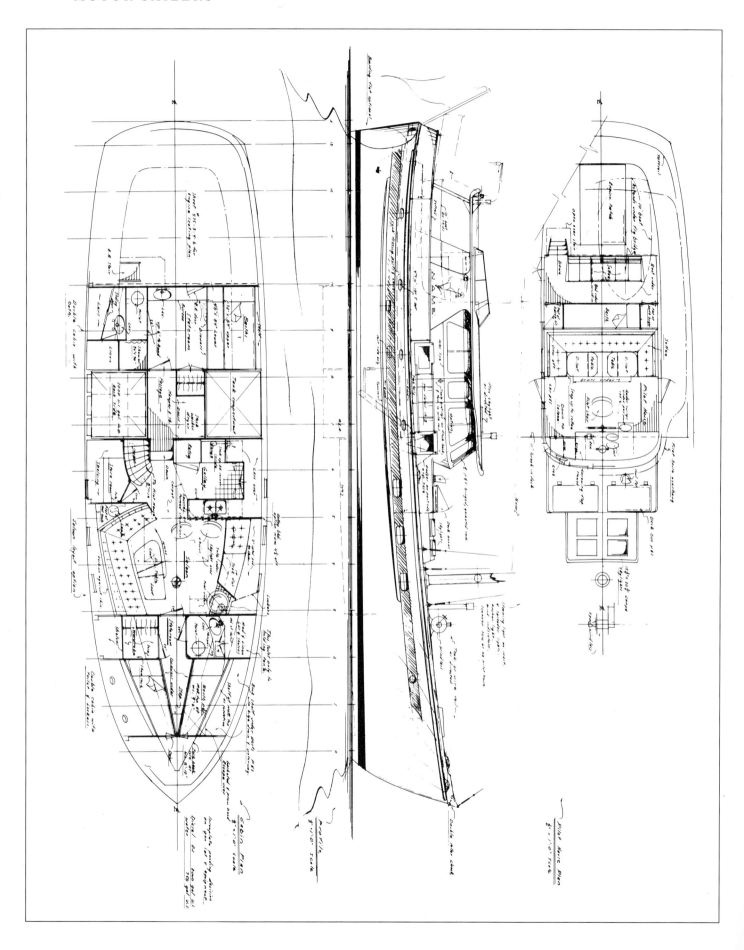

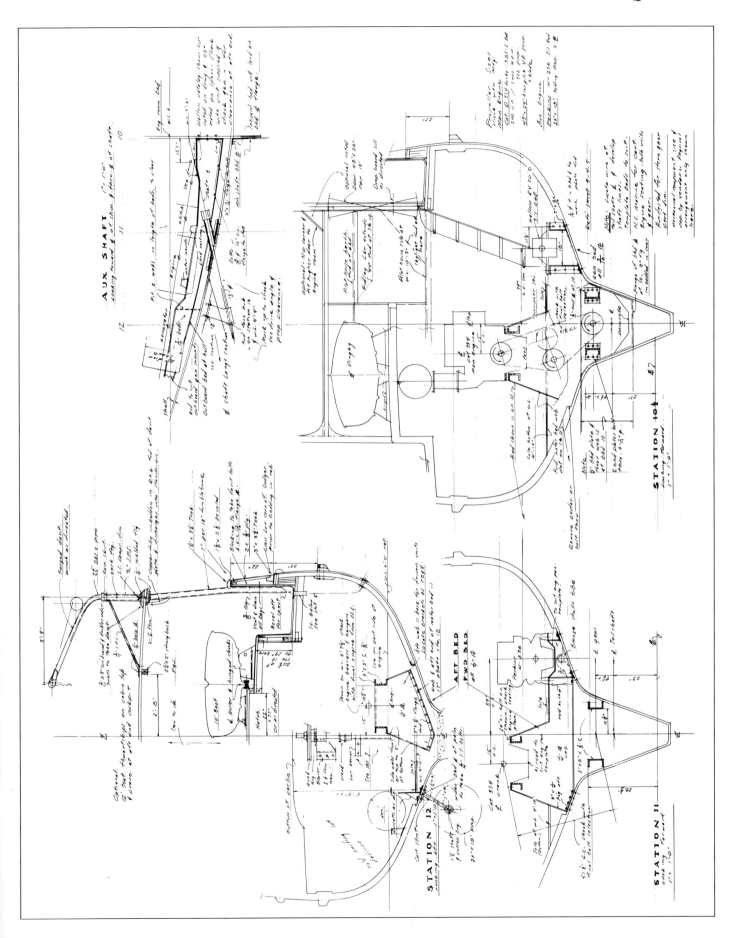

25

Mikado

LOA:	140' 0"
LWL:	120' 0"
Breadth:	30' 9"
Draft c.b. up:	9' 6"
Draft c.b. down:	20' 0"
Ballast:	120,000 lbs
Displacement:	640,000 lbs.
Sail Area:	7,154 sq.ft.
Mast Height:	156'
Power:	twin G. M. diesels (400 b.h.p. at 1,200 r.p.m.)
Speed Continuous:	12 knots

Mikado was built by Hitachi-Zosen at their Kanagawa Shipyard in Japan. She was built for a Guernsey-based company, with a hailing port of London.

Producing a yacht of this complexity takes many months of planning, and involves a great number of people. It's a long stretch for a small office to be involved, since detailed attention must be given to every phase, from the original concept sketches right on through each of the multitude of systems.

Mikado was designed for very experienced owners who had cruised extensively for many years in U.S. and European waters with their previous boat, a 99' ketch. They were great people to work with, knowledgeable, interested in every detail, and good friends through the good times and the worrying times required to produce a major yacht. The builders did their usual conscientious job with unfailing courtesy. All involved were good chaps who were intensely interested in creating *Mikado* from original concept to delivery.

In hull form *Mikado* is a full-bodied double-ender. Although encumbered by thrusters, skin-mounted cooling grids, stabilizers, and the bulky propulsion group, she moves quite well under sail. During trials in Tokyo Bay she slid along at 12.2 knots close-hauled in 28-m.p.h. apparent wind, with 14 degrees of heel. Unfortunately, on a yacht of this size there isn't much feeling of speed, due to the distance from the sailing station to the water.

For privacy when desired, the deck arrangement allows for two sailing stations. Under sail, usually she is handled from the flying bridge. When that station is used by the owner's party the sheets and trim can be managed from the forward cockpit, directly above the crew quarters and crew's on-deck access.

The Marquipt rig allows for sail-handling by a small crew. Sails are from the Hood loft in England. Roller furling and reefing of the four lower sails is handled hydraulically from either station.

Two centerboards are fitted, with the aft board for directional stability and downwind tracking in lots of wind and a big sea. While these boats seem large by normal yacht standards, they are tiny things on deep water in a gale.

A study of the accommodations will indicate the room afforded in a sailing yacht of this size. As an indication of the painstaking detail taken by the owner, the entire interior was mocked up full-size during the design development. The

mockup proved to be of great value in fine-tuning the interior, particularly in understanding of the galley work flow, and in previewing the interior spaces generally.

Something on cost always seems to be of interest. About 190,000 man-hours, depending on finish, are required to build a yacht of this complexity. The labor cost can in turn be about equalled by the cost of material, so a yard's labor billing rate will be a reasonable basis for total cost estimating. Initial cost plus upkeep costs result in a leaky-pocket operation for anyone but a really substantial owner.

For electric power, three 90-k.w. generator sets are installed, two of them available during peak loads, with parallel switching at about 70 percent load; generator number three is on standby.

The electronic package included every item of navigation and communication equipment available when *Mikado* was built, from gyro to satcom, along with an underwater viewing camera and complete state-of-the-art audio and video systems.

Construction is of aluminum to A.B.S. scantlings and finished to auto-body quality.

An interesting comparison of rig size with Mikado *alongside a tea clipper of the 1860s.*

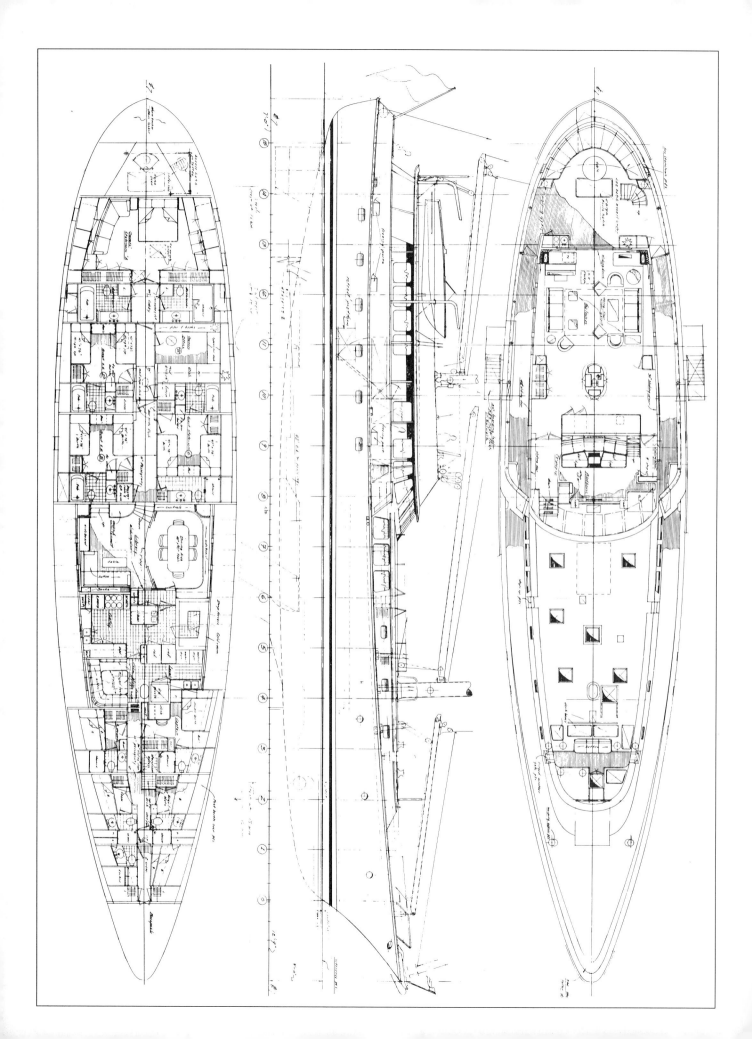

26

Chanel

LOA:	93' 4"
	(104' 0" as revised)
LWL:	85'0"
Breadth:	23' 9"
Draft:	9' 0" board up
Draft:	18' 0" board down
Displacement:	234,000 lbs. loaded
Ballast:	57,300 lbs.
Sail Area:	4,050 sq. ft.
Mast Height:	116'
Power:	Volvo Penta T.M.D.
	121c turbocharged
	diesels, 360 b.h.p.
	each, 2:1 reduction

Chanel was designed for New Zealander Neville Crichton, who will be remembered by competitive sailors as an Admiral's Cup contender with *Shock Wave* a few years back. *Chanel* was built of aluminum at Phil Thackwray's shops in Auckland. You will note that she is a development of *Shalimar*, but with greater sail-carrying power, a larger sail plan, and a draft of 18' with the board down, Neville being a highly competitive character who wanted top performance under sail or power.

Chanel's roller furling rig was by Marquipt of Vollenhove, Holland.

The layout is reminiscent of *Shalimar*, but the added length and breadth have loosened up the interior somewhat for an improved arrangement.

I should comment that on these boats ample engine-room space is an all-important feature, and often overlooked in an original design concept. The lavish accommodations occasionally seen on sailing yachts of this size are invariably at the expense of the space allotted to the engine and to the auxiliary equipment needed to make

The sailplan with deckhouse as proposed is shown here; on the next page is the deckhouse as built.

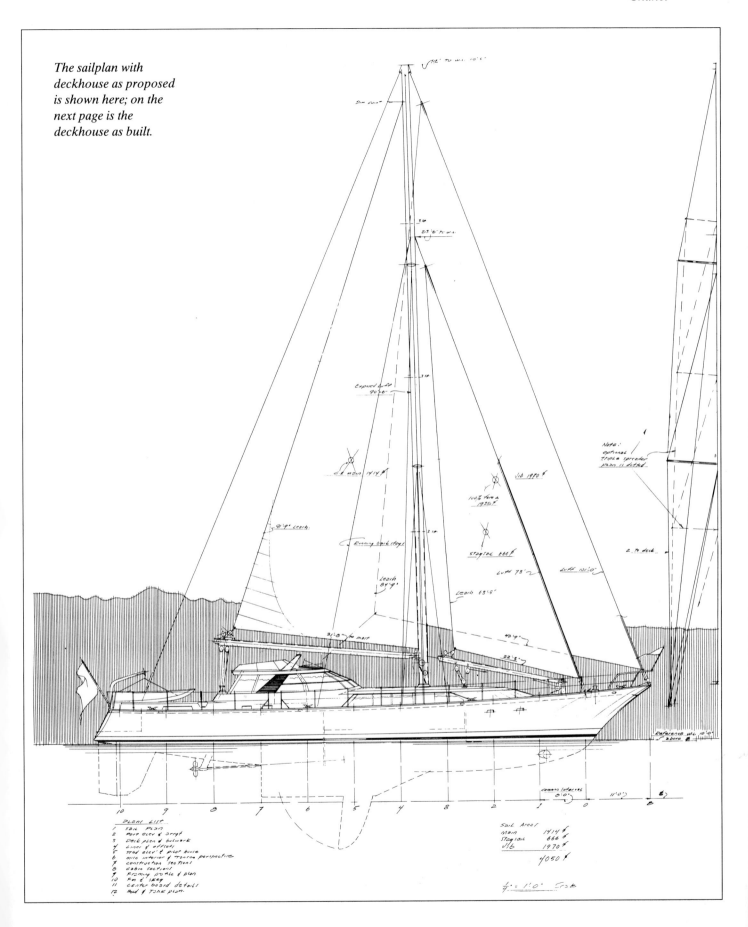

Chanel *as built in 1983.*

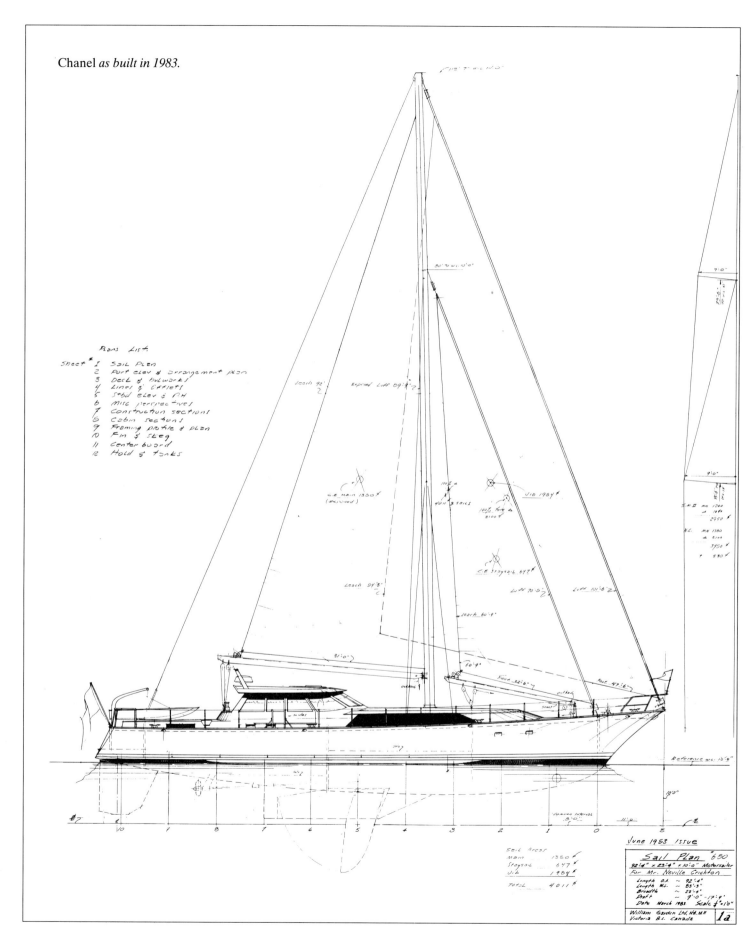

the systems operative. A tight engine room in a 90-100' boat, for instance, means batteries under berths, air conditioning, etc., squirreled away into inaccessible spaces, with pumps and other essentials positioned to baffle Sherlock Holmes. By contrast, *Chanel*'s engine room takes up 24', and is about the minimum length for a boat of this size. Space also must be provided for the mass of equipment essential for yachts of this complexity — room not just to shoehorn things in, but room for their proper maintenance and eventual repair.

The displacement required to float all this gear is another facet that is often underestimated when it's compared to a maxi or to a minimum-equipment sailing yacht. Stability or sail-carrying power is also a problem that we often see. Boats of this size can't carry a complement of tree-stump-sized characters to line up along the weather rail to keep her on her feet. Furthermore, the operating characteristics of a motor sailer dictate adequate stability so that she'll stay reasonably upright under a press of sail.

Three profiles are shown: the black-windowed view as she was built; the shaded background view as I wished her; and the lengthened extra-cabin-aft view as she is shown in the photos. Bless

the main boom for inhibiting the urge to emulate many of the modern three-story motor yachts.

After Neville sold *Chanel*, the second owner required another cabin aft for an office and retreat, so we had her drawn out 9' to a more conventional overhang. The revision was made at McMullen & Wing, in Auckland, to their usual high standards. Fortunately, these short-ended motor sailers usually can accept the addition of a longer stern, although it restricts the aft boarding that is so handy while at anchor. On the plus side an owner's office and radio room has been developed with access from the master stateroom. The office area is nicely laid out complete with satellite-communications terminal, fax, radios, telephone, air-conditioning, and extensive file and drawer storage areas. There is also access from the owner's stateroom through the office via a companionway ladder to the large open after deck.

A large lazarette has been added with a 6' x10' hydraulically-operated hatch, and this space accommodates windsurfers, wave runner and inflatables. A hydraulically-activated boarding platform folds out to replace the original permanent boarding deck.

Motor sailers seem to accumulate many miles

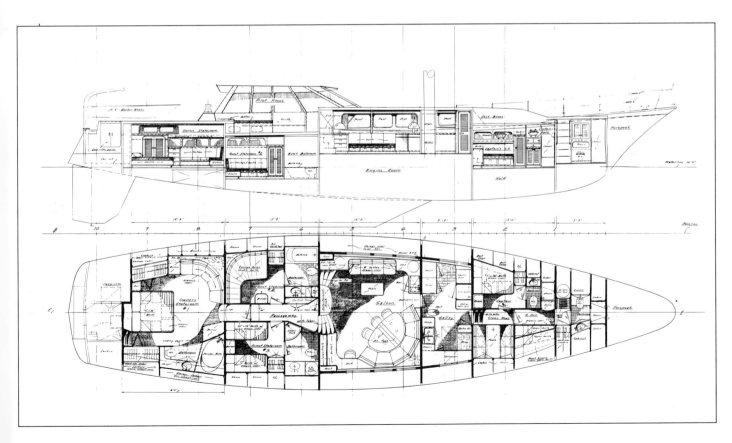

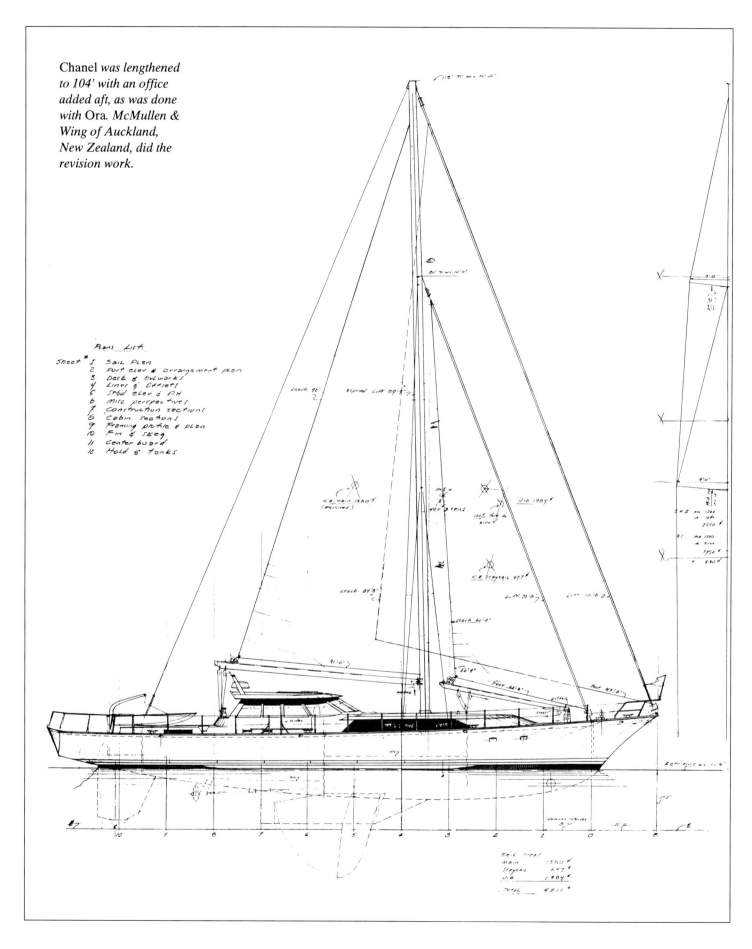

Chanel *was lengthened to 104' with an office added aft, as was done with Ora.* McMullen & Wing *of Auckland, New Zealand, did the revision work.*

The top photo shows Chanel as Arni A while cruising on the French coast. In the bottom photo she's on a good reach in a fresh breeze.

under their keels. The photos were taken in France, and kindly furnished by David and Esther Jordan, her current skipper and mate, who sail her in the early 90's under her present name of *Arni A*.

The photos will give an impression of her under sail. She's made some fast passages and has proven to be an ideal cruising yacht.

Evidence of this is that in 1988 she averaged a speed in excess of 10 knots from New Zealand via Cape Horn to South Africa. She's cruised from Alaska to the Tropics and the Mediterranean, and in 1990 she won the Ruban du Rose for the fastest time from St. Tropez to St. Barts. So *Chanel* has lived up to expectations under sail as one of the world's fastest true motor sailers.

PART THREE
Powerboats

27

Power Yachts

The smells of hard coal, cylinder oil, and hot steel in a steamer's engine room should start this section on powerboats, for these smells typify the beginning. The pre-diesel, pre-electricity era that we can read about with nostalgia did seem to have lots going for it in the way of a less-hurried existence. So let's forget about the lack of penicillin, and the prevalence of diptheria, tuberculosis, measles, and other almost-forgotten maladies, and look around in the dim light of a snug engine room of about 1883.

In truth, the temperature in the engine room is 110 degrees, but a good flow of air comes down from the deck cowls. At the gauges the light from the oil lamp shows the revolution counter at 150 turns, and steam pressure is steady at 100 lbs. The boiler room is brightened momentarily by the opening of the firebox door. We hear the shovel scrape a load of $4-a-ton coal and then the door clangs shut, while the nicely-balanced engine continues its rhythmic oscillations.

Coal bunkers are fitted port and starboard, boiler on the centerline, an up-and-down engine direct-coupled to the tailshaft, pumps, condenser, and an octopus of piping.

Galley and lavatories are served by simple manual plunger pumps, with replacement

On watch — a deck scene from the Victorian era, sans smoke. Drawing by Bourgain.

leathers in an engine-room drawer. Toilets pump overboard in the biodegradable days of the 19th century. Ventilation is attained with big adjustable cowls pushing the air below. But even with the cowls' air it's really too hot down here, so we'll say goodnight to the engineer in his wicker chair, and climb up the smooth steel ladder for a stroll out on the counter to watch the phosphorescent slashing of the screw's wake.

Check the taffrail log, light a good cigar, then forward again, running a hand along the moist teak railcap, to stand outside the wheelhouse door and sense the night. The sea is calm with an easy swell. The only sounds are the hiss and swash of the bow wave and the murmur of the machinery underfoot as the ship knifes along, each hour slicing through 11-1/2 nautical miles of ocean.

Two steps up and we are in the wheelhouse. A polished brass rail and brass-bound teak wheel are dimly outlined by the glow of the binnacle lamp, its wick well down, the low light forming patterns in the dark. The occasional creak of the steering ropes, the yacht's slow pitch and roll, and the shadowed, almost motionless back of the helmsman give life to the quiet room. On the starboard side the voice tube and the big brass Laughlin engine-room telegraph are the only connections with the engine room's orderly commotion below. Abaft the binnacle and steering standard, a polished mahogany chart table can be made out, its brass fiddle pins faintly reflecting the shielded chart lamp.

Navigation is by a big compass, a lead line, and a whistle, along with the taffrail log, the revolution counter, the sextant and chronometer.

In the galley the icebox holds a half-ton of ice, insulated by six inches of sawdust behind a zinc liner. Coal fires the big black cast-iron range. The heating system consists of a little Scotch boiler with piping connecting the cast-iron radiators. Fuel to the boiler is delivered by a coal scoop from a zinc-lined bunker, the heat controlled either by the fire or by the bypass valves at each radiator. There are no pumps to fail, the system being dependent on natural circulation and the coal heavers' enthusiasm. Oil lamps are fitted throughout, with a lamp locker and coal-oil tank in the forepeak.

Up in the fo'c'sle, ten off-watch, $30-a-month men are sleeping, their bellies full of $8-a-ton potatoes. We sold out at the top of the market, and dawn should reflect its rosy glow on a tropical peak above the southwest horizon.

For the pioneer steam yachts of the last century it was basically "fire out" by the beginning of the First World War. The internal combustion engine had literally exploded on sea and land. It was a mechanical development that brought greater change than that foreseen by all the philosophies. The slow-turning Union, Atlas, and other heavy-duty diesels replaced the large engine-room crew, and the smoke of the steam yacht's brief 50-year era dropped below the horizon astern.

These new heavy-duty diesels turned over at 350 to 400 r.p.m., not with steam-slippery smoothness, but with the near-reliability of a heartbeat. It was a measured *boogledy-boogledy* — an easy sound to live with and a great interesting pile of iron to contemplate: busy pushrods, rockers flopping back and forth, reciprocating pumps, the satisfying swoosh of air-starting, and the hypnotic pump and drip of a Mansell lubricator feeding through its spider-legged piping to the bearings.

The best feature of these engines was their simplicity. Installing one was a matter of boring a hole in the garboard strake for the cooling water intake, and another hole under the guard for overboard discharge. An air cylinder was chocked off alongside the engine, plus a standby air compressor. Feed lines from the tanks were led to the fuel pump. The fuel pump's return line led to a tank in the stack for gravity feed to the galley range, and from that tank's overflow back to the main tanks.

The engine exhausted up the stack via a heavy dry muffler. Pilothouse controls were connected to a repeat station in the engine room, and the ship was ready to sail. Give it the air! The powerful sigh of the air starter brings a satisfaction equal to the ultimate in mechanical sounds. The golden age of Babitt bearings and simplicity — the result was a big pile of iron, but certainly less bother than the various status-symbol systems that we lean on in today's electrical and mechanical yachting cocoon.

Thinking through the systems involved in the simpler boats of yesteryear, I wonder if those more basic boats didn't give greater pleasure and relaxation. Today we must fit in a multitude of interconnecting systems, all subject to failure if they lack expert attention. We have dozens of systems to cause concern, from the automatic ice-cube maker packing up so the mariners can't leave the marina, to the equally ridiculous postponing of an Alaska cruise until the backup radar is fixed. God help us when someone finally figures out how to pull the main switch on a world so dependent on electricity.

As we chug steadily away from the simpler yachting of decades past, our onboard systems must include a heat-exchanger-cooled, compact high-speed engine that develops the required torque through reduction gears. We'll have a water maker, hot and cold pressure water, holding-tank toilets, stabilizers, and electrical systems fed by a pair of diesel light plants. Add converters, compressors, transfer pumps, air conditioning, intercom, microwave oven, disposal, compactor, washer, dryer, refrigerators, deep freeze, broiler, electric range, crisper, and a half-dozen other appliances. Stay with me now, we are about to get the ship under way, which will require: radar, sonar, loran, GPS, ADF, radio Sat Com (good for ordering parts), recording fathometer, anemometer, sea-water thermometer; not to mention the alarm systems for lube oil, jacket water, exhaust, burglars. The list is lots longer, but I'm too sensitive to continue.

Revolutions are up and weight is down. The higher-frequency sound is more tiring, and a skilled crew, including an all-around electrician and a mechanic, is needed to attend to all this stuff that happiness is supposed to be made of. The crew is much smaller than the crew required for grandpa's boat. It will, however, get about the same pay in number of small dollars that 15 men got in the days of the big dollar. With it they will live perhaps twice as well — if we balance the loss of the hot cylinder-oil smell against the introduction of Medicare.

Yacht toilets have gone through a parallel development, from the ornate pump water closets of the 1890s to the holding-tank or treatment systems of today. While the modern toilets are compact, tidy, and highly efficient, I've always felt that the ultimate toilet was achieved with the continuously-circulating, constantly-flushing rim hopper located in a neat toilet room opening off the main deck. A warm seat was ensured by the engine's cooling water flowing through the hopper rim, thence down the soil pipe and back to the sea. It was a marvel of simplicity and comfort, the 4" pipe discharge impossible to plug,

even by a crew of giants. With the door open, this toilet room was a wonderful place to sit on a sunny morning, the engine turning over at about 320, and the great arc of sea and horizon to contemplate.

I often believe that the present-era owner has lost his way as the breakdown-prone systems sail off with him (probably in search of parts and someone to install them). An old sailor friend told me that in the Med, when he walks the quay sides where the big ones are moored end-on, he keeps well along the shoreside buildings with eyes averted, for fear some harrassed owner might rush ashore and *give* him a yacht.

To complete a proper broad-brush picture of the horrors of complicated yachts, the initial cost of the boat is equalled every six or seven years by the cost of maintenance and operation, not including the interest lost on the money invested. It's a costly way to ride.

But boats are a wonderful compulsion, so let's proceed now with the steam yacht *Firefly*, then on with the powerboat section of this book, while looking on the bright side — all systems percolating, good company aboard, steamer chairs out, warm sun on the bright blue sea, and the polished metal glistening like a silver star.

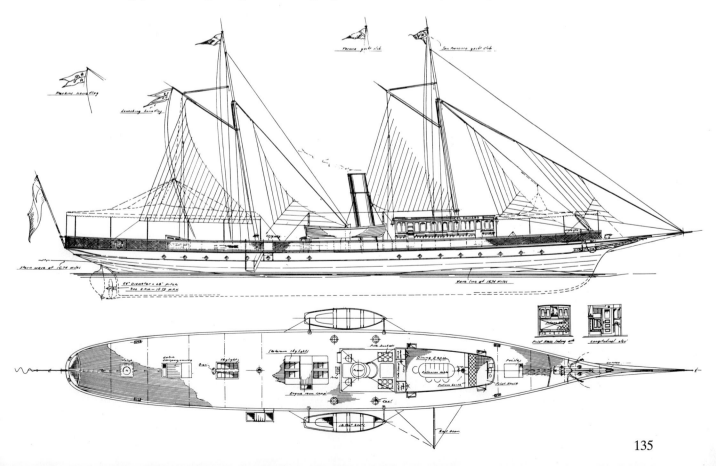

28

Firefly

LOA: 151′ 0″
LWL: 129′ 6″
Breadth: 17′ 6″
Draft: 8′ 0″
Displacement: 170 tons
Speed: 10.8 knots

You may have gained the impression that steam yachts have always had a strong attraction for me. I'll inflict you, patient reader, with one more of these smoky and cramped, but, despite all, really elegant yachts from the pre-income-tax era of private rail cars, fast horses, and — for some — three-month summer holidays.

Firefly is an imaginary ship designed as an interesting study of what an ideal coastal cruiser of the 1880s might be. With her and my crew of stalwarts, plus McPherson in the engine room and Capt. Astrolabe Duck at the helm, I would go voyaging to my heart's content. As illustrated here I've clewed up the awnings, stowed the deck furniture, and filled the bunkers with good hard coal. With steam up we're ready to point the bowsprit south across the bay, away from the winter gales and cold seas of the north.

In the drawing, the starboard steam launch has yet to be swung inboard over the engine-room fidley. The port cutter we'll stow on the boat skids over the deck saloon aft, abreast of the pulling boat, while steaming down the estuary. Then, with gear secure, we'll head off over the horizon on a long slant to the next coaling port.

The foresail is brailed up at present, and the forestaysail still covered. Along the way, we'll carry the five lowers to dampen the roll and save some coal. It's a snug rig, but it will give a real boost as the taffrail log spins off the miles in our wake — an easy, economical 40 nautical miles with each four-hour watch.

In the sunny south the awnings will be spread fore and aft, the wicker steamer chairs brought out, and wind sails rigged to the deck cowls. With the launch and cutter overboard and on the boat booms, we'll lie happily to 20 fathoms of 3/4" stud link chain, sloping off to a white sand bottom. Time then to swim in the clear waters, and in the steamer chairs sip tall drinks of local rum and juices. With the cutter under sail or the starboard launch under an easy head of steam, we'll explore the islands — a century before the coming horde of fat, black-windowed pushwaters.

My daydream has carefully glossed over the stokers who, four-on-and-eight-off, shoveled me south, and who I suspect dropped the piece of ballast through the bottom of the cutter after raiding the booze locker and making their escape.

So much for the steamers of yesteryear and back to reality.

A lovely conveyance to southern ports — but spend the day ashore when she's coaling.

29

Express Cruiser *Kalitan*

LOA:	42' 0"
LWL:	36' 0"
Breadth:	10' 0"
Draft:	3' 4"
Displacement:	14,650 lbs.
Power:	Twin Isuzu
	120 b.h.p.
	@ 2300 r.p.m.
Reduction:	1.5:1
Propellers:	20" x 20"
Fuel:	200 Imp. Gal.
Water:	50 Imp. Gal.

For a one-off boat of this sort aluminum is a good material to work with, resulting in a logical structure, without questions of the moisture content, leaks, and decay of wood, or the involved tooling process of a one-off glass boat. After careful layout work the pieces go together on a simple jig like a cardboard kit. Material standards are precise, and with aluminum the waste is minimal. What scrap is left doesn't go up the shop chimney but can be gathered for recycling. Construction time for the one-off metal boat is normally less than the time required for wood or glass. If you can find a good shop familiar with aluminum boatbuilding techniques, the light-metal boat is worth a long look.

John Beales is another old friend who seems able to put his hand to most things mechanical, be it boats, airplanes, or whatever. For this chapter I've included *Kalitan*, an aluminum express cruiser that John built when operating Beales Steel Fabrication Co. a few years back. On an overall length of 42' she has somewhat the appearance of a big *Katherine*, the wooden commuter illustrated in my earlier book of yacht designs.

Kalitan, however, lacks the zip of the 36' *Katherine*, due to limited power for her weight and size. Nevertheless, *Kalitan* ran along at well over 20 knots, but always seemed to cry for some real horsepower under the hatches. About 1,000 h.p. and 40 knots would be the way to go.

Along with greater power, John and I have discussed the best features to incorporate in a No. 2 version. *Kalitan's* layout is Spartan, for one thing, so another 18" of breadth would allow a vast improvement in accommodations. Side decks could be narrowed about 25 percent to further improve saloon width, and a layout fitted that would allow three to be seated abreast facing forward. Water plane area would be increased about 12 percent to retain optimum stability with the greater deck weights.

So it goes. John is scheduled to fly over soon for a high-level pow-wow on things in general, which brought *Kalitan* to mind as an interesting boat to review.

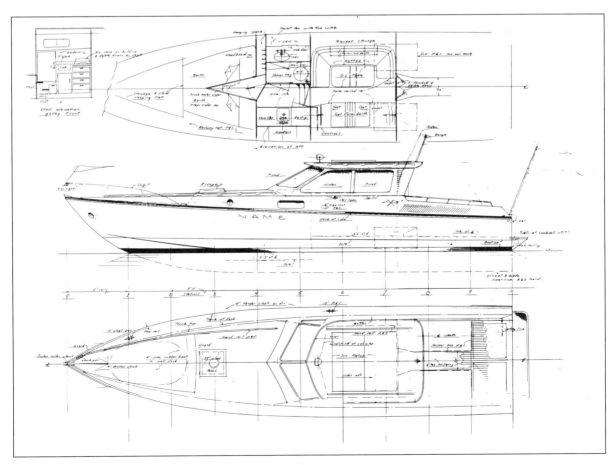

Despite the longitudinals not being shown in this plan, the relative simplicity of metal construction is apparent.

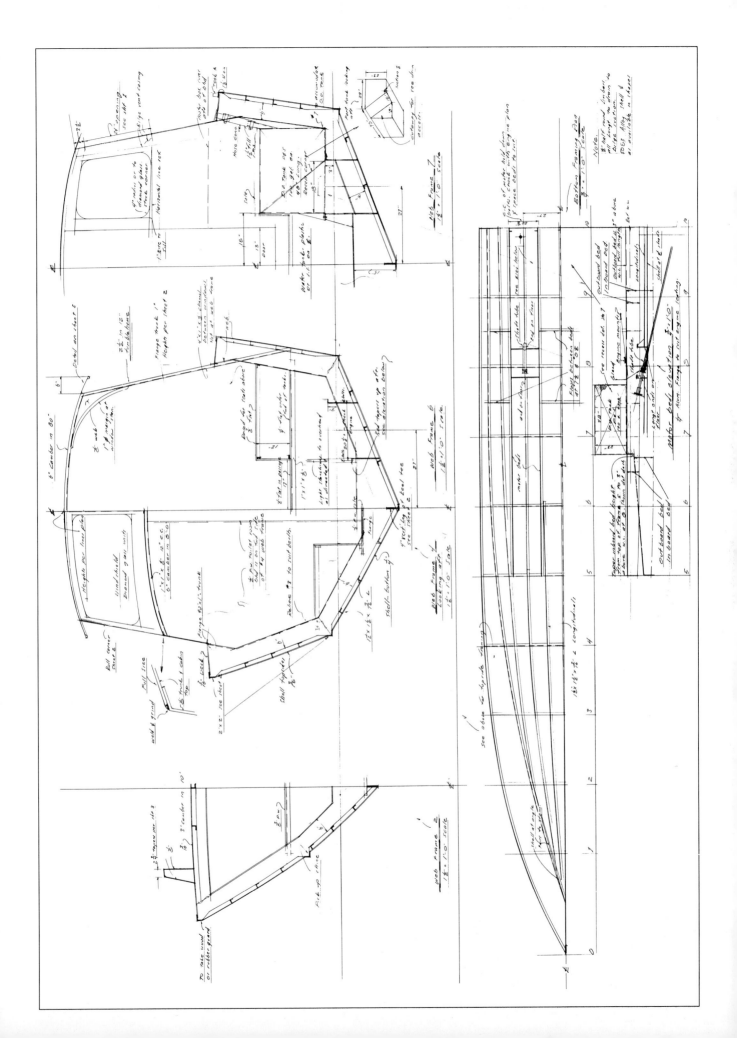

30

Wanderer 42'

LOA:	42' 6"
LWL:	39' 3"
Breadth:	14' 0"
Draft:	4' 0"
Ballast:	31,200 lbs.
Speed:	8-12 knots
Power:	150-300 b.h.p.

The Wanderer model was one of the early shipshape-appearing double-cabin motor yachts developed for Northwest cruising. A bunch of them were built from the 1950s on. Power then was usually a war-surplus G.M. 6-71 diesel, while many of the later ones had Cat or Cummins engines. Any one of these engines, along with 500 or 600 gallons of diesel oil and about 300 gallons of water, would take one a long way.

The layout is very practical for two couples or for a family, since reasonable privacy is afforded by staterooms in opposite ends of the ship. Uppers could be fitted forward to handle either a family of kids or locker overflow.

With such a layout, the midships on-deck galley and saloon also provide a central community space, with nearly 360-degree visibility. The view aft is restricted only by a big vegetable cooler and the flying bridge access ladder on the port side. For the fisherman while trolling, a view forward through the deckhouse windows is a reassuring feature. For the times when you want to escape from the crowd, the sleeping cabins fore and aft offer solace. Ease yourself below, take a nip of Old Grandad, and relax with a quiet book

to regain perspective.

But let's hop up on deck again and count the good things. A great dinner is under way in the galley, the sun has broken through for relaxing on a flying bridge steamer chair, the guests are off drowning themselves in the sailing dinghy, and the sun-washed cove is glistening after the rain.

These boats are of carvel wooden construction with bent-oak frames on a heavy backbone. Stem, propeller post, shoe, caps, and guards all are hardwood. The planking is yellow cedar, the keel, stringers, and beams are fir, and the entire superstructure is covered with fiberglass for a tight, easily-maintained surface.

Varying arrangements were tried in the dozens of this 447 series that were built, but the arrangement shown here seemed to be the most practical. The walk-around under-cover decks are particularly appealing for Alaska cruising. Side curtains can be lowered, enclosing the after deck area to afford a snug, cushioned lounge over the top of the after stateroom — a fine place to stretch out on some fat cushions for mellow contemplation as we motor up some glassy fjord.

But as we contemplate, the ugly worm of "if-only" starts to move. A vision of her comes to

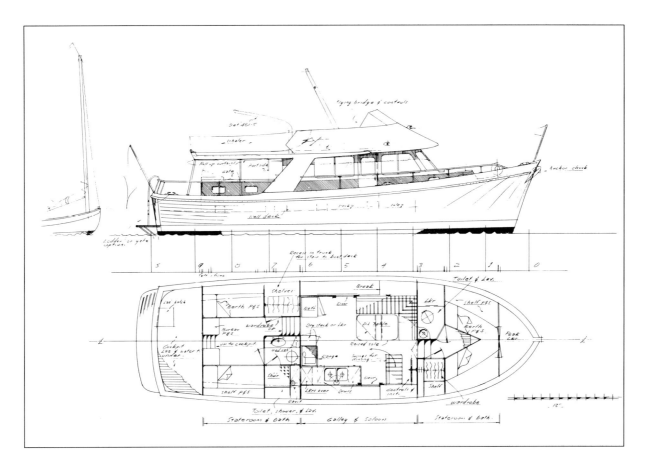

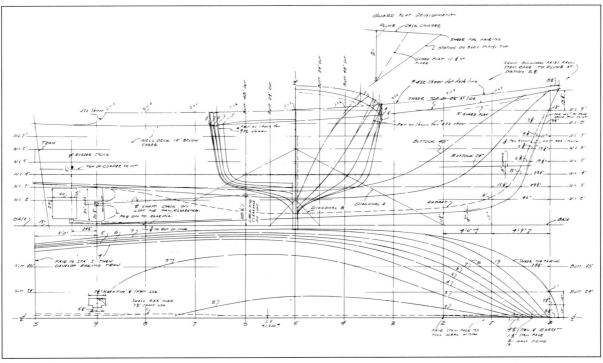

mind with another six feet added forward of the pilothouse for a loosened-up forward stateroom, and with a washer/dryer worked in at the foot of the companionway. This would be great — do away with the clothesline and three-day-old shirts. A quick decision this fall and the new ship will be promised in May, launched in July, and ready to head north in mid-August.

Then comes the thought of another 10 feet in the middle, plus a couple feet more beam, and twin engines. Lots of fuel and a summer out in the Aleutians.

31

Orca

LOA:	51' 0"
LWL:	47' 4"
Breadth:	15' 0"
Draft:	4' 3"
Displacement:	35,000 lbs.
Fuel:	300 U.S. gal.
Water:	200 U.S. gal.
Power:	Cummins V-8
Propeller:	28" x 18"
	3-blade
Speed:	12 knots

Another one from the 1960s that I'm going to inflict on you is *Orca*, a 51' motor yacht designed and built in 1962. She's a nice little ship, well built to Vic Franck's good standards, so we'll reserve a spot for her in this ramble through small-boat plans. *Orca* was the forerunner of a whole fleet of fast cruisers such as *Zest* and *Shining Hour*, plus many copies and developments of the theme.

Kline and Margaret Hillman of Seattle had her built, and with their decorator they created a most pleasant and peaceful interior color scheme and decor. In thinking back over the project, I recall an early lunch visit to Hillman's club, to inspect colors of the newly-redecorated dining room. Following some rather upper-crust munching, and not being a club type, I was taken on a tour of the premises. The locker room took me back with a jolt to high-school times. A couple of once-familiar faces were lacing up their shoes, and I was struck with the thought that perhaps they hadn't heard the bell ring at the end of the

period. I had a similar recollection when our kids were small and we visited their old Crown Hill School on open-house night, and were met with the half-forgotten school smell of waxed wooden floors, damp cloak rooms, blackboard chalk, and shining scrubbed faces — all of them thoughts that this boat brings to mind.

Most yachts of this type today are twin-screw. However, the waters of the Pacific Northwest, particularly in the 1950s and early 1960s, were noted for drift. Timbers, logs, and stumps were waiting to be run over, so a single-screw arrangement was chosen to minimize the chance of propeller damage.

Power was a V-8 Cummins developing 220 h.p. at 2600 r.p.m., turning a 28" x 18" cupped 3-blade right-hand propeller. This delivered 14.7 knots maximum and an easy 12 knots cruising speed when she was new and light. The engine is under the pilothouse with tanks aft, so the center of buoyancy is 56 percent of the L.W.L. from the bow. This is near the forward limit for her speed/length ratio of 1.75. The desired layout,

Orca's big bright pilothouse is shown at the top of the page; above is the view aft from the deckhouse to the cockpit with its sweep of cushioned seating.

with a low saloon sole, moved the position forward and dictated the position of the center of buoyancy, so she has a fuller forebody than I normally would have developed. Ideally, the machinery and tank weights should be located to trim with the boat's center of buoyancy at about 58 percent of the waterline length from the forward waterline. Alternately, with twin screws and a service speed of 21 knots, the weights would be moved aft and the center of buoyancy at rest would then be nearer the 61-percent mark to match a speed/length ratio of 3.

The usual pushwater cruiser seen plowing along with its spectacular bow wave is often the result of a failure to properly position the centers — that, plus the tendency to pack too much power and weight in a given waterplane. Computer analysis tells me that 68 percent of all motor-

A port-bow view of Orca *at cruising speed.*

driven boats are the result of misthinking in varying degrees, the printout ranging from "try again" to "abandon." Unkept political promises, I am told, run as high as 84 percent, but as with the boat ratio a five-star gov't galley for handouts and the right drapes make it all acceptable.

Orca's layout worked out well, but lacked the double bed that seems to be the status symbol today. Each stateroom has a private bath, one of them with a shower. A pilot berth, or passage berth, which as I remember ended up as a washer/dryer space, is located aft to port. The saloon was a most pleasant area, space being achieved with minimum-width side decks and the study-type galley finished in dark wood. This decor gave continuity to the room as a saloon when the galley activity was shut down. The wide saloon doors opened the room out into the cockpit.

Decor was a simple, functional, meat-and-potatoes approach compared to today's beautifully done but somewhat garish interior designs.

The pilothouse, four steps up from the saloon, had 360-degree visibility, a wide settee, controls, electrical panel, and pilot seat. A flying bridge wasn't requested, so the profile is low and pleasing — although for my own use an upper control station on the boat deck would be worthwhile.

A Whaler was carried on stern davits rather than topside as drawn. This is an excellent feature for simple, one-man launching, and ideal for the Northwest, where anchoring out is daily practice in remote areas.

For construction we used bent-oak frames, with the chine log outside, and yellow-cedar wedges to fair in for the 1-1/8" red cedar planking. No. 2 of this model was similar, but with a 1/2" diagonal skin and 5/8" fore-and-aft over, with hard glue between.

Today, in the 1990s, my friend Ed Richardson tells me that she's the well-loved possession of Mike Bain, in immaculate condition and hailing from Newport Beach, California, under the name *Summer Place*. She was *Cloud Burst* when owned by J. B. Youngblood. So she's had good owners over the years, and with luck another 35 years stretches ahead.

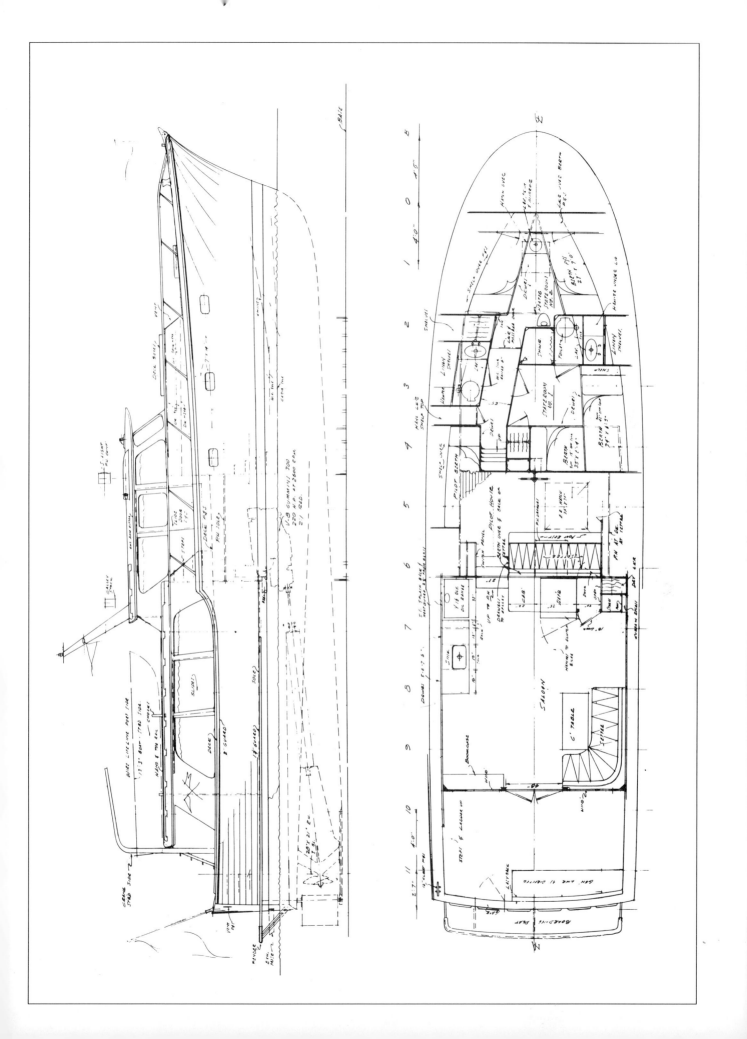

32

Beach Boy

LOA:	32' 0"
LWL:	30' 0"
Breadth:	10'6"
Draft:	3' 9"
Displacement:	16,000 lbs.
Power:	Caterpillar 3160
	203 b.h.p.
	@ 2800 r.p.m.
Reduction:	2.5:1
Propeller	27" x 18" 3-blade
Fuel:	250 Imp. Gal.
Water	40 Imp. Gal.
Service speed:	9 knots

B*each Boy* was a real gold-plater among Canadian log-salvage boats, so I'll slip her in here as an interesting work boat that could double as a cruiser. She was produced for Gordon Reid, who had her built at Philbrook's yard in the early 1970s. At the time, I thought the cost estimate would cancel the project, but Gordon didn't blink, so a few months later *Beach Boy* was off and working and earning her keep.

The usual and more practical log-salvage boats are of steel or fiberglass. They are heavily built, since they work right on the shoreline. Steel is the most practical for the service. The logs to be salvaged often end up high and dry on the shore, and must be jerked off by a boat with some real beef and heavy towing bitts. When a stray log from a broken boom is spotted, the boat runs in and a line is taken around it. Then, with a steady pull or with a run at it, a 40' stick some

30" in diameter will come bouncing down to tidewater at a great rate.

Gordon is happiest with a wooden boat, so *Beach Boy* was built to the heavy scantlings needed for her service. She is sheathed with gum, and fitted with massive underwater protection. You will note the log comb on the stem band, with a step on top for reboarding. Anchor bill boards of gum wood protect the bow, and the gum sheathing extends all the way aft and across the transom.

A run through *Beach Boy*'s scantlings will be

The profile and plan of Beach Boy *indicate a no-nonsense boat with on-deck space laid out for hard work.*

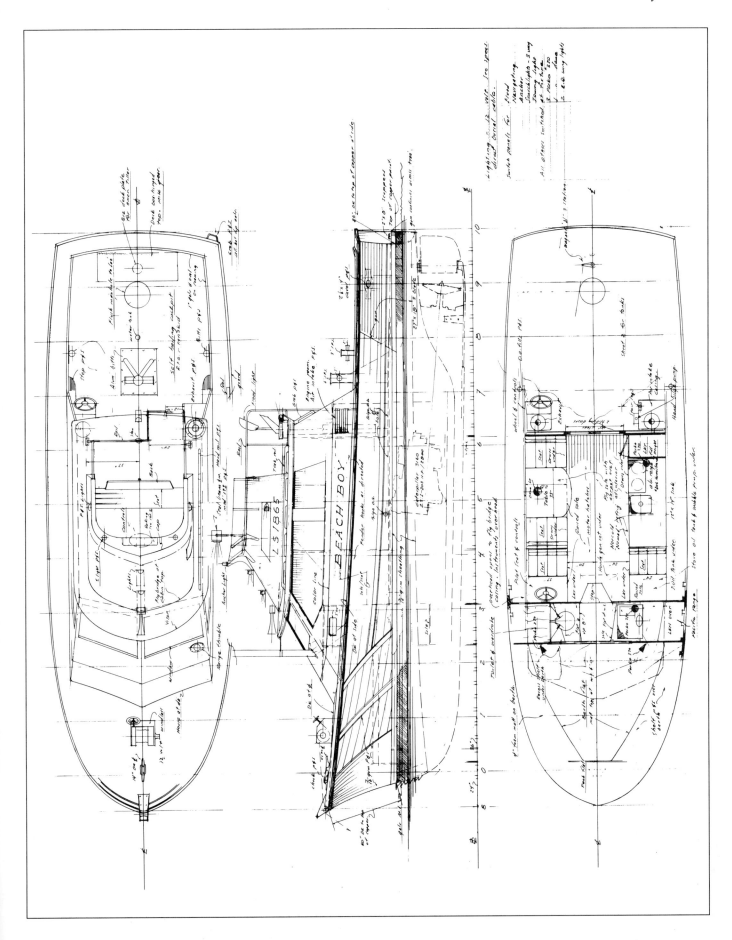

of interest. Planking is 1-1/4" Douglas fir on 1-7/16" white-oak frames spaced on 9" centers, and the balance of the members are as follows:

Keel:	4-3/4" x 9-1/2" fir
Stem:	4-3/4" x 9-1/2" gum
Forefoot:	4-3/4" x 9-1/2" gum
Stern post:	5-1/2" x 9-1/2" gum
Shoe:	1-1/4" x 4-3/4" gum
Decks:	Double 3/8" ply, fiberglass over
Shaft log:	5-1/2" x 11 1/2" yellow cedar
Sheathing:	7/16" gum

The framing plan generally outlines the construction method. Remember that she has to take more abuse in one season than a yacht would take in a lifetime. The third Cat engine is in her now, the first two having been run to major overhaul time prior to replacement.

The body plan shows the full reverse curve required to take the engine seating and to provide buoyancy for the weights involved. The buttocks are carried out in a flat run, and the deep vee'd forward sections under water allow her to slide through a head sea with a minimum amount of fuss and spray.

The photo shows her coming up to my float. It's a good shot to show her general appearance underway.

So that's about it for *Beach Boy*, a good rugged boat, and certainly a more interesting way to pay the bills than a nine-to-five routine.

Gordon Reid and Beach Boy *coming up to the Toad's Landing float for a stopover en route south.*

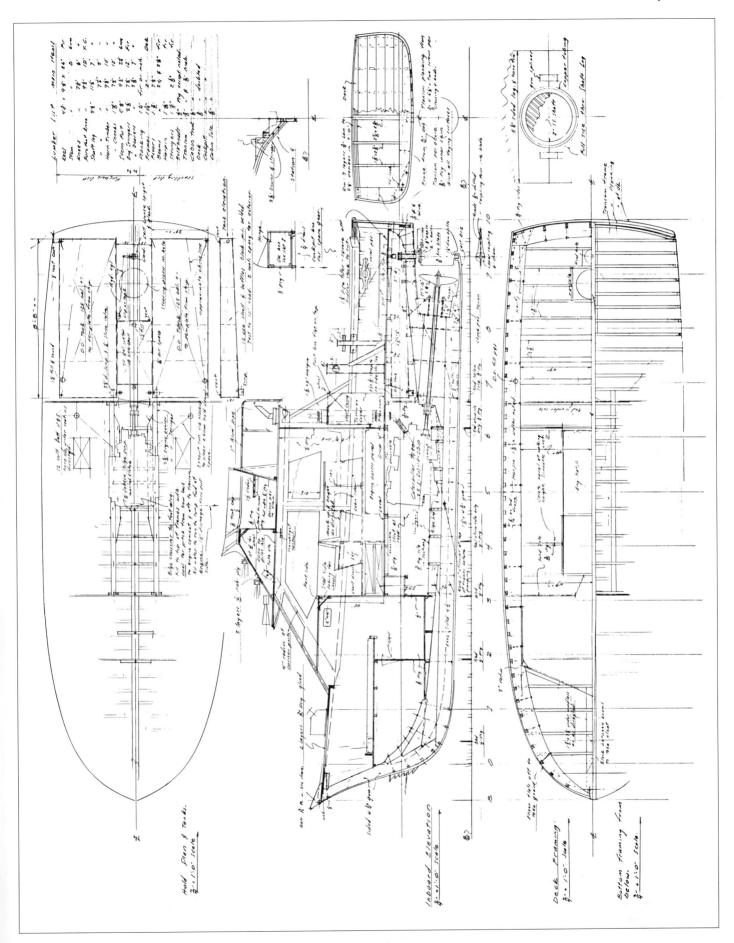

33

Katherine III

LOA:	92' 3"
LWL:	80'7"
Breadth:	20' 9"
Draft :	4' 6"
Displacement:	135,000 lbs.
Power:	Twin 16-92
	G.M. Diesels,
	1,350 h.p. each
Cruising Speed:	28 knots
Maximum Speed:	30 knots

Fast yachts seem to be the way to go in this era of excess. Speed does something to us all, and at about 30 knots I've noted that a somewhat glazed look comes into the eyes. The advancing throttles tend to convert a man into the personification of the do-or-die flotilla commander on a flank-speed mission through enemy waters, alert for action, a glass of nerve balm close at hand. Speed, as great as it can be, is costly, and it converts most of us into instant damn fools. An exhilarating way to go with a clean wake at full plane but unfortunately with a host of smaller and slower boats rolling in the wash.

Ninety feet is about the size limit for practical operation by an experienced man-and-wife team. In this case the owner is competent to maintain the systems, although things are fairly complex. In fact, compared with a 90-footer of 50 years ago, this boat has spaceship complexity. The systems and equipment add up to a ship of great technical interest (when it's all working). Moderate displacement, rugged foam-core fiberglass construction, an easy-lined hull form, and efficient power combine to make *Katherine* a good all-around fast cruiser.

This *Katherine* was designed for my long-time chums, Jack and Kay Hughes, as a larger, faster version of the 68-footer illustrated in Chapter 35. No. II had a pair of Stewart & Stevenson 8-92 Detroit Diesels, while this latest *Katherine* is powered by the 16-92 D.D.E.C. engines.

The Hughses will use her for the same commuter service from Skyline to Roche Harbor in the San Juan Islands. This with summer cruising in northern waters will keep her busy for most of the year.

The arrangement plan can be followed on the drawings. Basically, the boat has a single-level accommodation layout with a minimum of stairs. The interior is finished in a light, pleasant decor by Norm Warsinski, the N.W. decorator. She was delivered in 1990 by Knight & Carver of San Diego, with Howard Buller as project chief.

The hull is of double Airex foam-core construction with decks and house of Divinycell. F board was used on all vertical surfaces. Cabinetry is of Nomex-cored veneers, all in the interests of weight-saving and speed, although another five tons could be taken out of her without loss of

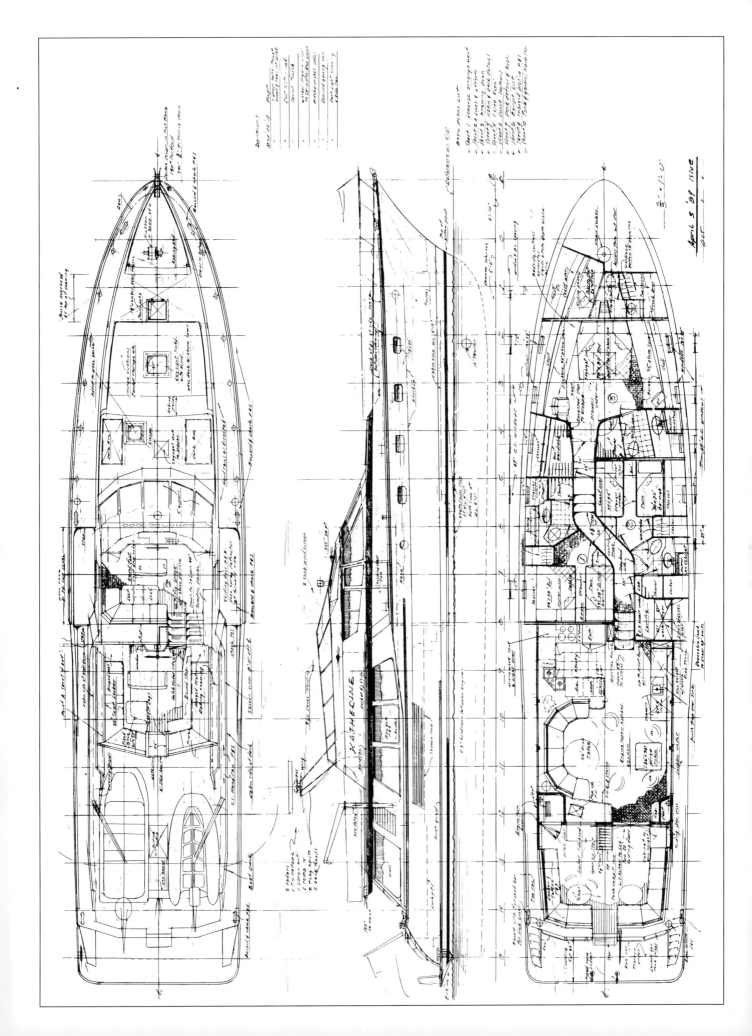

Katherine at about 28 knots, her cruising speed. A clean entry without the snowplow effect so prevalent with today's motor yachts is in evidence.

Neil Rabinowitz

A pilothouse with a touch of Darth Vader. Tivoli lights always seem a bit much, but the overhead windows are appealing in the often-overcast weather of the Pacific Northwest coast.

strength with a more sophisticated construction procedure.

Although the basic structure is somewhat over-built, the strength is reassuring during adverse conditions. Offshore, this sharp-forefoot model can maintain an easy 22 knots in a fairly rough sea state.

The running photo shows her at about 30 knots, en route to a weekend in the islands. An elegant way to travel.

156

34

Czarina

LOA:	97' 0"
LO Deck:	93' 6"
LWL:	82' 0"
Breadth:	19' 0"
Draft of hull:	4' 0"
Draft max.:	5' 10"
Displacement:	105,000 lbs.
	(plus fuel and water).
Power:	Twin 1,000
	h.p. Cat diesels
Fuel:	2,000 Imp. gal.
Water:	400 Imp. gal.
Max. speed:	30 knots
Cruising speed:	25 knots

zarina is included as a favorite boat. She was designed for Gene Greczmiel, an appealing and highly imaginative client, whose basic ideas were developed into a most attractive express cruiser. Of the fleet, this is the one I would cherish, given the bundle required to build and maintain a sophisticated 90-footer.

The drawings will give an idea of her general arrangement and construction features. You will note that the plans don't match. The "as-built" profile has been revised from the original framing plan to keep up with Gene's restless imagination and his constant re-thinking as work progressed. "Changitis," this usually is called, a symptom of being unable to comprehend a three-dimensional form on a flat sheet. In Gene's case, his comprehension is 100 percent, but his head won't leave things alone.

To be specific as to the changes here, you will note after a casual scrutiny that the pilothouse windshield jog has been smoothed out on the profile. To my eye it is cleaner and less contrived on a boat of this sort. The saloon glass extending to within a foot of the sole is another feature noted on the profile, and not changed on the framing plans. The low sill will increase the feeling of apparent width and space in the saloon, despite extending below the bulwark height. These and a couple of dozen other revisions were made during construction, all of them adding to an imaginative yacht several steps above the off-the-shelf models.

The result of scale is a factor often lost in today's boat styling. Along with the craze for black windows goes the inability to judge boat size without a background scale. For example, a friend excitedly pointed out to her husband a new cruiser anchored some distance away with tiny people having a barbecue on the flying bridge. A look through the glass brought them out as being full-size humans rather than Tom Thumbs. With design elements proportional to those of a 30-footer, the 100-footer minimized the human scale, with the folks hopping around onboard seeming to be half-sized

Watch the next one go by, particularly a view from astern, and have a chuckle at the tiny people lined up on the flying bridge. All must have come to the pier in miniature cars roaring happily up to the curb, or been disgorged en masse from one normal-size sedan to tumble onboard a blown-up 30-footer.

Anyhow, when a head pops up on *Czarina* it should look in reasonable proportion to the scale of the structure.

The layout shows a basically one-level plan, similar in this respect to the layout of Knute Qvale's *Kristina* that we did in the 1970s. Steps lead up to the pilothouse and again up to the flying bridge. Cabins are light and airy, with windows and skylights.

On deck *Czarina*'s cockpit leads to side decks at saloon height, with two rises forward up to the forward deck. A 5" bulwark extends around the forward deck, and is finished with a wide teak cap.

The long cabin trunk furnishes nearly 7' headroom in the staterooms, plus light and air below. Forward is a companionway hatch to a one-man fo'c'sle, fitted with toilet and lavatory. This fo'c'sle will be used on the rare occasions when a hand will be carried. Normally in the Northwest an experienced owner will run a boat of this sort with his family, upkeep being accomplished in a boathouse by home-port personnel.

The starboard pilothouse door opens to the deck. The port side has a gate and a step over the passageway door. The sketch shows the pilothouse port-side arrangement. The engine room door and trap allows standup access to the engines. The wheelhouse has a bridge above that will be a great place to ride. Basic controls are there, a shipshape teak grating, a signal mast, and a radar tower.

Construction details can be followed on the framing plans and sections. Basically, the hull is a bent-frame, hard-chine express-cruiser form. The hull is built upside-down to facilitate the triple-skin gluing, etc. — all downhand work this way — and then she's turned over for completion of the deckhouse.

Floors, stringers, harpins, beams, etc. all were prefabricated prior to framing, so the hull was complete when she was rolled over. Meanwhile, the propulsion group, tanks, steering components, etc. were being fabricated.

McQueen's shipyard in Vancouver, B.C. were her builders. A first-class job of wooden boat-building by an experienced yard.

Czarina is most impressive when flat out in a seaway. However, the photo above will give an idea of her appearance afloat.

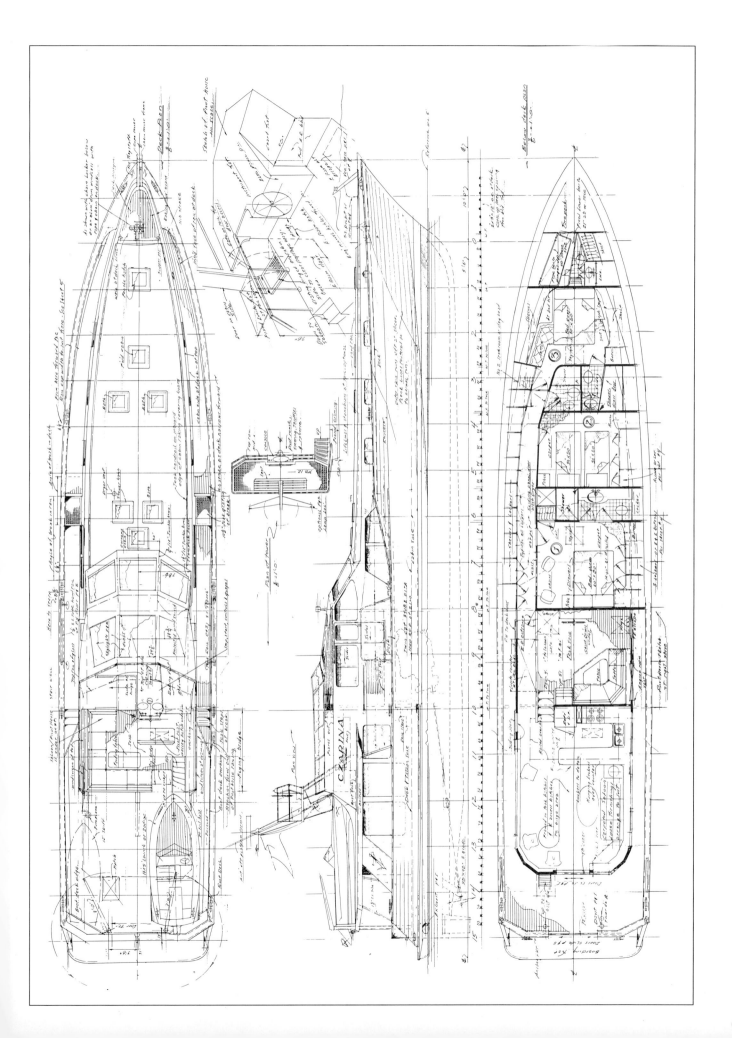

CZARINA

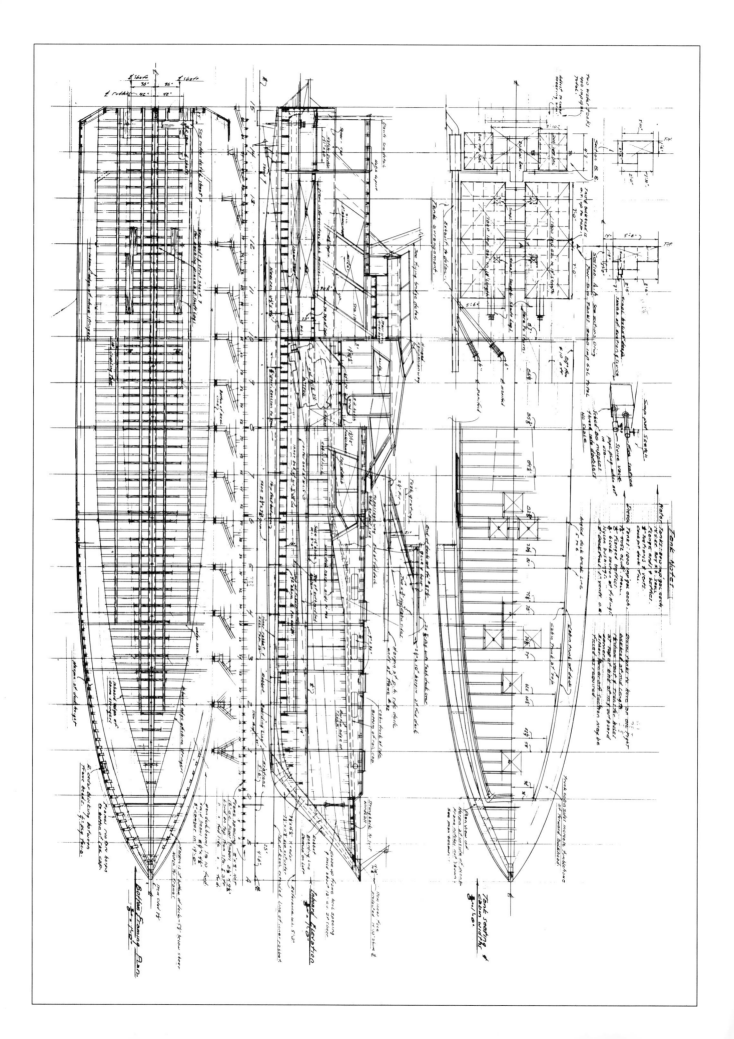

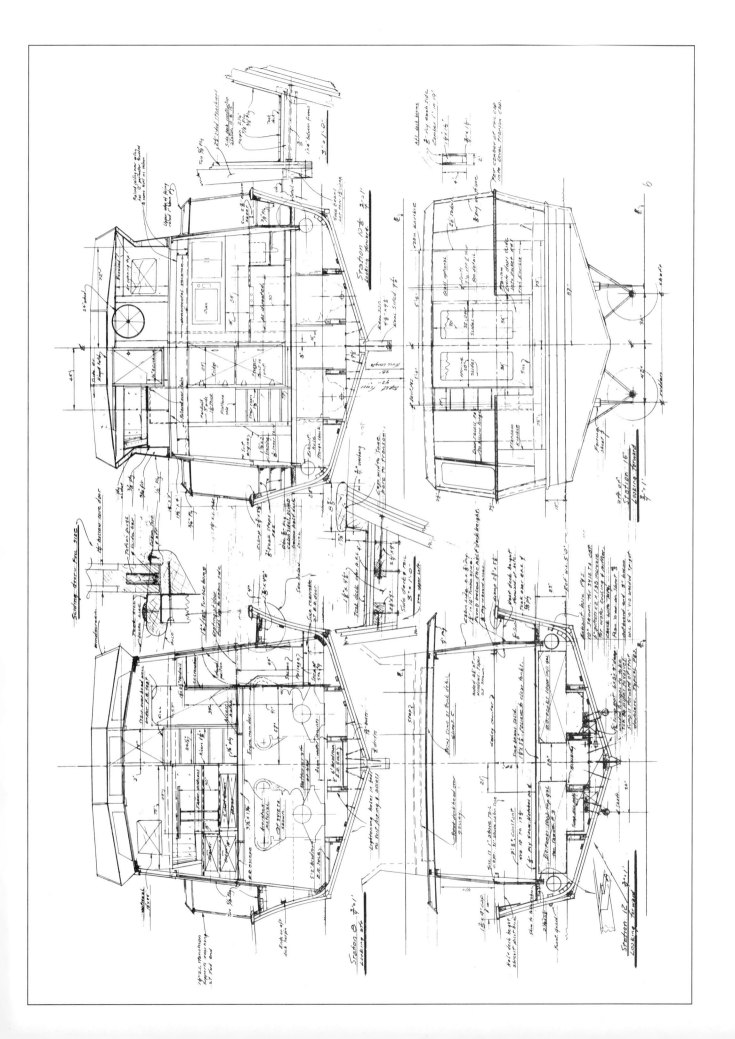

35

Bayliner Express

LOA:	67' 9"
LWL:	61' 9"
Breadth:	15'0"
Draft:	4' 0"
Displacement:	60,000 lbs.
Power:	Twin G.M. Stewart & Stevenson 8-V92T diesels, 650 h.p. each, 1.5:1
Maximum Speed:	28 knots
Cruising Speed:	24 knots

In the late 1970s two of these tri-cabin model 68-footers were built as prototype express motor yachts by Bayliner at their Arlington, Washington, plant. They are an interesting study in the maximum-performance-for-a-given-power approach, as opposed to getting the most accommodations in a given length — the results of the latter approach being the sluggish three-story floating condo models so prevalent in today's yacht market.

These designs have proven to be excellent sea boats, with rough-water performance unmatched in most stock motor cruisers. This is an endearing feature for the man who wishes to go places in any normal boating weather. A rough-water run will convert the owner of a chunky push-water model to the possibilities of a boat of this sort. As an example for the Northwesterner: Victoria to Princess Louisa Inlet is an easy 5-1/2 hours, and it's less than two days' running time all the way around Vancouver Island. A cruising speed of this sort puts the whole coast within holiday range.

Since the model is long and lean by today's standards, the resulting layout is elongated, but has resulted in an interesting and practical three-cabin plan.

Starting aft, the cockpit has a teak sole, high coamings, and a pair of gates for access to the wide transom step. Port and starboard over the engine casings a lounge area is fitted with cushioned tops, and with vinyl hassocks which double as sleeping-bag covers. The wide saloon door connects the aft cockpit with the main saloon lounge, making cockpit and interior an integrated area in good weather. Vinyl side and end curtains can enclose the cockpit from the inclement weather often encountered in the Northwest.

The saloon settee to port is 12' long, which will give scale to the drawing. A teak drop-leaf dining table is fitted to starboard, and there's space around it for loose furnishings. These are flanked by lockers, optional fireplace, bar, sideboard, and stereo. Next, forward to port and down two steps, is the galley, and opposite the galley a third double stateroom with washer/dryer at the forward end. As an alternate, this third stateroom could be fitted as a breakfast area.

The galley has excellent working space and lockers, and is open to the saloon through an

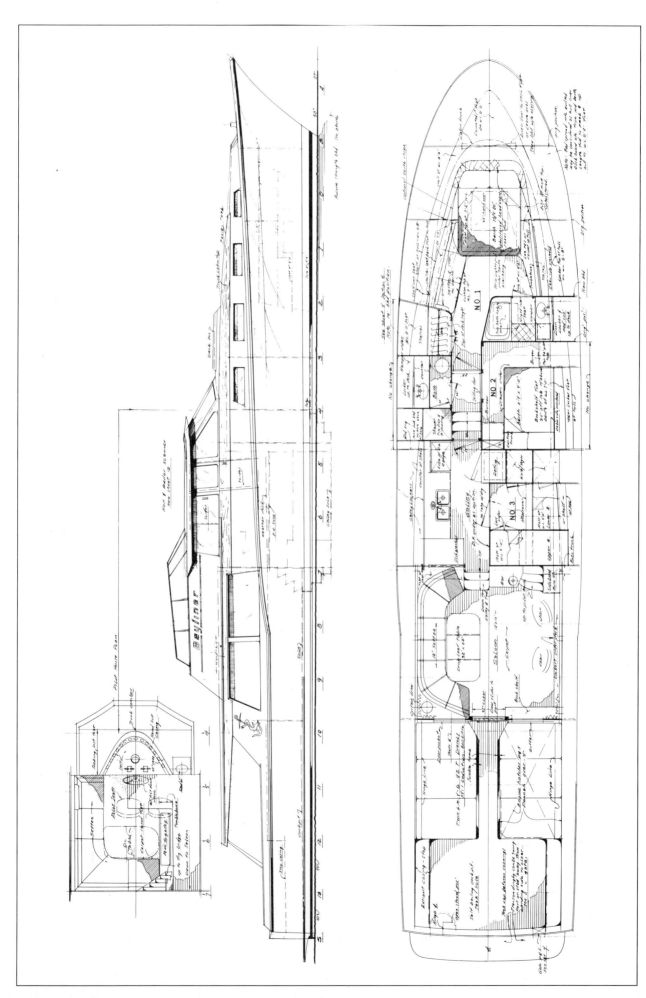

The general arrangement of Jack and Kay Hughes' earlier Katherine II.

arched bulkhead at station 7.

Forward of the galley is the no. 2 stateroom, with double bed. Across the hall from the no. 2 stateroom is a roomy toilet and bath. The owner's stateroom in the bow has a huge double bed with upholstered horseshoe-form headboard, and a divan to port. The roomy bath is fitted with a sunken tub, drawers, and Corian countertops.

The pilothouse sole is four steps above the main saloon. The pilothouse is an excellent area for lounging under way or for piloting during the off-season. The settee will seat a large party, and the table allows this area to be used as an optional dining space while under way. The settee is raised to give complete vision forward, with a glass bulkhead along the pilothouse passage below for additional light and for an open feeling in the galley. Pilot seats are fitted for the skipper and an observer.

Steps extend up from the aft end of the pilothouse to the flying bridge and another control station. At the aft end of the bridge is a boat deck, with davits for a Bayliner tender and one of Ray Richards' sailing dinghies. For an ardent fisherman another boat can be carried on stern davits. The two transom gates give float access outboard of the davit boat.

One of these tri-cabin models, named *Avanzar*, was built for Orin Edson, who was then Chairman of the Board of Bayliner. Another, called *Katherine II*, was built for John Hughes, who also owned the express commuter *Katherine*, illustrated in my first book of yacht designs. John Hughes' latest *Katherine* is described in Chapter 33 of this book. Both Orin Edson and John Hughes are long-time friends and connoisseurs of high-performance boats.

Mollie

The third version illustrated has just been launched by Sam LeClercq from his shipyard in Seattle; the hull is from the same mold as *Katherine* and *Avanzar*. The layout can be followed in the plans. *Mollie* is fitted with Arneson drives and a pair of 1,000-h.p. M.A.N. diesels. Maximum speed is 40.8 knots, and cruising speed is 32 knots, so for a 68' boat she is a real galloper.

Performance and accommodations in a motor yacht have always been in conflict. The more common semi-square yacht model's proportions allow the most practical and economical use of space — hence its logical selection for all-round sheltered cruising. At the marina the three-story look fits right in, but long, lean, and elegant will perform. For sheer go, and for the man who can afford it, the thin look is beguiling at all speeds.

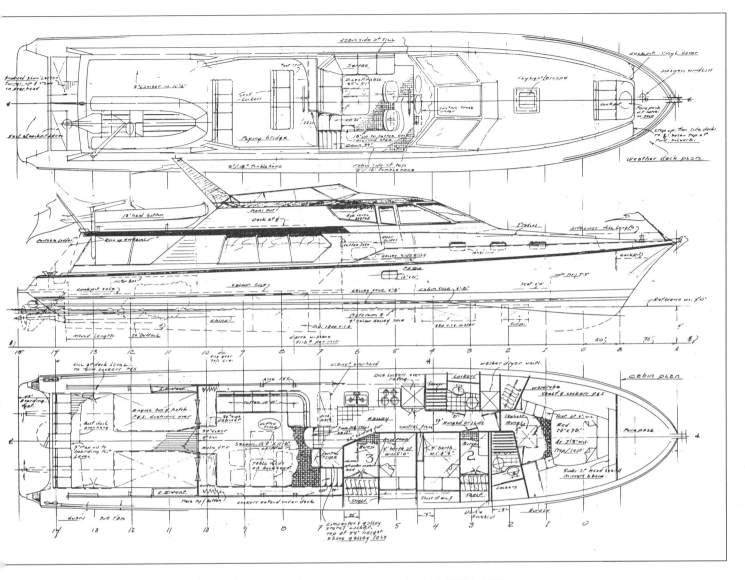

Neil Rabinowitz

Shown on this page is Mollie, *capable of 40-knots-plus and a cruising speed of 32 knots.*

Her dimensions:

LOA:	73'0"
LWL:	61'9"
Breadth:	15'0"
Draft of hull:	3'0"
Displacement:	60,000 lbs.
Power:	twin 1000-hp M.A.N. diesels

36

Mud Thumper, a Steel Motor Cruiser

LOA:	37'
L.W.L:	33' 8"
Breadth:	12' 2"
Displacement:	36,252 lbs.
Power:	Hundested 39 b.h.p. @ 425 r.p.m
Fuel:	300 U.S. gal.
Water:	60 U.S. gal.
Speed:	7.2 knots
Range	850 n.m.

Years ago, before practical stock fiberglass boats designed for mass appeal were available, boats seemed to be of more shipshape form, or were just plain boatier-looking. Today, cookie-cutter boats and even cookie-cutter boat people appear to predominate — people who ride from one marina to the next on the tide of affluence in off-the-shelf lookalikes. Just this morning when I was coming past the marina on the way out to work, the floats were filled with summer visitors up on their two-story boats. The "occupants," I'll call them, seemed to be of a stamp: ladies looking somewhat harassed as they walked down the float, usually followed by a blue poodle and a heavy-displacement skipper — a skipper whose gait suggests a mood that might best be dispelled by seeing the lady walk the plank. I distinctly heard some farm talk from one boat as a lady leaped off the boarding platform with the entire stern line tangled over her arm.

Attire seems about the same on all the boats, the more formal being in evidence as the length and number of decks increase. No bib overalls or straw hats as in the days of yesteryear.

Deck houses too have become higher and wider. Designing from the inside out is the new world. Small versions of cruise-ship bulgy proportions will finally reign.

But before I get too depressed, it was an absolutely beautiful calm summer morning. The 3-cylinder Vivian in my little *Merlin* was knocking off its 450 r.p.m. on the way out to the island, and on arriving at the office I had the *Mud Thumper* plans shown here to finalize.

For some background: Ted Williams, the chap we designed her for, phoned one spring day and asked if we would look over some drawings of a boat he planned to have built. The hook before referring him to someone closer at hand was his comment that he had in his barn a 39-h.p. single-cylinder Hundested diesel, about two tons of new

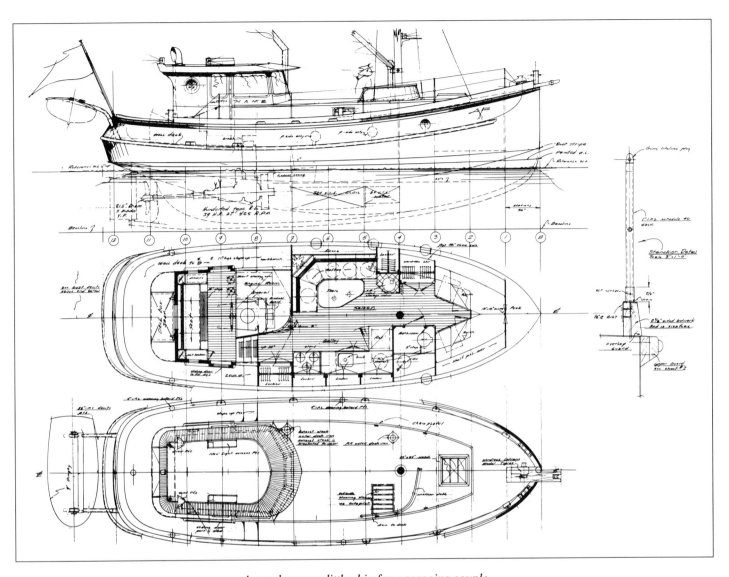

A good, roomy little ship for a seagoing couple.

engine, sitting there and waiting.

His other requirements were equally appealing, so we ended up scrapping Ted's first plans and designing *Mud Thumper* — a sort of marine aspirin to take after seeing too many look-alikes.

As finished, I believe *Mud Thumper*'s layout will appeal to the cruising man. The open, roomy cabin contains a good galley, an L-shaped settee/lounge for the dining area, and a fireplace that is great for wet-weather cruising.

A roomy stateroom is forward. One head serves the entire ship. The towering engine is *right there*, where one can give it a salaam on passing. The engine room sole is down 8", and the engine is protected by a curved see-through plexiglass door, plus a flywheel guard and a polished brass rail for the loiterers who like to watch

things run. To port is a workbench with lockers for tools, and to starboard under the pilothouse is the air bottle for engine starting, plus batteries and storage. The auxiliary generator is aft, followed by a roomy lazarette.

The hull form is a developed-surface chine model, with a box deadwood aft fairing into the propeller aperture, and affording width down low for the 34" flywheel and engine beds.

Construction can be followed on the framing plan. Webs are on 3' centers, with longitudinals on close intervals.

From the sheer up, the superstructure is wood with Dynel over it to give a good painted finish. A good shipshape form of superstructure, rather than ornamentation, to provide interest.

The pilothouse is arranged with a high for-

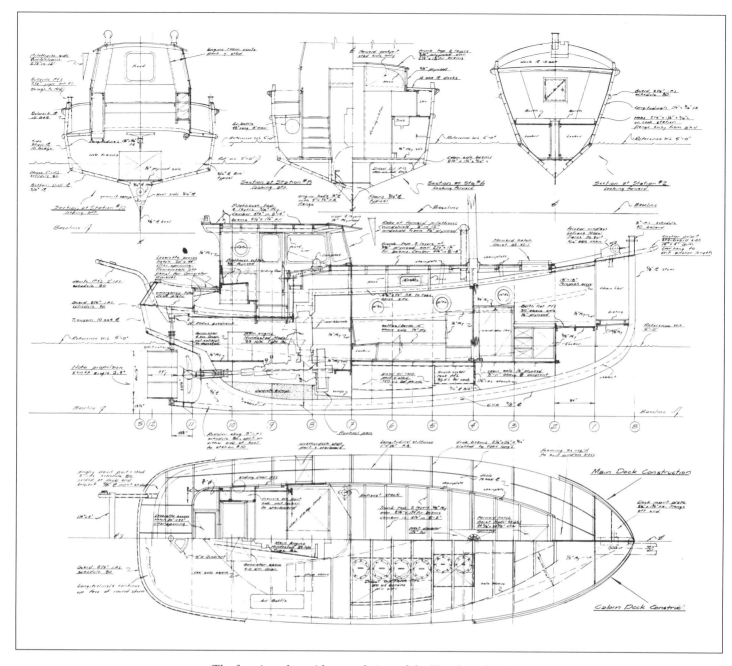

The framing plan with a good view of the Hundested engine.

ward viewing settee across the after end, flanked by drawers to port and a wet clothes locker to starboard, utilizing heat from the engine room for drying.

Sliding doors are fitted port and starboard, and controls for the engine are to port — two more big brass hand wheels to polish. Reach rods drop down to the engine via U-joints.

The chart flat extends to the windows forward, with a slight fall to allow for easy reading. Under the hinged flat is a bin large enough to take a couple dozen charts.

On deck *Mud Thumper* has good roomy passageways alongside the trunk cabin. The foot-

well steering station forward, you will note, is recessed in over the refrigerator space. The weather cloth will form some shelter here, and two can take their ease on deck, with the autopilot remote for control. It's a nice place to sit with a cup of coffee as she plugs on up the Gulf on a sunny morning.

The windlass drops the chain into a self-bailing chain locker directly below in the forepeak, high lifelines surround the deck, and a deep bulwark affords security in the well deck aft.

One boat is carried on davits aft, and the mast and boom will lift a rubber boat to stow on the trunk top amidships.

37
Southerly

LOA: 64' 9"
LWL: 56' 0"
Breadth: 18' 6"
Draft: 3' 2"
Displacement: 94,500 lbs.
Power: Twin 760-h.p.
                M.A.N. diesels
Fuel: 1,500 U.S. gal.
Water: 400 U.S. gal.
Cruising Speed: 20 knots
Max. Speed :   23 knots
Range: 36 liters/hr.
                @ 9 knots

Based in Auckland, New Zealand, this aluminum motor cruiser was designed and built as a stock boat for its home waters. McMullen & Wing, an Auckland firm noted for excellent quality whether sail or power, are the builders.

The Porters, the owners of McMullen & Wing, are specialists in aluminum, steel, fiberglass, or wooden construction. *Southerly* is an example of the expertise and care that they put into each project. Brian Riley was the foreman on the structural work, and we're fortunate now to have him relocate here in Victoria, B.C., where at Vision Yachts Ltd. he continues to produce yachts to the same high standards.

On this stock hull the builders offer a variety of overall lengths and layouts, so the basic form can be used as a passenger, charter, or sport fishing boat. Various interior layouts also have been developed, making the model adaptable to an owner's particular needs and wishes.

Sixty-five feet is a nice size for a family cruiser,

a boat able to make quick work of the Auckland/Bay of Islands run in any normal conditions. Stretched about to the limit of her endurance, she has made the turbulent passage across the Tasman Sea to Sydney.

Sixty-five feet is well within the range of management for a man and wife or a family to handle without a paid hand, while the size will allow ample space for a half-dozen people to live onboard without getting on one another's nerves (any more than usual).

The layout shown was the rough draft for the prototype, and has been utilized with variations developed during construction. Basically, the plan allows a four-cabin layout, with the two forward staterooms accessible from the pilothouse companionway. The owner's stateroom access is from the saloon, while the aft cabin enters from a flush hatch fitted with an easy-opening gas ram like the tailgate opener on a van or station wagon.

In a hull of this depth and freeboard, the

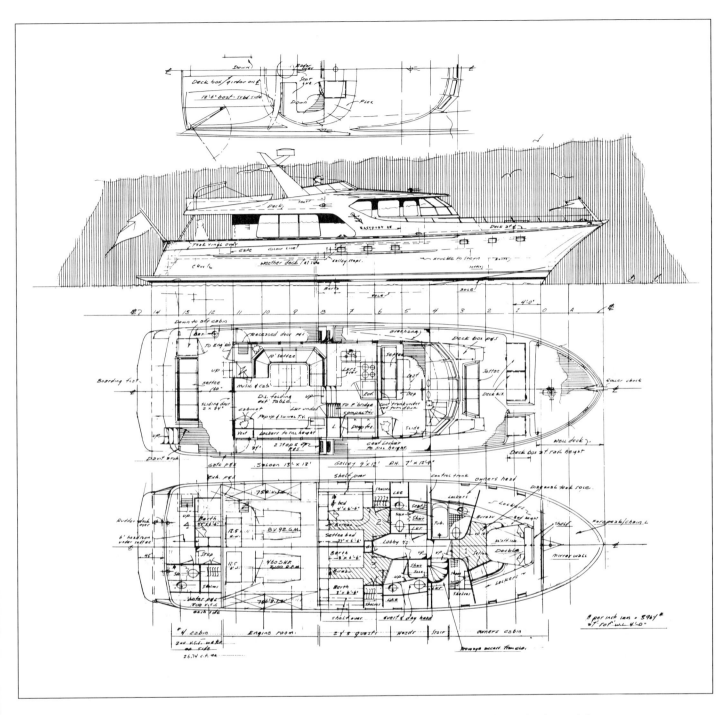

Shown above is one of the optional layouts for the New-Zealand-built Southerly *models.*
At left are details of these clean-lined little vessels.

lazarette affords space for an aft cabin. Alternatively, the space could be used for general stowage, with lots of room for scuba gear, stores, spares, and the multitude of equipment a serious cruiser accumulates. A watertight door can lead out to the boarding platform for easy access to the skiff or swimming ladder.

On deck every effort has been made to keep her clean-lined and simple. Walk-around decks are fitted, with two breaks leading up from the aft-deck saloon level to the fo'c'sle height.

The general deck layout can be followed on the plan. The boat has good lounging areas, from the forward settee with its 180-degree visibility and bulwark shelter, to the pleasant flying bridge settees. A good deck plan for a small motor ship.

38

Merlin

L.O.Deck:	25' 1-1/2"
Hull breadth:	7' 3"
Max. breadth:	7' 10"
Draft:	2' 6"
Displacement:	5,300 lbs.
Power:	18-h.p. Vivian
Propeller:	21" x 21" 3-blade
Cruising speed:	5.6 knots @
	450 r.p.m.

This is something more on the launch *Merlin*, the hard-working island office tender mentioned in my first book of yacht designs. *Merlin* was built in 1904 as an open boat, powered then by a Lozier gasoline engine, and built for Mr. Francis Barrow, of Shoal Harbour, near Sidney, B.C. I have heard that she was built by Hinton Electric Company of Victoria, and others say she was built by Dafoe in Vancouver.

Whoever the builder, he had a good eye for a boat, and did a simple, strong job of it that has lasted for nearly 90 years. *Merlin* has survived shipwreck, worn out five engines, and has sailed countless miles in her travels. As a little white launch she was known to many during her first 60 years as *Toketie* — a major character in Beth Hill's excellent book *Upcoast Summers*, the story of some of the Barrows' cruises during the years that followed World War I.

For many years the boat made annual cruises in northern B.C. waters, these during the golden days when yachts were scarce and upcoast residents still looked forward to summer visitors.

Judging from old photos of her voyaging in those quieter days, the yachting garb on board *Toketie* was bib overalls, a print housedress and straw hat, or fisherman's pants and a woolen pullover. Cooking was accomplished over a gasoline stove, and a dishpan was the sink. A bucket on board served for a toilet, otherwise one rowed to the beach. The engine was the only source of dry heat. All in all, a simple style of voyaging — not for everyone, but a way of cruising with few things to break down.

My old friend Dennis Ashby first pointed *Merlin* out to me when she was under Joe John's ownership, the Johns having acquired her from the Barrows' estate. She was still in service then, but understandably tired. Over the years she had been used for everything from cruising to transporting island sheep.

Eventually the Johns sold her, and occasionally I saw her limping past the island, out of trim and looking really tired, obviously on a slow cruise to the knackers. The next meeting with her was in Sidney, when I was on my way to meet my wife at the ferry. I came across poor old *Toketie*, renamed *Hobo* and looking the part, propped up in a backyard, quite forlorn and headed down the last mile.

The ferry was 10 minutes late, and the lady at the house said they wanted a thousand dollars for her. After a three-minute survey I bought the tired little vessel — if delivered afloat (more or less), and with the engine running to get her home. Too much money, but the nice, shapely form was there and the hull was reasonably sound.

My chum Snuffy Roark was visiting that next weekend, so we picked up *Toketie/Hobo* at the Sidney wharf. She was leaking, and her Universal engine was hitting on three cylinders. "Shambles" would have been a more fitting name than *Hobo*. Anyway, off we went, Snuffy steering and I having a great time throwing rusty spanners and miscellaneous junk equipment over the side.

I've written about using rocks for ballast, and sure enough old *Hobo* had a big one under the gas tank forward, right in the bow. I suppose the rock was put there in a misguided effort to prevent squatting under way when wide open, since the Utility Four with a 2.5:1 reduction was more than adequate power. This was the second engine of that model she had worn out after going through the original 1904 Lozier and a 2-cylinder Scripps. I slid the big rock back from the bow and we eased it overboard as we went along. The boat seemed happier for it.

We renamed her *Merlin*, after my kids' old cat, since *Hobo* wasn't fitting and *Toketie* was reserved.

That summer saw some rot come out of the cabin, leaks tightened up, and a general bandaid treatment given her, including new piston rings, the head planed off, a new fuel tank, and the dozens of fix-ups for an over-the-hill boat.

Each year since she has received a dividend. One year Bill Trenholme made some handsome teak windows to replace the worn-out 1919 pine windows. Another year I shortened the house to allow better cockpit space, and in later years a pot-bellied stove was fitted, a bronze stem band, bronze skeg and rudder castings, sponsoned-out guards — an endless list of improvements to the old girl.

Meanwhile that second Universal engine was wearing out. A friend up in Tahsis had all the

pieces of a 3-cylinder, 18-h.p. Vivian that was retired from a West Coast gillnetter, and I talked him out of it. That engine went in after a half-way rework. The Vivian wore itself out again after a run of four or five years. At that time it came out for a more complete rebuild, including new timing gears and all the rest. Shipmate Gerry Lazzara cast three beautiful stainless steel heads in his foundry to really make a job of it.

The Vivian was a popular engine on the B.C. coast for many years. The manufacturer, who built both gas and diesel engines, was located in Vancouver. As I am informed by the old catalog sheet, the engine was advertised in the 1930s as their high-speed model, probably in response to inroads from the marinized automobile and industrial engines that were steadily replacing the heavy, slow-turning machines that had been developed for marine service. With few exceptions, in the next few years the lighter, faster-turning engines would replace them all.

The old engines, though, were of simple design, easy to work on and nice to run, and the Vivian seems to be a good match for *Merlin*. Now lest you think that old boats, engines, cars, houses, or whatever are the way to go, you should be forewarned. Nothing can take more time, cost more money, or cause more headaches than rebuilds, as anyone who has fixed one up will tell you. Television programs extolling the virtues of fixing up old houses should be put in the catagory of pornography, banned and replaced with a bulldozer ad.

But admittedly there is an appeal about old things if well-proportioned — an appeal that hooks even people who are otherwise sane. In the case of boats, the time and money endlessly trickles out as the bilge water trickles in, until finally the boat is brought back to serviceable condition. An audit, however, would certainly be a shock. The cost of restoration is usually far more than the cost of building new, but the satisfaction of pumping the water out and the life back in would be lost.

As *Merlin* slides away from the float, headed for town, the Vivian idling steadily at 210 r.p.m., the cylinder heads polished, the rocker arms methodically nodding away, and with the smell about her of fresh paint from another spring

173

SPECIAL HIGH SPEED "VIVIAN"
BUILT IN SIZES 2 TO 6 CYLINDERS

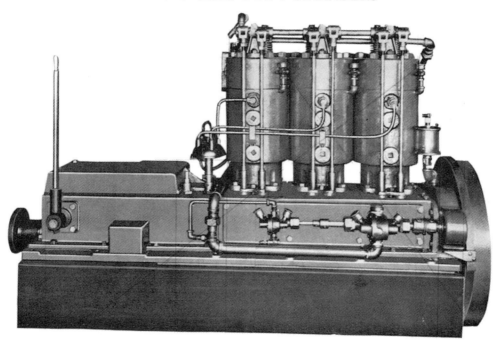

A good, buoyant little ship — well-matched with her 3-cylinder 4-1/2"x5" Vivian gas engine. Merlin *provides steady, reliable transportation in almost any weather, including the boisterous southeaster in these photos.*

overhaul, the whole thing seems worthwhile.

My office now and since the late 1960s is on a small island about a 15-minute voyage each way from shore base, and *Merlin* has been our transport for many years, through good weather and bad. The photos, which were taken by my neighbor, Capt. Walrus, probably give the wrong impression of the normal homeward voy-

age, but I like the way she looks, chugging along, headed home out of the pass against a winter southeaster. Usually, of course, our trips are a real pleasure, with the constant movement of tide, the sea birds to watch, an occasional killer whale pod, and the weather in all its moods. So *Merlin* gets her daily workout, back and forth. A hard-working little ship.

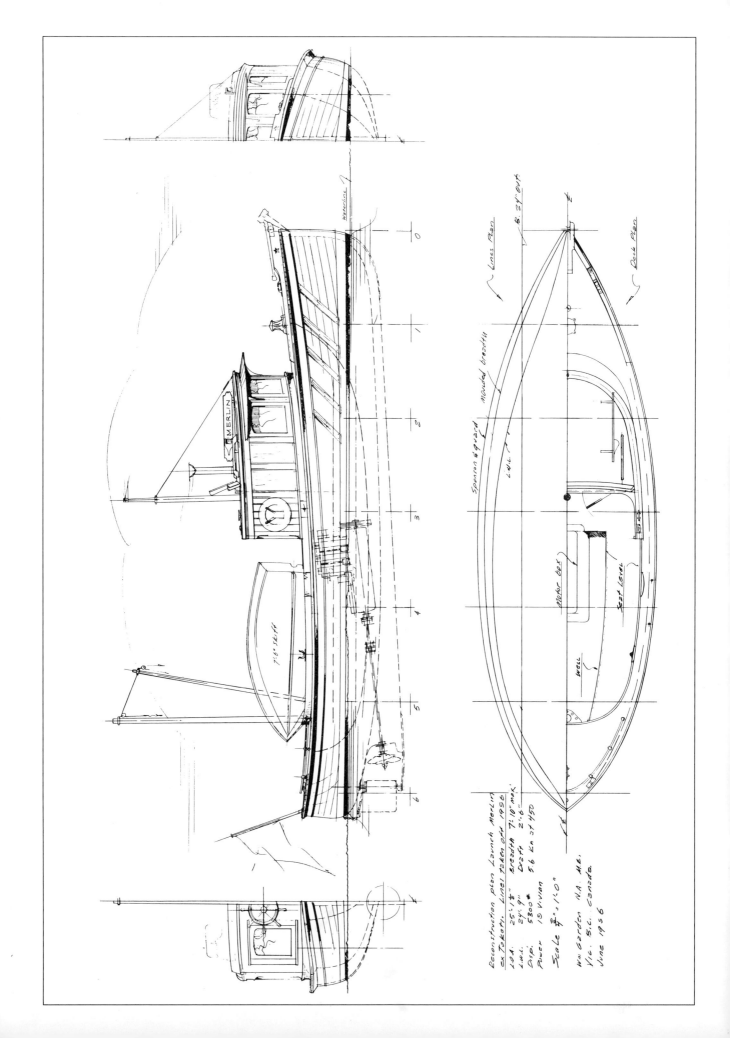

Reconstruction plan Launch Merlin
ex Tokoti. Lines taken off 1956
L.O.A.   25'4"   Breadth   7'10" max.
L.W.L.   24'9"   Draft   2'6"
Disp.   5300#   S.A.   56 sq.ft. 450
Power   18 Vivian

Scale 3/4" = 1'·0"

Wm. Garden N.A. M.E.
Vic. B.C. Canada.
June 1956

39

Tlingit and Two Dories

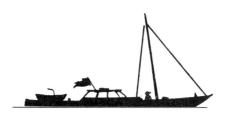

Tlingit

LOA:	62' 0"
LWL:	55' 0"
Breadth:	7' 6"
Draft:	3' 6"
Ballast:	2,500 lbs.
Power:	Easthope 20
	h.p. @ 550 r.p.m.
Propeller:	24" x 26"
Speed max.:	9.75 knots

Y ou may remember *Tlingit* from my first book of yacht designs. She was designed and built for my summer neighbor Dick Stewart, who used her as a commuter launch to his Sheep Island landing farther out in the Gulf.

In the fall of 1989, the Stewarts decided to cut down on their fleet. *Boreal*, an 80' steel motor sailer we designed for them a few years back, sailed off to New Zealand and her new owners, the Porters; miscellaneous small boats went in all directions; and *Tlingit* ended up in my hands.

For several years I've had an urge to convert *Tlingit* from a purely day boat to an economical cruising launch. So shipwright Kurt Frost came back on the payroll for a few weeks, and we

reworked her deckhouse into a more practical cruising arrangement. This, plus rewiring, engine work, and the dozens of other upgrading items that always seem necessary on an old boat, took up most of the winter.

Shortly after I acquired *Tlingit*, my long-time friend Orin Edson got the bug and we decided to share her — Orin's half as a step back to basic boating, and as penance for owning a 105' Italian motor yacht. So work proceeded.

Tlingit's power is still the same 463-cubic-inch, heavy-duty 3-cylinder Easthope gasoline engine. Idle is about 150 r.p.m., and maximum is 550 r.p.m. An economical cruising speed is 8.5 knots, burning about 1-1/2 gallons an hour. The Easthope is 1800 lbs. of long-lived iron, with all sorts of neat things to oil. Most of the lively parts are right out in the open. Busy rockers, the solemn stroke of the water pump, a Manzel lubricator — all are good things to see and enjoy as she ker-chunks the slippery hull along with minimum wake and fuss, but admittedly with a fair racket from all the moving parts.

We've added a trunk cabin forward under a new three-panel windshield. The trunk cabin houses a couple of good bunks and a tiny galley, with stove and sink. The portable ice box is under a cockpit seat. A toilet is fitted between the berths forward, and the main saloon has four folding chairs for seated visibility while lounging or underway. The saloon overhead is low, but the floorboard on the centerline forward lifts out for standing headroom at the wheel.

On deck forward of the trunk cabin is a deep cockpit for quiet running on the sunny days afloat. Less engine noise up there, and a great

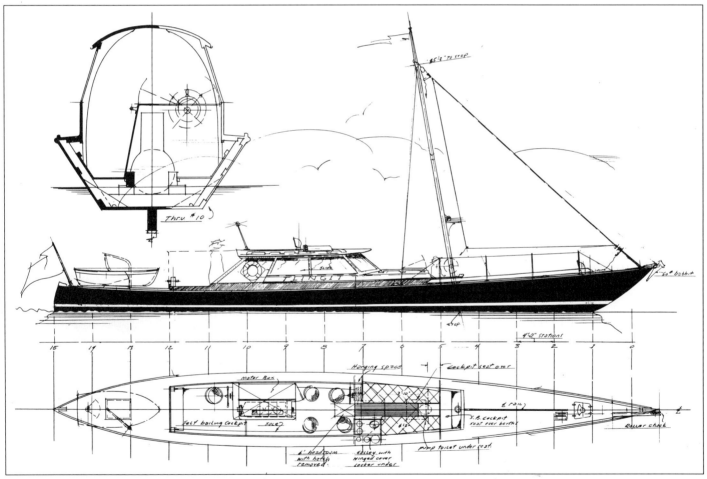

view along the bow up to the stemhead — the same appeal as the view forward along the hood of a 1939 Bugatti.

So *Tlingit* has ended up about as shown, an economical day boat doubling as a simple, clean-running cruising launch with Spartan accommodations. It makes for a more interesting life down at the water's edge, without the high freeboard required to house today's more commonplace cocoon of breakdown-prone accessories.

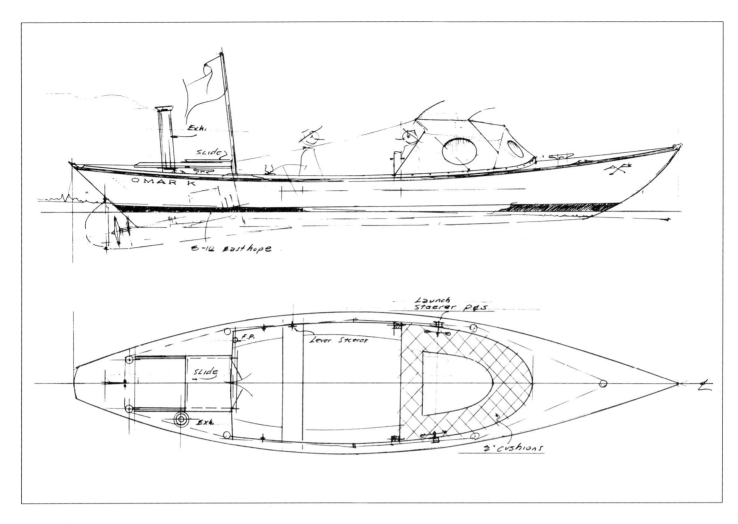

An old-time power dory has always seemed to be a pleasant way to travel.
Simple to build, handsome afloat, and six easy knots at 450 r.p.m.

A 30' Power Dory

LOA: 30' 6"
LWL: 25' 0"
Breadth: 7' 0"
Draft: 2' 0"
Displacement: 4,500 lbs.
Ballast: 900 lbs.
Power: Easthope 8-12
Propeller: 17" x 16"

This little fellow, along the same theme as the 88-footer shown next, might be termed a picnic-launch dory designed for pleasant excursions afloat. She is powered by an 8-12 Easthope 2-cylinder gasoline engine tucked well aft, in the manner of Alaskan power dories of the past. Under way, the rising stern wave gives ample propeller immersion, while 900 pounds of ballast settles her down nicely to a good running trim at six nautical miles per hour.

For day-boat accommodations she has pleasant curved seats forward under the melon hood cover. They make a nice U-shaped area for us to face each other and tell lies while we chug along down the inlet — a big flag flying aft to proclaim a holiday, and a fat hamper of stores chocked off amidships.

An 88' Power Dory

LOA:	88' 0"
LWL:	70' 0"
Breadth:	15' 0"
Draft:	5' 0"
Displacement:	78,000 lbs.
Ballast:	10,000 lbs.
Power:	6-71 G.M. diesel
Speed:	10 knots

A big gin palace with the modest name *Magnificence* was in port last week, which made me pleased that I had known people who gave their boats names such as *Walrus, Clam Hound, Ocean Plunger,* or *Mud Thumper* — people whose yachting attire sometimes had shoulder straps attached to bib overalls, people who wore straw hats that later could be relegated to a pet horse, people who were on good terms with priming petcocks, big flywheels to roll, and a Johnson bar linkage to the reverse gear.

The triple-decker *Magnificence,* moored at the fuel dock, had smoked glass windows, so I couldn't look inside to see the inhabitants. I was told they were quite nice, although further disguised with smoked eye glasses.

Now, I don't want to appear overly critical, since I know the fascination of both boating worlds: the heartbeat thump of an old-timer with a big clinker skiff towing astern, and its opposite number, the high-tech (as some call it) ultra-modern yacht with its beautiful array of sophisticated, vulnerable electronic marvels across the control surface.

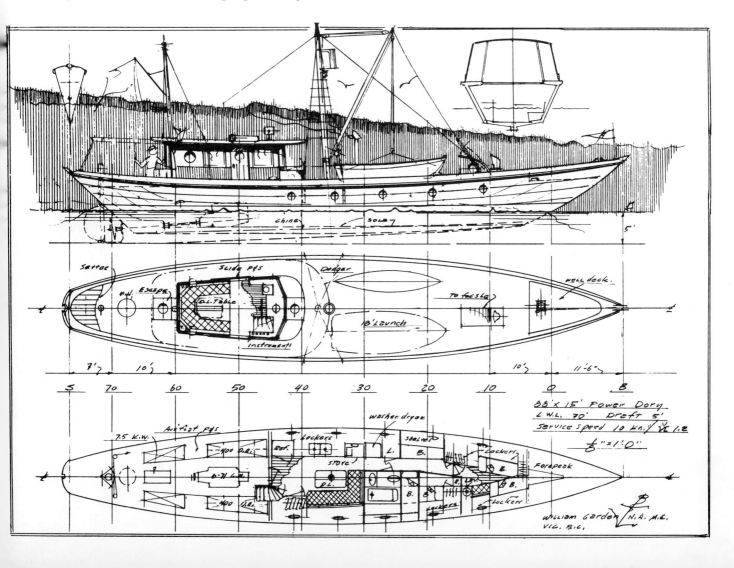

Each way to go is equally fascinating if the ship is well-proportioned. Too many have a beautiful linear polyurethane finish on an uninspired, chopped-off shoe-box-shaped hull and deckhouse. But it's nice to know that the poor old tortured globe is generating sufficient wealth to produce them, however gelatined the flavor.

Back to names for a moment. They have changed with the times, certainly, but come to think of it, the *Valiant*, *El Primero*, and *Courageous* names that seemed so good in years past are simply variations of today's superlatives. Even so, "*Magnificence*" would seem a little much on my sailing overalls.

As part of the final barrage in the losing battle for more boat-shaped boats, this big power dory will be of interest to the few remaining backward-looking boatmen who are still out of step.

Eighty-eight feet by fifteen feet admittedly is a big dory, but the dory form is always appealing to the eye, and it's a simple hull structure to erect. Framing for this one is sawn from 2-1/2" fir, set up on a double-diagonal 3/4" fir bottom.

In construction, the first step is to cut the bottom frames with the modest deadrise required to run bilgewater down to the sump. The bottom frames then are placed upside-down to the bottom curve on a simple jig, and then the chines and longitudinals are fitted.

The double-diagonal bottom is made up with glue and either screws or galvanized nails. A 2-1/2" x 9-1/2" keel batten that has been let into the frames along the centerline will take the hood ends at midpoint.

After planking the bottom, the external keel is bedded on the bottom layers, with through-bolts at each frame crossing to tie the assemblies together. Then the bottom is ready to turn over for erection of the side framing. These side frames are 2-1/2" x 5-1/2" at the chine, and taper to 2-1/2" x 4" at the sheer, with a heavy chine gusset to tie them to the chine and to the bottom frames.

This being an 88-footer, the bottom assembly is a heavy piece to turn over, but much easier than turning the entire hull. When right-side-up, the topside frames are glued and bolted to the bottom frames as noted above. Then the hull is ready for deck beams and side planking. Deck beams are first glued and bolted to the frame heads, then lined up with a sheer batten that is let in as another chine piece in order to form a backup for the deck/hull joint and for the sheer-guard bolts.

Topside planking is also double-diagonal 3/4" fir, set at about 45 degrees from horizontal, or as flat an angle as possible to utilize the maximum available lengths. Decks can be diagonal in the same manner, or else laid with staggered-butt double plywood. In either case the decks and superstructure will be encapsulated in fiberglass in the interests of maximum watertight integrity and minimum upkeep.

As to arrangement, a basic flush-decked layout is dictated, since the narrow-bottomed and easily-driven dory form lacks the stability to carry the weight of a large deck house. Below decks we have a simple elongated interior that will keep you in good walking trim, while on deck it is 40 round trips to the mile.

On deck forward is a well for anchor storage. The windlass is located there, with forepeak and chain locker directly under. From this point aft, she's flush-decked back to the pilothouse. Just abaft the well deck is a booby hatch leading to the fo'c'sle via the bulkhead ladder. Amidships the 18' launch and the canoe are handled by a short cargo boom and mast.

The pilothouse has a settee observation lounge with the control station located above the engine room. Eight hundred gallons of fuel are held in port and starboard wing tanks. Water is carried in wing tanks aft at station 60', and the 7.5-k.w. generator is located between them on the centerline. Steering is by wheel, sprocket and roller chain, via 3/8" 7 x 19 wire to a 26" quadrant, with deck plate above for an emergency tiller.

From the pilothouse forward is a companionway to the roomy galley and saloon. Between stations 15' and 30' is a good stateroom, plus passage berth, lockers, and space for a washer/dryer. On the original plan, which was designed as a small freighter, this area was a cargo hold with about 10' x 15' of floor space. With cargo she trims slightly by the head, which improves pilothouse visibility somewhat. The pilothouse settee is on a raised flat, thus maintaining a fairly constant eye level, whether standing at the wheel or seated. Bone simple throughout, but still about 8,000 man-hours and many dollars from concept to reality.

40
Three Large Yachts

Once upon a time, a wealthy merchant of Antioch, while gazing across his groves on the slopes of Mount Silpius, reflected, "By Jove, I'm bored. My holdings now include a goodly piece of Antioch, the third-largest city in our known world. I have chariots for all occasions, villas for all seasons, servants, stables, and civic power. Why not a pleasure villa afloat? It would be mine to command on coastwise jaunts — nothing ostentatious really, something with perhaps fifty oars. A neat pleasure version of a government trireme would do, but cut down to a bireme in order to fit nice accommodations. Some columns, baths, and other knick-knacks. What a way to elicit the admiration and envy of my friend Usurius! I'll build a pleasure palace afloat, and recycle a few amphoras full of gold into the pleasures of coastal voyaging."

So shipbuilders were brought in and plans and prices worked up amid an endless coming and going of nautical specialists.

"Nothing really ostentatious," our friend decreed at the onset, but with no concept of the complexity of such a project, nor an inkling of the pots of gold required.

It came to pass that the requirements were settled. Our friend bit the arrow, so to speak, and presently loads of aromatic cedar and gopher wood and whatever were forthcoming. The decorators in particular shook our merchant to the core, with cost estimates of the thin marble dictated by the shipbuilder's weight requirements, the gold inlay work, the fountains, sculpture, drapes, carpeting, lamps, and furnishings.

All this, plus cages for the odd tiger, the peacock housing, and the need for another 20 oarsmen — plus the greater hull length to maintain speed with the heavier accommodations, fountains and such — proved to be a shock, but finally the project was a reality. Some 300,000 hourglasses of work were required, and the gold accumulation was somewhat thinned down. Finally she was afloat, with flags snapping in a fresh morning breeze, ready to salute the power plant, which was being marched down from the local jail. To a man, they were sullenly prepared to develop trial-run calluses — a crew problem, incidentally, that will give the owner of today's large yacht an idea of how bad things could be.

So the ship was readied for sea, and guests boarded. As Antioch's port of Selvecia, shining in the sun under the serene slopes of Mount Silpius, slipped off in her oar-patterned wake, an envious guest named Libelius sipped his drink and thought of how his trireme would outdo this one in speed, in peacocks, in hand maidens, with even nastier chaps manning the whips on the catwalks to speed the stroke. *The mega-yacht era was born.*

Despite wars and plagues, the fall of empires, the Dark Ages and other miscellaneous setbacks, the big yachts persist. Today's incredibly luxurious vessels often equal in size the palatial yachts so common in the early years of this century. In numbers of vessels 60' and larger they surpass anything imaginable at that time.

"Show & Tell" boats they often are, with the systems that propel them well-encapsulated in an ornate and generally non-waterproof decor, reflecting varying degrees of ostentatiousness. The modern equivalent of peacocks, apes, and structure is but a minor contribution to the burnout of our dear planet, however, so we proceed.

Big boats or little boats — all are interesting to develop on the design board, to build and sail. In addition to the many smaller boats we have produced, we have done many studies and designs for larger yachts. The ones I've felt the most interesting were usually based on a workboat theme. For me, the workboat thread has always appealed, although for the black-sunglasses group the vaguely boat-shaped tarts of the nautical world provide a better stage on which to perform. Ornate capsules many of them, about as far from seagoing reality as one can get while afloat. Their popularity, however, indicates a need fulfilled, so we'll leave them alone.

For the amateur mariner who loves to actually go to sea, a more waterproof boat is the practical choice. Happily, we still have a few people who want more of a small ship for their voyaging, so some of the plans herewith might kindle a spark and set one or two off on the fascinating but often trouble-strewn passage of new construction.

Given the difficulties, a practical meat-and-potatoes approach to structure and machinery seems best-fitted to the small shipyards that specialize in medium-size craft, such as pilot boats, tuna boats, and small motor ships. These are boats that must survive at sea, both from a seakeeping and an economic standpoint. Such a small ship, supplemented by commercial-quality heavy-duty machinery, and a practical water- and wear-resistant interior decor, is probably the best approach to a happy life on the deep blue sea. Let's look at a few possibilities.

136' x 23'6" Motor Yacht

LOA:	136' 0"
LOD:	132' 6"
LWL:	123'6"
Breadth:	23' 6"
Draft:	8'4"
Power:	Twin Caterpillar 3512, 1,250 h.p. each @ 1300 r.p.m.

Given a reasonable bundle of cash and the time to go voyaging, a fair approach to the ideal might be something like this 136' motor yacht. She combines seagoing ability and good accommodations, a size that will fit into most small harbors, and she's big enough to be a fairly comfortable sea boat.

The layout has some good features. The hold in particular is a great place for the overflow of gear that always seems to occur, and a good spot to store scuba gear, spares, and miscellaneous mechanical components.

Direct access is arranged between the engineer's stateroom and the main engine rooms. On the starboard side, adjacent to the engineer's stateroom and off the engine room, is an insulated double-glazed control room. To port is a shop area with lathe, milling machine, and miscellaneous other tools for repairs.

In this review we seem to have started at the mechanical heart of the ship, which I suppose is fitting in these days of complicated mechanical equipment required to keep us operational.

The engineer's cabin in this case is also the choice spot from the standpoint of easy motion. Peter Lee's *Khalidia*, which we once used as the basis for features that her owner wished to be

This nicely arranged and proportioned mega-yacht is a medium-sized one by today's standards. At 136'x23'6" she's a nice size for extended voyaging.

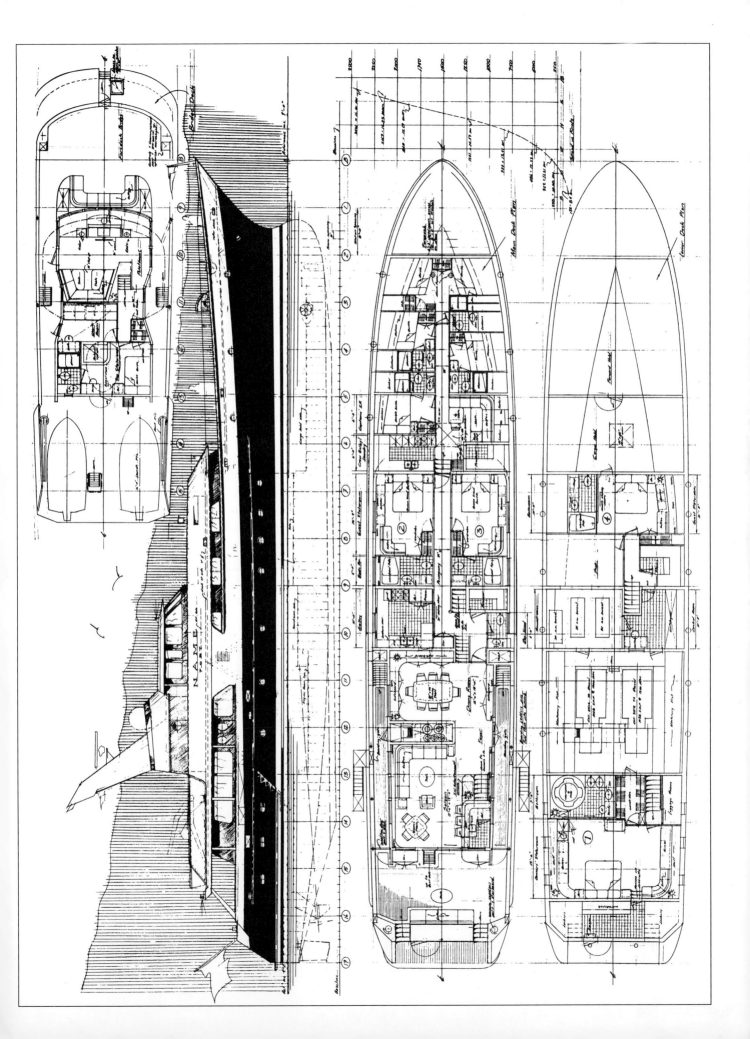

incorporated in her replacement, was originally built for a man confined to a wheelchair. His stateroom was in about this same area of least motion, the owner in his wheelchair having access to the upper decks by elevator.

So we'll leave the happy engineer with his easy access to machinery fore and aft, and — in this best of all possible worlds — a wife who is an accomplished electronics technician, and go up on deck for a general look around.

A sea cabin is directly abaft the bridge, adjacent to both the chart room and the bridge. This cabin is the captain's choice at sea, although it has a livelier motion than his cabin below. Moving aft on the boat deck, the two launches are handled by a pair of hydraulic cranes (although two sets of davits would be my choice for real control of a boat while lowering in a seaway).

A quick walk-around in dry dock gives an idea of hull form. A semi-bulbous bow fairs into a round-bottomed hull with firm bilges, five degrees deadrise amidships, stabilizers, bilge keels, and a long straight run aft terminating in a slightly immersed transom stern. Twin screws are fitted, each impinging on an ample spade rudder for good tracking downwind in a seaway. The transom stern also allows a usable boarding platform with easier access than that provided by an amidships accommodation ladder, particularly when anchored and rolling with the swell of an open roadstead.

So we get to the owner — the poor chap who has to pay the bills. His quarters are aft below decks or abaft the bridge in the skipper's sea cabin, in which case the skipper uses guest cabin no. 2 or 3 below.

Double staterooms for guests are fitted amidships. On a long cruise three couples seem to be about the limit for compatibility, so accommodations have been kept spacious but limited in number. The crew area is liveable with good accommodations for seven.

We'll sail off with a congenial afterguard of six in this able small motor ship manned by a crew of stalwarts. If you keep her on the go to interesting places for about nine months of the year, she'll be a home afloat. For short-time voyaging, it's best to charter, since a ship such as this is only for the completely dedicated.

236' Motor Yacht

LOA:	236' 0"
LWL:	216' 0"
Breadth:	38' 0"
Draft:	12' 0"
Speed:	17 knots

This small ship will appeal to those of us who remember the comic strips of the good old days, when Daddy Warbucks would return to harbor from some exotic but unexplained adventure required to recoup his fortune. His yacht would be shot full of holes as big as ash cans, but Daddy's egg-sized diamond stick pin was still sparkling as they steamed past the amazed Harbor Master's office. "Great Scott, Warbucks has made it," the Harbor Master would exclaim. With seven-foot-tall Punjab and The Asp as his bodyguards, Warbucks would load a big black double-length limousine with boxes of mysterious loot. Then they would roar away off the page, leaving us yearning for the next installment.

The arrangement and accommodations of a yacht of this size and complexity will take a week's cruise to unravel, while for a new engineer a year might be needed to become thoroughly familiar with the systems. Electronics in particular seem to be unlimited, and I often think that if all the wiring involved were stretched end-to-end, it would be a good thing.

Let's give the drawings a brief look. Then, in the mind's eye, we'll retire to the bar for a depth bomb and a snack. She's a lovely thing, but 236 feet is a lot of boat, and somewhat beyond our needs for carefree summer cruising. For those upset with the idea of one man corraling this much of the world's material things, I should observe that such a yacht represents some 30 million dollars channeled into direct shipyard construction jobs with an equal amount spent on material and its required manufacturing. This plus year-'round employment for the yacht's crew, as well as shoreside technicians, shipyard workmen, suppliers, and the host of satellite enterprises upon which the well-being of the yacht depends. So I suppose that, whether or not you agree that the dollars should be redistributed

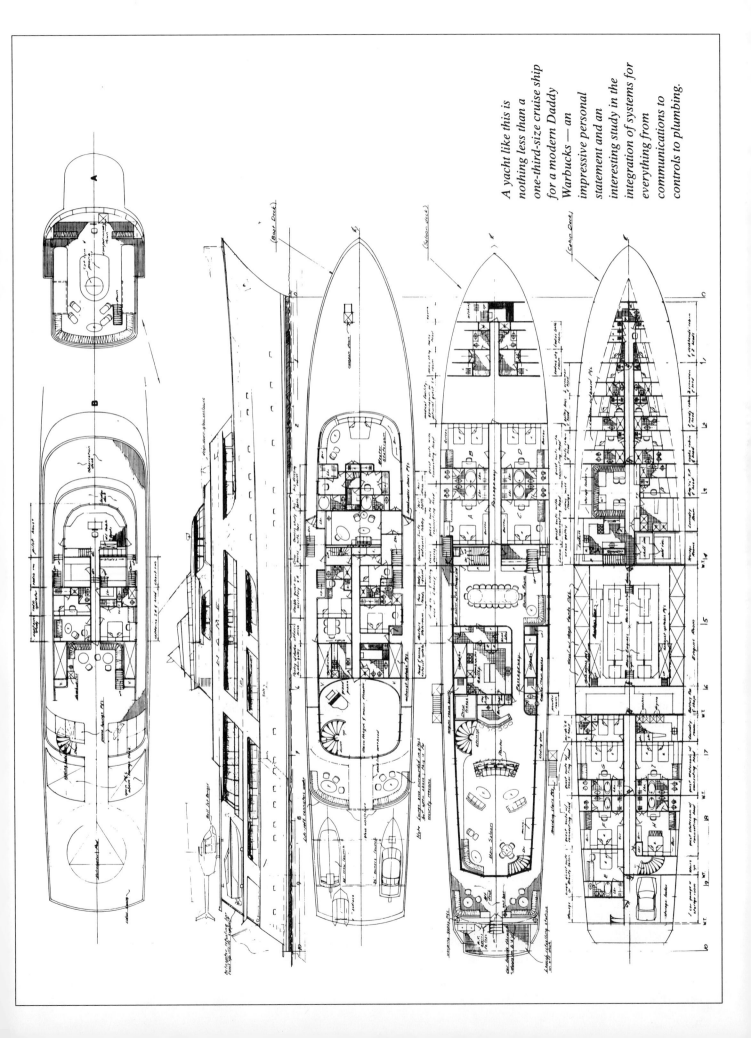

A yacht like this is nothing less than a one-third-size cruise ship for a modern Daddy Warbucks — an impressive personal statement and an interesting study in the integration of systems for everything from communications to controls to plumbing.

in this imperial manner, it all spells recycled money and work in the world beehive.

And, on the other hand, a way of life requiring armor plate, ballistic nylon drapes, one-way bulletproof glass, and a Webley-toting shadow. All this could make one think that low-profile is perhaps the way to go...

196' Motor Yacht

LOA:	196' 6"
LWL:	182' 0"
Breadth:	34' 0"
Draft:	10' 6"
Displacement:	900 tons
Range:	7,000 n.m.
Power:	Twin M.A.K. diesels
Speed:	16 knots

The 196-footer shown here is closer to reality, embodying as it does less chance of getting lost during an exploring expedition through the ship. It has a good layout for a man who loves a crowd and wants room to entertain.

This vessel was designed around the mechanical components of a tuna clipper from the Tacoma shipyard of J. M. Martinac. Twin M.A.K. main engines are specified, along with the same long-lived, stay-at-sea equipment that Martinac has developed during the building of dozens of major clippers.

The layout can be followed on the plans. A practical layout for her size, allowing flexibility, whether cruising at sea or entertaining in harbour. The photos of her model will give a good three-dimensional idea of her outward appearance. Again, a huge project — so in the next chapter we'll taper off on something closer to reality.

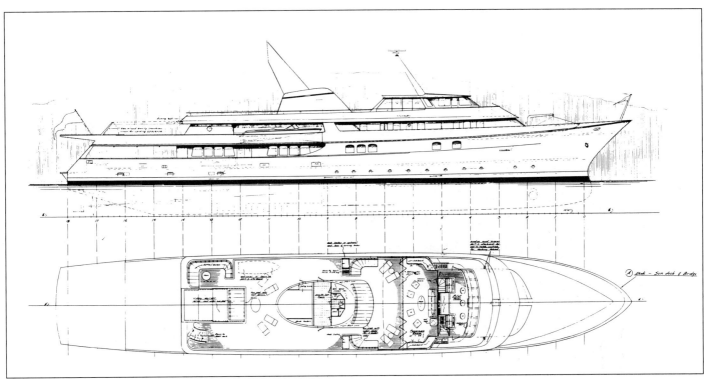

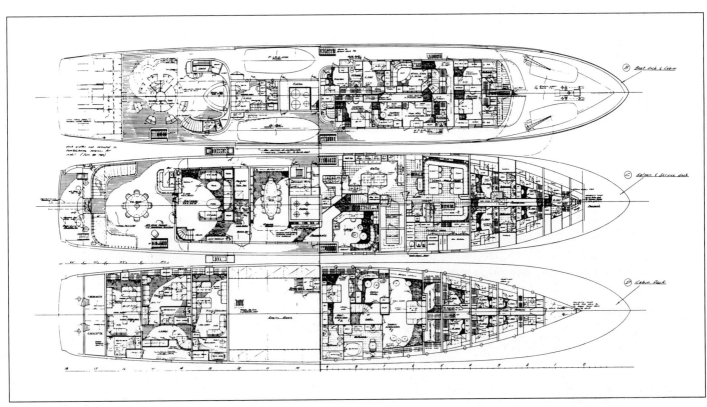

*Two sheets of the
196-footer are shown.
Unfortunately, the
reduced large drawings
will require a strong
glass to follow details.*

41

Cricket

LOA:	90′ 0″
LWL:	76′ 6″
Breadth:	17′ 0″
Draft:	
Max.	5′0″
Hull	3′6″
Displacement:	110,000 lbs.
Power:	2000 b.h.p.
Speed Max:	28 knots
Fuel:	3000 U.S. Gal.
Water:	400 U.S. Gal.

In this last chapter it's my turn to have a powerboat for northern cruising, so herewith is an amalgam of the more elegant style of yesteryear and today's technology. The marriage of light weight, a stepped fantail stern and one of our express-cruiser underbodies has resulted in a non-condominium appearance but still with real performance for leisurely cruising or for a fast run. Something like this is a change of pace from today's usual pushwater in both style and performance. A handsome boat to look at when at rest, combined with a hull form that has lots of go when required.

Speed is great to have in the bag when faced with a long stretch of relatively uninteresting water, particularly so when it can be combined with an easily-driven hull form of fair ecomony when throttled back to a more relaxed rate. High speed seems to be all-important in today's boat-ing world but the desire seems always to have been with us. As long ago as 1903 in *Rudder* magazine, W.P. Stephens wrote a commentary on the trends in large power yachts:

"A comparatively high service speed, upward of twenty knots on continuous runs of some hours, is at least demanded by business men who take their pleasure at high pressure and may want at any time to get from Newport to Wall Street in less time than train connections would permit. At the same time, when free from business for the moment, they expect on board a yacht the same comforts in the way of space, light and ventilation and many of the same luxuries of cuisine and household service that they would enjoy at a city club or hotel or a private home."

Given an equal period of affluence generating a bloom of large yachts, there seems to be little change in the act, only in the players.

Of the half-dozen motor yachts that I've designed over the past couple of years, the top speed has ranged from 20 knots to 52 knots, nary a one happy with boats of the 10-12-knot speeds that kept us on the go in the 'forties and 'fifties. No more happy, pokey powerboats seem to be built, although quite often an unhappy, pokey, boat seems to sail by.

As to the styling of motor cruisers, the "auto boat" themes have long been with us and acceptable to the average marine motorist. Sort of short and fat to fit the box they came in — but for the few out-of-step purists some of the shipshape elegance of the old fantail steam and diesel yachts has a lasting appeal.

The general theme of our ship can be followed on the plan and elevation drawing. The hull is of vee-bottomed form with the chine spray knocker dying out forward at station 1. The entry is sharp with the chine dropping aft in almost a straight line to the knuckle at the stern. Construction is of triple-skinned wood on longitudinal framing with a glass skin over all superstructure.

A run through the arrangement plan might help to clarify the general features. This boat came to mind during a cruise last summer in Glacier Bay, Alaska, on friend Orin's Azimut 110, an Italian yacht appropriately named *Avanti*, a most practical and well-conceived ship but a real bullfrog from some angles. Something with speed combined with looks seemed to be an interesting study. The cruise also brought back some of the fast cruises we had with the 70' *Claymore* (Illustrated in *Yacht Designs #1*) using about the same amount of fuel that *Avanti*'s generators burned, so the 90-footer herewith developed as an idea of how gracious voyaging might be accomplished.

To start with the layout, reasonable space is provided in the long, lean hull for two or three couples or for a family. For my own use the middle stateroom would be mainly for overflow of cruising gear or occasionally for another guest. Lots of stowage space is available along the port passageway, the heads are of reasonable size, and the one-level layout forward works out quite well. Staterooms 2 and 3 share one head in the interest of a good washer/dryer locker.

Moving aft the steps lead up to the galley whose lockers and stowage are supplemented by the stowage bins forward. Along the passageway, a Dutch door opens out to port for stores loading and general deck access.

The steps up forward from the galley lead to the pilothouse. Here we have a raised L-shaped settee high enough for easy visibility over the bow. Opposite on the port side is access to the boat deck plus a drying locker with the top at sill level for visibility over. Racks are here for coat and sweater drying during the wet days met with in northern cruising. This and the washer/dryer located off the forward passageway will be most welcome after a wet tramp ashore.

Engine room access is via flush hatches to the port and starboard sides of the wheel, plus repair hatches in the pilothouse and in the overhead. The engine room has 7' of headroom between the engines, lots of bins, a bench and good light and ventilation. A pair of 30-k.w. generators are fitted aft.

Out the pilothouse door and forward is a great open bridge, about 200 square feet of good-weather lounging space. A hinged wind-screen protects the helm station forward. Wing control stations are fitted port and starboard for control in maneuvering the vessel while mooring.

The deck area has room for proper steamer chairs, 36" rails all around, a laid-teak deck and a proper mast to carry the headlight and radar. All this on one level without having to climb up on top of the cabin to the flying bridge. For the wet days or for sun shelter while at anchor a light awning can be extended from the pilothouse visor to an awning bar across the mast. Fender lockers are fitted at the forward end and under two seats ahead of the pilothouse.

Forward again through the rail gate is deck space for an inflatable, along with a shallow well deck at the bow with a spool windlass that carries 40 fathoms of 9/16" S.S. wire rope plus six fathoms of 7/16" chain and a 250-pound Babbitt anchor. The anchor is self-stowing in a rocking roller chock at the stem head. The clipper bow allows the anchor rode to fall well clear of the bow.

Back again to the saloon area which is separated from the galley by some open stanchions. A couple of easy chairs are fitted to starboard, an 8' settee is to port, and on the aft bulkhead are cabinets for music and books. To starboard note that the saloon windows, a pleasant feature here,

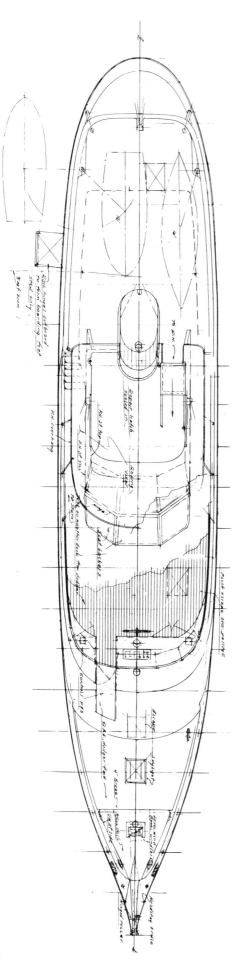

drop down to nearly deck height to open up the saloon. The forward one also slides open as a door adjacent to the tail gate for optional boarding access, and both the low sill door and matching window look out through the hinged bulwark platform opening when at anchor. Some steel is worked in here at the gate for longitudinal strength continuity. The sheer also dips down through the waist for maximum visibility while seated in the saloon. The saloon table can be used for dining while at anchor, or it's an easy pass up from the galley to the pilothouse table for dining while under way.

And finally to the fantail with its great curved settee, a real source of contentment with feet up while enjoying a sundowner. Lockers are under the settee, and a companionway ladder to port of the centerline leads up to the boat deck. Warping winches are fitted here port and starboard on the rail-height cabinet bases. During a spell of bad weather the drop window curtains will convert the aft-deck area into a snug addition to the saloon. The doors port and starboard along the weather decks also form windbreaks to close in the after deck. So that's about it for *Cricket*, a reasonable conveyance for Glacier Bay.

As to construction date, my anticipated lottery winnings one day should be more than adequate to do the job right. Since I started to buy a ticket my evenings have been spent in working out this great scheme for dispersal of the winnings, although the odds of 13 million to one have kept her size within reason.

The deck plan of Cricket *is reminiscent of a small motor ship. She is, in fact, a small motor ship for voyages north to the glaciers or south to Coconut Land.*

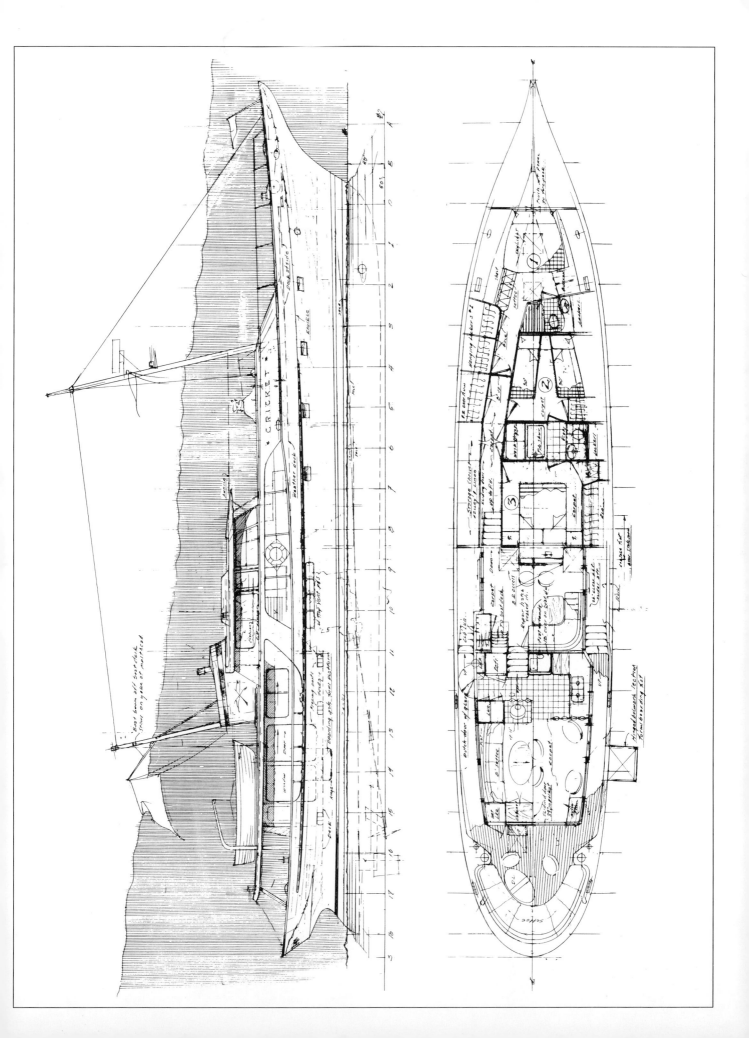

INDEX